BUILDING
DEMOCRATIC
INSTITUTIONS

BUILDING DEMOCRATIC INSTITUTIONS

GOVERNANCE REFORM IN DEVELOPING COUNTRIES

G. Shabbir Cheema

Kumarian
Press, Inc.

Building Democratic Institutions: Governance Reform in Developing Countries
Published in 2005 in the United States of America by Kumarian Press, Inc.,
1294 Blue Hills Avenue, Bloomfield, CT 06002 USA

The text of this book is set in 10/14 Caslon

Copyedited by Lynne I. Lipkind
Proofread by Beth Richards
Production and design by Victoria Hughes Waters
                    Hughes Publishing Services, Worcester, MA

Printed in the United States of America by Thomson-Shore, Inc.
Text printed with vegetable oil-based ink.

♾ The paper used in this publication meets the minimum requirements of the American
National Standard for Information Sciences—Permanence of Paper for printed Library
Materials, ANSI Z39.48-1984

Library of Congress Cataloging-in-Publication Data

Cheema, G. Shabbir.
Building democratic institutions : governance reform in developing countries /
G. Shabbir Cheema.
    p. cm.
Includes bibliographical references and index.
    ISBN 1-56549-197-1 (pbk. : alk. paper)—ISBN 1-56549-198-X (cloth : alk. paper)
    1. Democracy—Developing countries. 2. Developing countries—Politics and
    government.
I. Title.
    JF60.C487 2005
    320.9172'4—dc22

                                                                 2004022706

14 13 12 11 10 09 08 07 06 05   10 9 8 7 6 5 4 3 2 1   First Printing 2005

TABLE OF CONTENTS

KEY TO ACRONYMS USED IN THE TEXT

ACE Project Administration and Coordination of Elections

ALG Alternative Law Groups

ANC African National Congress (South Africa)

ANFREL Asian Network for Free Elections

BCAP Balilihan Country Action Program (Philippines)

BELA Bangladesh Environmental Lawyers' Association

BNWLA Bangladesh Women Lawyers' Association

CALS Centre for Applied Legal Studies

CARERE Cambodian Resettlement and Reintegration Program

CBO community-based organization

CDF Capital Development Fund

CEDAW Convention on the Elimination of All Forms of Discrimination Against Women

CEDOH Centro de Documentación de Honduras

CHEs complex humanitarian emergencies

CIDA Canadian International Development Agency

COPARMEX Confederación Patronal de la República Mexicana

CPC Criminal Procedure Code

CPIB Corrupt Practices Investigations Bureau (Singapore)

CSO civil society organization

DANIDA Danish International Development Agency

DCEC Directorate on Corruption and Economic Crime (Botswana)

DFID Department for International Development (United Kingdom)

EC-ESA Economic Committee of the Economic and Social Affairs

EMB Electoral Management Body

ESAMI Eastern and Southern Africa Management Institute

EU European Union

FEPADE Special Prosecutor for Electoral Crimes (Mexico)

FINNIDA Finnish International Development Cooperation Agency

FIS Front Islamique du Salut (Algeria)

FLN Front de Libération Nationale (Algeria)

GDP gross domestic product

GERDDES-Afrique Study and Research Group on Democracy and Economic and Social Development in Africa

GNU Government of National Unity (South Africa)

ICAC Independent Commission Against Corruption in Hong Kong

IEA Indian Evidence Act

IEC Independent Electoral Commission (South Africa)

IFE Instituto Federal Electoral

IFES International Foundation for Election Systems

IFP Inkatha Freedom Party (South Africa)

IIDEA International Institute for Democracy and Electoral Assistance

ILO International Labour Organization

IMF International Monetary Fund

INTAN National Institute of Public Administration (Malaysia)

IP Integrity Pace (South Korea)

IPC Indian Penal Code

IPU Inter-Parliamentarian Union

IRI International Republican Institute

IT Information Technology

JIPA Jordan Institute of Public Administration

KPU Indonesia's independent election commission

LDCs Least Developed Countries

LIFE Local Initiative Facility for the Urban Environment

LRC Legal Resource Centre

MAMPU Malaysian Administrative and Manpower Planning Unit

MCA Millennium Challenge Account

MDGs Millennium Development Goals

MIT Massachusetts Institute of Technology

MLAA Madaripur Legal Aid Association

MP Members of Parliament

MSD Management Services Department

NAMFREL National Citizens Movement for Free Elections

NDI National Democratic Institute for International Affairs

NEDEO Network of Domestic Election Observers (Ghana)

NEP New Economic Policy (Malaysia)

NGO nongovernmental organization

NORAD Norwegian Agency for Development Cooperation

NP National Party (South Africa)

OAS Organization of American States

ODA Overseas Development Assistance

OECD Organization for Economic Cooperation and Development

OSCE Organisation for Security and Co-Operation in Europe

PACT Partnership for Capacity Building in Africa

PAP People's Action Party (Singapore)

PBRC Pacific Basin Research Center

PCIJ Philippine Centre for Investigative Journalism

PPI Indonesia's National Election Committee

PRI Institutional Revolutionary Party (Mexico)

PRODERE Area Development and Peace-Building in Central America

PSIS Program for Strategic and International Security Studies

PVT Parallel Vote Tabulation (Indonesia)

SALs Structural Adjustment Loans

SIDA Swedish International Development Cooperation Agency

SPE Professional Electoral Service

TA Technical Assistance

TI Transparency International

TQM Total Quality Management

UAE United Arab Emirates

UN United Nations

UNDESA United Nations Department of Economic and Social Affairs

UNDP United Nations Development Programme

UNESCO United Nations Educational, Scientific and Cultural Organization

UNHCR United Nations High Commissioner for Refugees

UNICEF United Nations Children's Fund

UNMIK United Nations Mission Interim Administration in Kosovo

UNRISD United Nations Research Institute for Social Development

USAID US Agency for International Development

WHO World Health Organization

WSP War-torn Societies Project

PREFACE

Over the past 50 years, the world has experienced many positive changes—the end of the Cold War, the impact of information and communication technologies on the way individuals and nation-states interact, the recognition of global public goods such as environmental improvement and the protection of human rights, global reach of the civil society to promote the interests of the poor and vulnerable groups, and concern for gender equality. These positive changes, however, have been accompanied by widening income gaps between the rich and the poor, inadequate access of the vast majority in developing countries to such basic services as shelter, water and sanitation, primary health care, and economic opportunities; increased intra-national conflicts, drug cartels, and trafficking of human beings. Terrorist and extremist organizations, as exemplified by the September 11, 2001 terrorist attacks in the United States, pose the most serious challenge to peace, security, and personal safety.

Many of the above changes are influenced by globalization, a dominant force in the twenty-first century. It has led to a greater and faster increase in the exchange of goods and services, greater access to knowledge, shrinking time and space, and the emergence of new actors, tools, and rules. It is providing new opportunities for economic activities, technological advancement, and human development. However, many developing countries have not been able to benefit from the opportunities provided by globalization.

How does a country effectively respond to these changes and take full advantage of the new opportunities provided by globalization to improve human development? It is argued that effective, transparent, and accountable governance at the local, subnational, and national level enhances the collective capacity of the country to face the challenges of the twenty-first century. Countries that attract higher levels of investment and trade are those that have relatively better government systems—where rules and policies are predictable, where law and order is maintained, where the governments invest in human capital including in health and education, and where property rights are protected. Governance is the process through which actors from the state, the civil society, and the private sector articulate their interests, exercise their rights and obligations, and mediate their differences. It has three interrelated dimensions—political, economic, and social.

Governance for the twenty-first century has many attributes: It is transparent and accountable to the people; it is based on the separation of powers between the executive, legislative, and judicial branches; it derives its legitimacy from free and regular elections; it devolves power and resources to subnational and local governments; and it provides for multiparty system and freedom of the press. It is based on the paradigm shift in the role of the state from controlling to providing a macroeconomic and microeconomic environment that creates incentives for efficient economic activities; establishes and enforces institutional arrangements such as law and order, rules, and property rights to domestic and international investment; and provides basic social services and a framework for human resource development.

The centrality of governance in promoting development has been recognized by policymakers and development practitioners in developing countries, as well as by bilateral donors, multilateral organizations, and the global civil society. Over the past few years, the series of United Nations conferences and summits, the landmark Millennium Declaration of the United Nations, and the Millennium Development Goals highlight governance as the necessary condition for alleviating poverty, improving access of the poor to services, providing economic opportunities to all segments of society, and creating a framework for political and economic participation of people in the development process.

Three factors prompted me to write this book: (1) the need to learn from practice in governance and public sector institution-building in developing countries, (2) the need to examine the role of globalization and international development in spreading ideas of democratic governance, and (3) the need to identify conditions that make democratic governance possible. My objective is to contribute to the theory of governance by examining innovations and good practices, thereby reducing the existing wide gap between theory and practice. The sources of data are published case studies of governance practice or those available through the Internet, academic studies undertaken by scholars, and my own experience over the past 25 years in working with institutions and entities in developing and developed countries to design and evaluate urban development, rural development, and institutional reform and governance programs.

Over the years, I have learned a great deal from my colleagues, policymakers and development practitioners from developing countries, and scholars of democracy and development. I am grateful to many former colleagues for discussions about the determinants of governance practice and their points of view concerning alternative conceptual frameworks to understand the phenomenon of governance. I would particularly like to thank Linda Maguire, Robertson Work, Mounir Tabet, Kristinn Helgason, Pratibha Mehta, Georges Chaplier, Samina Kamal, Randi Davis, Thord Palmlund, Ken Sherper, Bahman Kia, Rebecca Rios-Kohn, Pauline Tamesis, Fred Schenkelaars, Peter Blunt, Maria Zwanikken, Abdul Magid Osman, Carina Parelli, and Jose Cruz-Osorio. The views expressed in this book are entirely mine and should not be attributed to any of them. Adam Przeworski from New York University, Dennis Rondinelli from University of North Carolina, Chapel Hill, and Julie Fisher from the Kettering Foundation provided critical comments and suggestions on earlier drafts of the manuscript. Andrea Snyder assisted in the preparation of the bibliography.

I am grateful to my family—Sharon, Zach, and Yasmeen—to whom this book is dedicated, for their constant support and patience, which enabled me to work long weekends and holidays to complete the manuscript.

The views expressed in the book are entirely mine and do not necessarily reflect the views of the United Nations or its Member States.

G. Shabbir Cheema
Scarsdale, New York
January 10, 2005

CHAPTER 1

DEMOCRACY, GOVERNANCE AND DEVELOPMENT

Over the past two decades, considerable progress has been made across the globe in economic, technological, and social development.[1] As the speed, size, and integration of the global economy increases, the global community in turn has become smaller and more interconnected. Travel, the Internet, and multimedia advances make information more accessible to more people, faster than ever before. Global concerns such as human rights, the environment, and crime bring citizens from diverse backgrounds together to work for a common purpose. As a result, civil society has grown and become more globalized in its membership and agenda. Every region in the world reduced adult illiteracy rates from 1990 to 1997, with Sub-Saharan Africa seeing the largest (albeit still modest) reduction of eight percent.[2] The percentage of people living in extreme poverty in the world has been gradually declining from 29 percent in 1990 to 23 percent in 1999. There has also been an encouraging increase in the number of countries that has implemented antipoverty action plans at the national level.

However, despite these gains, serious gaps remain. Although the wealth of the world in general has increased, the gap between rich and poor has widened. In the past 10 years, a smaller and smaller percentage of the world's population has controlled a larger and larger percentage of the world's wealth. The figures are startling: the top fifth of the people in the richest countries enjoy 82 percent of the expanding export trade and 68 percent of foreign direct investment—the bottom fifth, barely more than one percent.[3] In 19 out of the 41 Least Developed Countries (LDCs), people were poorer in the 1990s than in the previous decade on a per capita basis. Disparities between rich and poor are also evident in how they access and use improved information, communication, and transit technology. For example, computer and Internet technology remains prohibitively expensive in many developing countries; and a quarter of the world's countries have not reached the basic minimum standard of one telephone for every 99 citizens.[4] The absolute number of illiterates in the world is increasing because of population growth. Forty-two percent of the poor (living on $1 a day or less) were in South Asia, 27 percent in Africa, and 24 percent in East Asia and the Pacific.[5] And it is still true today that regardless of where they live, the poor are more likely to lack access to goods and services, to live shorter lives and to be the victims of violent conflict.

Terrorists and extremist organizations, drug cartels and the trafficking of human beings are seriously affecting human security in developing and developed economies alike. The September 11, 2001 terrorist attacks in the United States have brought to the attention of the world the global reach of the extremist organizations and the frightening consequences of their actions concerning personal safety, peace and security, potential tensions among different segments of the society, and pressures on the state institutions to balance security concerns with the protection of human rights of all citizens.

There are many causes of human deprivation in developing countries—lack of income to obtain the basic necessities including food, shelter, and health and education services; and the low level of people's assets including skills, land, access to infrastructure, savings, credit, and networks of contacts.[6] Experience, however, suggests that the ability of the people to organize themselves to participate in the political process and influence national and local policies and programs is the single most important factor in improving human conditions.

Democracy and good governance—that is, the democratic institutions and the quality of the processes and practice of governance—are critical factors that influence the development process and human conditions. When governance is democratic—that is, infused with the principles of participation, rule of law, transparency, and accountability, among others—it goes a long way toward improving the quality of life and the human development of all citizens.

THE EVOLUTION OF DEMOCRACY
IN DEVELOPING ECONOMIES

Today we are witnessing an upsurge in the popularity of democracy as the most critical vehicle to fulfill individual aspirations, articulate interests and nurture the civil society.[7] Myriad political systems and cultures adhere to the fundamental values of respect for human dignity, justice, equity, participation, and accountability that underpin human rights, democracy, and good governance. Even as democracy proliferates, however, its nature and models diversify.[8] This is especially true for developing and newly democratic countries in which variables such as cultural and political differences, economic and social development, the history of democratic governance, and globalization impact the way in which (and the pace at which) democracy evolves.

For the first time in history, there are more democratic states than nondemocratic states. Indeed, some view the rise of democracy as perhaps the most important event to have transpired in the twentieth century.[9] The 2001–2002 survey of Freedom House—Freedom in the World—reports that about 65 percent of the world's population lives in free or partly free states that afford their citizens some degree of basic rights and civil liberties.[10] The survey also showed that of the world's 192 countries, 121 (63 percent) were "electoral democracies." This is a significant change from 1987, when only 66 out of 167 countries (40 percent) were in this category.[11] The Freedom House survey goes on to point out that human liberty steadily expanded throughout the twentieth century and, "when viewed from the perspective of the century as a whole, democracy and civil liberties have made important and dramatic progress."[12] The United Nations studies show that since 1980, "81 countries have taken significant steps in democratization, with 53 military regimes replaced by civilian governments."[13]

Significant advances in democratization have taken place during the last two decades of the twentieth century—including the fall of military dictatorships in Latin America such as in Ecuador and Peru, the emergence of "new democracies" in Central and Eastern Europe after the fall of the Berlin Wall, and the ousting of long dictatorial regimes in Africa and Asia including those in Mali, Malawi, and the Philippines. The progress in democratization has been the slowest in the Arab Region, with only four out of the 17 countries having multiparty electoral systems, though there have been increased opportunities for people's participation in Jordan, Tunisia, and Morocco. Furthermore, towards the end of the 1990s, some of the world's new democracies either reverted to authoritarianism or slowed down their democratization process—including Sierra Leone, Belarus, Cameroon, and Uzbekistan.[14]

This is not to say that democracy is inapplicable to more recent transitions. Indeed, as Safty points out, "from Poland to Yemen, from Bulgaria to Taiwan (province), from Mauritius to Guatemala, and from Albania to Nigeria, democratization seemed to respond to a universal human yearning for freedom and life with dignity, undiminished by our cultural diversity and ethnic differences."[15] Particularly because newer democracies face many challenges their older siblings did not, democracy has proven to be a flexible and adaptable system under a variety of circumstances.[16]

An expanding climate of consolidating and consolidated democracies gives way to the corresponding attempt to define democracy in a meaningful way.

Seymour Martin Lipset describes the two major current alternative definitions of democracy as "minimalist" and "maximalist." Lipset himself adopts a minimalist definition, viewing democracy as a "political system of political rights that specifies how leadership should be designated at the highest national level in a policy."

The maximalist definition, on the other hand, enumerates various rights and liberties that have to be associated with a competitive and inclusive system of government.[17] Larry Diamond uses the maximalist definition of democracy as encompassing "not only a civilian, constitutional, multiparty regime, with regular, free and fair elections and universal suffrage, but organizational and informational pluralism; extensive civil liberties (freedom of expression, freedom of the press, freedom to form and join organizations); effective power for elected officials; and functional autonomy for legislative, executive and judicial organs of government."[18] The process of developing democracy, however, leads to different forms and stages.[19]

In the late 1990s, it became popular to discuss the ascendancy of the "illiberal" strain of democracy over the "liberal"—the latter being defined in maximalist terms as "a political system marked not only by free and fair elections, but also by the rule of law, a separation of powers, and the protection of basic liberties of speech, assembly, religion and property," and the former being defined as the erosion of "basic constitutional practices."[20] If democracy is only defined in terms of elections, then it is possible to have an illiberal democracy—one in which the people freely choose a government that subsequently curtails their rights. This presupposes that constitutional liberalism and elections are two separable strands that make up democracy.[21]

As the following chapters show, the emergence of different elements of liberal democracy in developing countries may move in different directions and follow different routes and sequences. Electoral democracies can become more democratic or less democratic. Similarly, liberal democracies can improve or decline in their levels of accountability and responsiveness.[22]

THE CONCEPT OF GOVERNANCE AND GLOBALIZATION

When most people hear the word "governance" they think of "government." After all, both have "govern" as their root word. But governance is about more than just government. It is a complex yet universal force that exists in all societies. People use governance in their daily lives to manage human relationships, just as corporations and countries use it to manage their interaction and activities.

Governance is a neutral concept comprising the complex mechanisms, processes, relationships, and institutions through which citizens and groups articulate their interests, exercise their rights and obligations, and mediate their differences. Good governance addresses the allocation and management of resources to respond to collective problems; it is characterized by the principles of participation, transparency, accountability, rule of law, effectiveness, equity, and strategic vision.

In practice, these principles translate into certain tangible things—such as free, fair, and frequent elections; a representative legislature that makes laws and provides oversight; and an independent judiciary that interprets laws. They also translate into the guarantee of human rights and the rule of law, and into transparent and accountable institutions. Good governance also decentralizes authority and resources to local governments to give citizens a greater role in governance. Finally, good governance ensures that civil society plays an active role in setting priorities and making known the needs of the most vulnerable people in society. In sum, governance is good if it supports a society in which people can expand their choices in the way they live; promotes freedom from poverty, deprivation, fear, and violence; and sustains the environment and women's advancement.

When we speak of the quality of a country's governance, then, we mean the degree to which its institutions (such as parliament) and processes (such as the electoral process) are transparent, are accountable to the people, and allow them to participate in decisions that affect their lives. It is also the degree to which the private sector and organizations of the civil society are free and able to participate. "Good" or "democratic" governance is when the authority of the government is based on the will of the people and is responsive to them. It is when open, democratic institutions allow full participation in political affairs and when human rights protections guarantee the right to speak, assemble, and dissent. And it is when government and governmental institutions are pro-poor and promote the human development of all citizens. In short, it distinguishes between the institutions and processes of governance, and their content and quality.

In today's world, governance can no longer be considered a closed system. The state's task is to find a balance between taking advantage of globalization,[23] and providing a secure and stable social and economic domestic environment, particularly for the most vulnerable. Globalization, however, is placing governments under increasing scrutiny, something that may prompt improved state conduct and more responsible economic policies. In developed countries, globalization has also resulted in fewer state-supplied services in favor of private services. And, as the phenomenon of globalization spreads worldwide, it brings with it a proliferation in regional and global institutions that are neither elected by nor accountable to citizens. This has translated into the need for states to develop their capacity to maneuver within a new architecture and to facilitate policies that promote human development locally while protecting national interests globally. Developing countries sometimes lack the capacity to interact with global organizations such as the World Trade Organization, the International Monetary Fund (IMF), and the World Bank, as they sometimes negotiate from a position of weakness.[24] Inadequate access in developing countries to the global market and the high level of agricultural subsidies provided by the developed countries are having a negative impact on the livelihoods of poor farmers in Africa, Asia, and Latin America.

There is also a growing relationship between the quality of governance in developing countries and the aid and investment provided to these countries. Some democracy assistance providers and donors argue that the linking of conditionalities to assistance is a trend in the right direction, and that debt relief and other incentives should be used to prompt political liberalization, while others worry about separating the "winners" from the "losers" and leaving behind those very countries most in need of help.[25] It is important to recognize that external actors are always going to bring to the table certain concepts and conditionalities that are influenced by how they view governance and human development.

In short, good governance has become an important criterion for a country's credibility and respect on the international stage. There are compelling reasons to care about whether the quality of governance is good across the globe.[26] For the good of their own people and for the sake of our common aims, the capacity of weak states to govern should be strengthened because countries that are well governed are both less likely to be violent and less likely to be poor. A country that protects human rights and promotes inclusion is less likely to have citizens who are alienated enough to turn to violence as a means of addressing their problems. And a country where the poor have a voice in their government is more likely to invest in national policies that reduce poverty. When people's interests, needs, and human rights are at the center of governance institutions and practices, there can be real progress in combating poverty.

DEMOCRATIC GOVERNANCE AND DEVELOPMENT

Since 1959, when Seymour Martin Lipset[27] first presented an empirical correlation between a high level of economic development and stable democracy, the debate on the linkages between democratic governance and development has evolved considerably. We will first approach the issue in terms of economic growth alone, and not from a holistic human development perspective. According to Carlos Santiso, this debate has centered primarily on three issues: (1) whether democracy fosters wealth and growth; (2) whether higher incomes and wealth promote democracy; or (3) whether there is a synergistic, combination effect of both.[28]

Different scholars have come up with different answers to the question of whether democracy stimulates economic growth or vice versa. Adam Przeworski and Fernando Limongi conclude that they "do not know whether democracy fosters or hinders economic growth."[29] On his own and more recently, Przeworski has said that while the jury is still out on whether democracies generate economic development or vice versa, democracies are much more likely to survive in wealthy societies.[30] Robert Kaplan, on the other hand, concludes that certain prerequisites are needed in a society before democracy can take root, including a certain level of employment, economic stability, and civil peace.[31] In his view, economic development first will increase the chances that a democracy will be sustainable.

Still other scholars, such as Thomas Carothers, aver that political and economic development are synergistic and must not be artificially separated or sequenced. The argument for "sequencing" is seen by many as artificial and nothing more than a thin veil for authoritarianism. According to this view, it is the poor, and indeed all citizens of a society, who must decide whether they prefer to eat or to vote or to do both. This is a choice that they and no one else can make. And it is only through the exercise of democracy that such a choice can be made.

While it is often claimed that authoritarian regimes are better at bringing about economic development, comprehensive statistical analyses do not back up this hypothesis.[32] First, as Przeworski found, wide-ranging statistical analyses confirm that no linkage can be drawn between authoritarian regimes and economic development. Second, the recent economic crises in South East Asia proved that poor governance and lack of accountability and transparency can derail economic progress.[33] And third, even if nondemocratic governance were proven to promote economic growth, democratic governance has an intrinsic human development value in that it enables political and social participation. This is because human development is a measure of far more than just economic well-being. It is a process of enhancing human capabilities in a way that expands choice and participation.[34] In this way, democracy and its values go to the very heart of human development. Indeed, as Amartya Sen has pointed out, "since democracy and political liberty have importance in themselves, the case for them remains untarnished."[35]

Flowing from the above is the lesson that strategies to improve human conditions can only be sustained and effective in the long term where the affected group is involved at all levels of the decision-making process. Although many types of regimes including nondemocratic ones—such as present-day Cuba or Chile under Pinochet—have been able to reduce poverty in the short term, they have not been able to sustain such efforts. This can only be done through the effective participation of the poor in decisions that affect their lives, and this participation is most completely realized through democratic regimes.

This lesson has been reinforced with many examples from developing countries themselves. In Thailand, for example, local communities are planning their own development projects and mobilizing their own resources to bring them to fruition. In Bangladesh, entire villages, rather than just "the poor" segments, are mobilized to combat poverty through homegrown collective projects. In Bulgaria, local civil society organizations have trained unemployed workers in harvesting and other skills.[36] These are all examples of local government structures and civil society organizations, operating through the principles of democratic governance, directly impacting on the quality of life of disadvantaged communities.

Democracy is not a cure-all for human development and poverty alleviation. As Amy Chua argues in a recent study, elections and free markets in developing countries often lead not to stability and prosperity but to ethnic tensions, discrimination, and concentration of wealth in the hands of a "market-dominant minority" even though the political power of the impoverished majority is increased.[37] Despite the above limitations, democracy still holds more potential for achieving these goals than any other system of government. Democracy creates opportunities for and enhances capabilities of the poor and underprivileged.[38] As such, it has an intrinsic human development value. Moreover, most stable democracies tend to have lower levels of poverty, and, on the flip side, democracies that let their citizens remain in protracted poverty tend to be short lived.

Democratic governance has three distinct advantages over authoritarian regimes.[39] First, democracies are better able to manage conflicts and avoid violent political change because they provide opportunities for the people to participate in the political process of the country. Second, democracies are better able to avoid threats to human survival because of checks by the opposition parties, uncensored criticism of public policies, and the fear of being voted out of office. Third, democracies lead to greater awareness of social development concerns including health, primary health care and rights of women and minorities.

In the aftermath of the September 11, 2001 terrorist attacks on the United States, a debate is taking place in the United States and indeed the whole world about the determinants of the rise of extremist and fundamentalist movements within some Islamic countries. Though the causes of national and international terrorism are highly complex, one of the predominant views being expressed is that the lack of effective democratic institutions and processes in many countries leads to exclusion and fosters extremist organizations because their members do not have adequate opportunities to participate in the political process in the country. The 2001–2002 survey by the Freedom House, for example, showed the "democracy deficit" in the Islamic world, especially in the Arab region. Though the majority of the Muslims in the world live under democratic rule—because of the large size of such Islamic countries as Indonesia, Nigeria, Bangladesh, and Turkey and large number of Muslims in India—only 11 of the 47 countries (23 percent) with Islamic majority had democratically elected governments.[40]

Human development is aimed at expanding people's capabilities and choices that enable them to lead long, healthy, and creative lives and enable them to participate in decision-making affecting their lives. Its characteristics include people's empowerment, equity of opportunities, sustainability, and human security and freedom. By examining the set of these characteristics, a country's development performance and predictors thereof become clearer. These critical generic characteristics include life expectancy, adult literacy, school enrollment, and per capita income.[41]

Also critical to human development performance are characteristics in a society that are both more difficult to quantify and more revealing. These include access to services; participation in decision-making; income disparities; equality of opportunities; level of employment; economic growth by community; health and education indicators; and human security. This is why it is important to disaggregate, wherever possible, human development indicators so that they reveal development disparities along the basis of ethnicity, gender, age or other bases. In line with this, specific indices have been developed to measure such things as gender empowerment, human poverty (including access to water, health services, and sanitation), education, access to information flows, economic performance, macroeconomic structure, environmental status, political life, crime, personal distress, and other components of development.[42]

As we have seen above, democratic governance is the most human-development-friendly system of governance. Why and how do democratic governance specifically affect human development performance? To take first the example of generic human development indicators, democratic governance can help to increase life expectancy, improve adult literacy and school enrollment, and raise per capita income by providing a system of government that responds to the needs of the

and debated and policy options identified. Yet, elections as events are not sufficient to make a country democratic. It is the quality of the electoral process that
promotes democratic governance. Quality in this context implies multiparty
elections, active involvement of civil society organizations, frequency and regu-
larity of elections, and acceptance of election outcomes by the opposition. Also
important are the capacity of electoral management bodies as governing institutions to ensure efficient and transparent conduct of elections based on universally recognized standards. (See chapter 2.)

Promotion of Human Rights Through Inclusive Democracy

Human rights and democratic governance are closely interrelated. In order to
fully utilize their capabilities, citizens must have certain inalienable rights. They
must be free from discrimination, from want, from fear, and from injustice. And
they must be free to develop and realize their potential; to think, speak, and participate; and to work without being exploited.[45] Human rights are indivisible. All
types of human rights are important—social, civil, political, economic, and cultural. Democracy is compatible with all categories of rights—economic, social,
political, cultural, and civil. Democratic governance protects and promotes human
rights through the rule of law, through regular elections and through representative government that solicits citizen participation.

Institutions, mechanisms, and legislation are required both for promotion
and protection of rights by the state and of rights of the state.[46] Four key
defining characteristics of democracy are based on human rights—free and fair
elections contribute to political participation; freedom and independence of
media are conducive to freedom of expression; separation of powers among
branches of government protect people from abuses of their civil and political
rights by other individuals or the state; and encouragement of civil society and
political parties promotes the right to peaceful assembly and association.[47] (See
chapter 5.)

Democracy at the Grassroots Through Decentralization

Decentralization including devolution of power and resources helps to strengthen
the role and capacity of local authorities to become more responsive and accountable to the concerns of local communities and groups. Decentralization and local
governance enable local authorities to involve civil society organizations and the
local private sector in formulating, implementing, and managing plans and policies. Simultaneously, communities and their organizations are empowered to
become equal partners in local governance and development processes that are

pro-poor, progender, and environmentally sustainable. Urban areas present specific challenges and require specific responses in terms of providing for the needs and enhancing the opportunities of the urban poor. In recognition of the role of decentralization in people-centered development and promotion of the values of democracy and good governance, there is a global trend towards decentralization of power and responsibilities from the center to regions, and to local governments.

Decentralization can take four forms: deconcentration of functions from the central government departments to local areas, delegation of authority to semiautonomous bodies to perform specific functions, devolution of power and resources to local governments, and transfer to functions from the government to nongovernmental organizations including the private sector. Devolution of political power and financial resources is the basis of "democracy at the grassroots," though other forms of decentralization also facilitate people's participation in local decisions affecting them. (See chapter 6.)

Strengthening Parliamentary Processes

The legislative branch of government is the principal representative branch of a country's governing institutions. In democratic countries, it is the forum by which people's concerns are voiced in the governing of a country. The role of a legislative branch is generally associated with law making, representation, and oversight. Thus, legislatures play a critical role in shaping human development strategies; determining resource priorities for health, education, and the environment; and creating the enabling environment for the private sector to thrive.

In many developing countries, however, there are major gaps between the theory and practice of legislator-constituent relationships. Single party parliaments—still existing in many developing countries—are not conducive to discussion of alternative points of view. In addition, where parliaments are dominated by feudal groups, major reform efforts are thwarted because of the vested interests of these groups. Lack of education and low income levels prevent constituents from holding their representatives accountable to their needs and aspirations. (See chapter 4.)

Judicial Reform—Improving Access to Justice

Equal and fair administration of justice is among the first pillars of democratic governance. Strong legal and regulatory frameworks—including those pertaining to the constitution and electoral system—and equal access to justice are essential to establishing an environment in which human development can take place. Citizens need to know that laws will be enforced and that the administration of justice will be fair, in order to have faith in the system. In addition, the justice system needs to provide equal access to the poorest and most marginalized in society.

There are several dimensions of the judicial system and access to justice which have direct impact on promoting democratic culture and values: independence of the judiciary from the executive branch; structures and processes including planning for institutional development; human rights enforcement and related dimensions; legal aspects of the environmental protection process; public safety, and the prison system; and access to justice including a legal aid system, promotion of alternative dispute resolution, and public awareness campaigns through civil society and other mechanisms. (See chapter 8.)

The Role of Civil Society and Political Parties

Civil society and political parties play a vital role in deepening democracy and good governance. Civil society is a keystone of democratic governance in that it can act as a galvanizing force for positive social change. Civil society and its organizations represent different voices, perspectives, and values in a pluralistic society. A vibrant and active civil society is a critical element in human development, since it is the part of society that connects individuals with the public realm and the state. Civil society can provide checks and balances on government power, monitor social abuses, and offer opportunities for people to develop their capacities. Today there is a growing dichotomy between domestic and international politics in the sense that civil society is growing on a national level and, at the same time, clarifying its role through global issues such as environment, debt, human rights, crisis, and so on.

Like civil society organizations, political parties are an important vehicle responsible for articulating and aggregating the diverse demands of society. One of the key differences, however—and the reason they are addressed separately here—is that political parties compete for political power and have the ability to directly translate these diverse demands into public policy if voted to power. Where civil society organizations are often issue based, a political party must develop positions on a wide range of issues and approach those from its ideological standpoint. A vibrant multiparty system is essential to the health of democratic governance because it ensures that positions are established ideologically and provides a series of platforms for action that citizens can accept or reject.

Civil society organizations and political parties are directly involved in the electoral process; the functioning of the legislature; the promotion and protection of human rights; anticorruption strategies; decentralization; and local governance systems and governance in crisis and post-crisis situations. In this sense, they are crosscutting and are, therefore, examined in each of the related chapters.

Globalization and Public Sector Management Capacity

Public sector institutions and civil service systems are the institutional foundations of the state's capacity to govern, formulate, and implement development programs and to pursue human development towards poverty eradication. In today's globalized economy, public sector institutions must play new and demanding roles—such as abandoning central planning in favor of strategies that encourage private sector activity and increased investment, rewarding good organizational and individual performance, increasing productivity, and using and managing resources more efficiently. Public sector institutions today need to enable rather than control, to facilitate rather than interfere, and to manage less but more effectively.

Political institutions—electoral management bodies, parliaments, anticorruption bodies, court systems—are more likely to be effective when public sector institutions pursue complementary objectives at the national level and when local officials from the government departments have the capacity and orientation to improve the access of the people to such services as primary health care, agricultural extension, population welfare, education, and low-income housing. Thus, effectively functioning public sector institutions and the capacity of the public sector to lead the process of policymaking and implementation can deepen democracy and good governance and enable the country in question to benefit from globalization. (See chapter 7.)

Integrity in Governance—Combating Corruption

Integrity in governance and anticorruption strategies apply to and impact on not just public institutions but private and civil society organizations as well. The public sector is perhaps the most important, however, because it is responsible for managing and allocating public funds, international assistance, and public goods; therefore its effectiveness, efficiency, and transparency are critical to human development. Integrity in governance—including accountability of public officials, transparency of public decision-making, access to information, and enforceable ethical standards and codes—has significant impact on the institutionalization of democratic political institutions and processes as well as on poverty eradication. Investment by national and international interests are also very much dependent upon investors' confidence in the integrity of governance and the likelihood that someone will be accountable for their capital at the end of the day. (See chapter 3.)

Democratic Governance in Crisis and Post-crisis Situations

Many countries, especially in Africa, find themselves in situations of marked internal and external conflicts that result in social and economic dislocations. During and after crisis, democratic institutions and processes that protect the vulnerable are usually destroyed and need to be rebuilt. Countries in crisis and post-crisis situations must address peculiar problems of democratic governance to restore political legitimacy—the human rights, human security, and livelihoods of the people need to be protected; institutions dealing with the judiciary, police, and public administration need to be rebuilt; political reconciliation among fractured communities needs to be achieved; the displaced population needs to be rehabilitated and integrated; and new elections needs to be organized, usually under the supervision of international observers. Building democracy in such situations requires a holistic approach. (See chapter 9.)

Contextual Factors and the Sustainability of Democracy

And finally, Figure 1 captures contextual factors, which are intended to explore the impact that culture, ethnicity, history, and other factors have on the quality and content of democratic governance institutions and processes. Some suggest that certain cultures are inherently inhospitable to democratic values and institutions. However, a critical analysis of the evolution of the democratic idea and practices, and of the global advance of democracy in governance, suggests otherwise.[48] Democratic governance appeals to and grows out of the universal human values of dignity and freedom. Where democratic governance has failed, it has done so due to imperfect institutions or execution rather than to the "unripeness" of a given country. Indeed, countries possessing such diverse cultures as India, Costa Rica, Mali, Poland, and Indonesia have all come to the conclusion that democratic governance is a positive thing. This is not to say that the process of democratic governance will take the exact same form in each of these countries or that democracy will take root in different societies with the same speed. Local cultures and traditions will impact upon the way democratic values and systems are built and supported.

Independence of media is generally seen as a prerequisite of participatory democracy. Indeed, the media perform an important civic educational function in explaining political processes, positions, and events. Free access to information and ethical print, radio, and televised media are critical if citizens are to stay informed and if government institutions are to be held accountable for their actions. In many democracies it has been the media that have exposed corruption and other abuses of the public trust that have prevented citizens from realizing their full human development. (See chapter 10.)

In addition to internal factors, the pace of democratization is also affected by global forces and the roles of external actors. Bilateral and multilateral development partners are increasingly concerned with effectiveness of development assistance. They are emphasizing the centrality of democratic institutions and practices in promoting people-centered development. Rapid pace of globalization requires systemic changes in internal governance as well global governance architecture. This would ensure that globalization works for all and not for a few. (See chapter 10.)

Also an integral part of Figure 1 is the quality of democratic governance institutions and processes. This draws attention to the degree of access, participation, accountability, transparency, rule of law, etc. that these institutions provide. It is not enough merely to have the architecture of democratic governance in place. Democratic institutions and processes must be infused with the principles of democracy—the most important of which are liberty and equality—in order to work.

It is important when examining the linkages between democratic governance and human development to remember that there is no one size that fits all. That is to say, each country transitioning to or consolidating democracy faces unique contextual factors that will impact upon the pace and nature of change. These include the evolution of democracy (historical and colonial legacies) within a country; the class structure; the history and current status of civil-military relations; the past history of conflict and resolution; geographic and demographic considerations; and the role of international donors.

ABOUT THE BOOK

This book discusses the main issues in building democratic institutions in developing countries of Asia, Africa, Latin America, the Arab region, and Eastern Europe. It not only provides a framework for understanding how governance, democracy, and development are related but also for assessing the conditions that make democratic governance possible. Based on case studies and examples of governance practice, it examines the quality of democratic institutions and processes. It analyses contextual factors—internal and external—that influence the quality of democratic institutions and processes. Institutions are defined as "rules of the game" that emanate from laws, informal norms and practices, and organizational structures.

Chapter 5 examines the relationship between human rights and democratic governance and identifies key elements of the "rights-based approach" to development. After presenting the global framework for human rights, it discusses the impact of democracy on economic, social, and cultural rights, the exclusion and rights of minorities, human rights in crisis situations, and the capacity of human rights institutions in developing countries. The chapter also reviews women's rights and the impact of globalization on human rights situations in developing economies.

The process and mechanisms through which decentralization deepens democracy at the grass roots are examined in chapter 6. It describes the driving forces because of which developing countries have been trying to decentralize decision-making authority and resources. It also presents some good practices of the recent decentralization policies and programs and the factors that influence the choice and impacts of decentralization programs.

Chapter 7 reviews key issues in the public sector capacity to cope with the rapid pace of globalization. It examines the magnitude and impact of globalization on developing economies, the changing role of the state and recent trends in new public sector management in different regions. The chapter presents case studies of public sector innovations as they relate to the changing role of the state and the agenda for reform to provide a conducive framework for democratic institutions.

Chapter 8 describes the experiences of developing countries in improving access to justice by designing and implementing legal and judicial reform programs. It examines the independence of the judiciary and the impact of political environment, and institutional and organizational factors that constrain judicial independence. It presents case studies of access to justice at the local, community level and the role of civil society organizations in providing paralegal services to the poor to protect their interests. Finally, it presents lessons learned from the judicial reform experiences in different regions.

Chapter 9 reviews governance in crisis and post-crisis situations. It explores the potential of democratic governance as a tool for conflict management and resolution, looking at specific components of each. Finally, it presents some examples of rebuilding fractured communities that bring together the issues of governance and conflict in a practical manner.

The contextual factors, internal and external, that contribute to the sustainability of democracy are examined in chapter 10. It starts with a review of the impact of culture and ethnicity on democratic governance with a focus on the relationship between Islam and democracy. It attempts to identify the role of civil-military relations in the consolidation of democracy, the role of the press and mass media, and the impact of poverty on developing democratic institutions. Finally, it analyzes the role and approaches of external partners—including bilateral donors and multilateral organizations—in supporting and promoting democratic governance and examines lessons learned from experience.

ENDNOTES

1. United Nations Development Programme (UNDP), *Human Development Report* (New York: Oxford University Press, 1999), 28–42.

2. UNDP, *Overcoming Human Poverty* (New York: UNDP, 2000), 41–52.

3. UNDP, *Human Development Report* (1999), 28–42.

4. Ibid.

5. UNDP, *Human Development Report* (2003), 53.

6. The World Bank, *Attacking Poverty* (Washington, DC: World Development Report 2001), 31–36.

7. T. Inoguchi, E. Newman and J. Keane eds., *The Changing Nature of Democracy* (Tokyo: United Nations University Press, 1998), 1–19.

8. Ibid.

9. Amartya Sen, "Democracy as a Universal Value," *Journal of Democracy,* 10, no. 3 (1999) 3–17.

10. Freedom House, *Freedom in the World 2001–2002* (December 18, 2001), News Release.

11. Ibid.

12. Ibid.

13. UNDP, *Deepening Democracy in a Fragmented World* (New York: Oxford University Press, 2002), 13.

14. It is important to consider some of the differences between democratic transitions today and those of the more established democracies. Older, Western democracies tended to have three things in their favor that facilitated both transition to and consolidation of democracy. These were economic prosperity and equality (enhanced by early industrialization); a modern and diversified social structure in which a middle class plays a primary role; and a national culture that tolerates diversity and prefers accommodation. Today, however, many countries—

particularly in the developing world—are struggling to consolidate democracies. In very poor and sometimes ethnically divided countries, the preconditions of the older democracies do not prevail.

15. Adil Safty, *The Global Advance of Democracy in Governance* (New York: Management Development and Governance Division, UNDP, 2000), 6. Long-established democracies face their own unique challenges. In consolidated democracies, there is a growing trend of apathy and disillusionment, with respect to politics, particularly among young voters, whereas in emerging democracies voter turnout tends to be high and many democratic movements are led by youth.

16. Ibid.

17. Seymour Martin Lipset, "Prospects for Democracy," Paper, Conference of New and Restored Democracies, December 4–6, 2000, 1–8.

18. Larry Diamond, *Promoting Democracy in the 1990s: Actors and Instruments, Issues and Imperatives: A Report to the Carnegie Commission on Preventing Deadly Conflict* (Washington, DC: The Commission, 1995).

19. Larry Diamond, *Developing Democracy: Toward Consolidation* (Baltimore, MD: Johns Hopkins University Press, 1999), 14. These forms and stages are "electoral democracy" with a minimum level of freedom of speech, press, organization, and assembly; "liberal democracy," which, in addition to elections, requires the absence of reserved seats for military or other groups, horizontal accountability of the office holders to one another, and "extensive" mechanisms and provisions for individual and group freedom and political and civic pluralism; "midrange conception" that falls between an electoral and liberal democracy including various degrees of freedom of expression but weaknesses in the rule of law; and "pseudodemocracies and nondemocracies" that are less than minimal democracies but are not like purely authoritarian regimes because they "lack at least one key requirement: an arena of contestation sufficiently fair that the ruling party can be turned out of power."

20. Fareed Zakaria, "The Rise of Illiberal Democracy" in *Foreign Affairs*, 76, no. 6 (Nov./Dec. 1997), 1–2.

21. Ibid.

22. Diamond, *Developing Democracy*, 19.

23. That is the rapid development and global proliferation of new technologies and telecommunications, and the continuing integration of the world economy through trade and investment.

24. UNDP, *Human Development Report* (1999).

25. Note on 2000 USAID Democracy and Governance Partners Conference, 30 November to 1 December 2000, Washington, DC.

26. Furthermore, good governance provides the setting for equitable distribution of benefits from growth. In short, more peaceful and more prosperous nations contribute to a more peaceful and more prosperous world.

27. Seymour Martin Lipset, "Some Social Requisites of Democracy: Economic Development and Political Legitimacy," *American Political Science Review* 53 (1959), 69–105.

28. Carlos Santiso, "Democratic Governance: Economic and Political Development in New Democracies," Background Paper for the International Institute of Democracy and Electoral Assistance (Stockholm: IIDEA, 1997).

29. Adam Przeworski and Fernando Limongi, "Political Regime and Economic Growth," *Journal of Economic Perspectives,* 7 (Summer 1993).

30. Adam Przeworski, *Democracy and Development: Political Institutions and Well-Being in the World, 1950–1990* (Cambridge: Cambridge University Press, 2000), 178–179.

31. Robert Kaplan, "Was Democracy Just a Moment?" *The Atlantic Monthly* (December 1997).

32. Indeed, some statistical analyses point to a weak negative relation between political rights and economic development, while others find a strongly positive one. The correlation seems to depend on a range of factors, including history, type of democratic transition, resources, societal structure, etc.

33. Sen, "Democracy as a Universal Value," 1–17. A recent study by the United Nations shows that there are reasons to believe that democracy and growth are compatible. The study points out that, with two exceptions, the world's richest countries with per capita income of $20,000 or more have the most democratic regimes. See United Nations Development Programme, *Deepening Democracy in a Fragmented World* (New York: Oxford University Press, 2002), 56.

34. UNDP, *Human Development Report* (2000).

35. Sen, "Democracy as a Universal Value."

36. UNDP, *Overcoming Human Poverty* (2000), 55–61.

37. Amy Chua, *World on Fire: How Exporting Free Market Democracy Breeds Ethnic Hatred and Global Instability* (New York: Doubleday, 2003).

38. IIDEA, "Democracy and Poverty: Is There A Missing Link?" Aide Memoire for 2000 Democracy Forum, Stockholm, 2000.

39. UNDP, *Deepening Democracy in a Fragmented World,* 56–58.

40. Freedom House, *Freedom in the World 2001–2002,* 2.

41. UNDP, *Human Development Report* (2000).

42. ———. *Human Development Report* (2000).

43. Ibid.

44. Lord Meghnad Desai, "Poverty and Governance," Unpublished paper, Management Development and Governance Division, UNDP, New York, 2000.

45. UNDP, *Human Development Report* (2000).

46. Ibid.

47. Ibid.

48. Safty, *Global Advance of Democracy.*

CHAPTER 2

ELECTIONS AND DEMOCRACY

Free, fair, and regular elections constitute one pillar of democratic governance. Such elections confer and sustain political legitimacy because they reflect popular participation and choice in the political process. As such, they are an important first step in crafting government of, by, and for the people. Free, fair, and regular elections also hold out the promise of leadership that alternates. That is, they provide losing parties and candidates with incentives to remain participants in the process, through, for example, the promise of winning future elections, or through power-sharing arrangements that incorporate the opposition. In this way, elections set ground rules for a game in which the winner cannot take all with finality. Elections provide the direct participation, choice, and, ultimately, accountability that translate into a higher degree of inclusion and, consequently, less alienation and cause for violent dissent.

Contested and regular elections may also bring about a "correspondence" between public policy and the wishes and aspirations of the voters. Many reasons for this can be discerned:[1] (1) The politicians who are seeking election or re-election are more likely to support public policies that the voters desire. (2) Voters can use the election as an opportunity to select good types as often reflected in the voter preference for principles and consistency. (3) The voters' ability to monitor the performance of the incumbents provides an incentive for the elected public officials to "listen" to the public policy preferences of voters.

This chapter describes the evolution of elections and the global norms and standards for their administration. This is followed by five recent case studies of elections in developing economies (South Africa, Ghana, Indonesia, Mexico, Kyrgyzstan). Based on these case studies and other literature, key issues in the electoral process are identified including the legislative framework, voter education, the use of information technology, the use of international observers, and the role of political parties, the media, and civil society organizations. The final section examines the role and the capacity of electoral management bodies in improving the quality and effectiveness of the electoral process.

THE EVOLUTION OF ELECTIONS

Over the past 25 years, elections have gained increasing recognition for their central role in democracy. If one argues that the democratic method is the institutional arrangement to arrive at political decisions in which individuals gain the power to decide by competing with others for the people's vote, then elections can be used as the central determinant for democracy. Along the same lines, in 1991, Samuel Huntington embraced this procedural definition of democracy because it focuses on elections as the practical manifestation of the two critical dimensions of democracy—contestation and participation.[2] He does go on, however, to give some qualitative aspects to his definition, stating that it also "implies the existence of those civil and political freedoms to speak, publish, assemble, and organize that are necessary to political debate and the conduct of electoral campaigns."[3]

Some argue that elections are necessary but not sufficient for deepening and sustaining democracy. While recognizing that elections are "an important virtue of governance" Fareed Zakaria, in his recent book on the future of freedom, states that "the heart of building democracy is building the institutions of liberty, not holding quick elections."[4] He adds that the "institutions of liberty" implies a functioning judicial system accessible to the people, free press, free speech, multiple political parties, economic reform, civic institutions—all of these anchored in a constitution supported by the main political forces in the country.

On a practical level, it is interesting to compare the evolution of elections—in terms of their phases and types—with the evolution of democracy over the past 25 years or so. Generally speaking, as democracy has improved so too have elections. First, in terms of frequency, there are far more elections taking place today than there were 25 years ago. This is due to a number of factors—i.e., that there are more states in existence, that more of them are democratic, and that democracy means holding fairly frequent elections. Electoral democracies today constitute 120 of the 192 internationally recognized independent polities.

A number of factors contributed to the rise of elections in the 1980s and 1990s, including newfound cohesiveness of opposition forces, liberalization by autocratic leaders and the collapse of the Soviet Union. The rise in the number of elections stemmed at least in part from the miscalculation of authoritarian leaders when faced with pressures to democratize. During the third wave, authoritarian leaders sought to "democratize" through elections because they did not think that they would lose these elections. At the same time, many of these first-ever multiparty elections were boycotted by opposition parties that feared co-option or the appearance of legitimizing possibly undemocratic processes. Huntington sums up these two tendencies in saying that "[t]he lesson of the third wave seems clear: authoritarian leaders who wanted to stay in power should not have called elections; opposition groups who wanted democracy should not have boycotted the elections authoritarian leaders did call."[5] One might say, then, that a true transition to democracy has occurred when there is a competitive selection of leadership and there is broad-based acceptance of the results of that competitive selection process (i.e., the rules of the democratic game).[6]

Intimately tied to the trend toward elections has been the international community's role in supporting the democratization process. Some place the significant beginning of the modern international interest in democratization with the Kennedy Administration in the early 1960s in the United States. Kennedy made a big push to link development aid and democracy[7] and this translated into the creation of the US Agency for International Development (USAID) and proactive democratic initiatives in countries emerging from decolonization. The 1970s witnessed a decline in the interest to promote democracy abroad, although this interest was resuscitated in the late 1980s and early 1990s. One phenomenon that contributed to the effectiveness of democracy promotion was the rise in international election observation. Indeed, the "emergence and prevalence of the foreign observer phenomenon was a major development of the 1980s and significantly enhanced the importance of elections in the democratization process."[8]

GLOBAL NORMS AND STANDARDS IN THE CONDUCT OF ELECTIONS

Any discussion of global norms and standards in the conduct of elections must begin with the United Nations Declaration of Human Rights, which was adopted by the General Assembly in 1948. Article 21, Section 3 of the Declaration states that "the will of the people shall be the basis of the authority of government; this will shall be expressed in periodic and genuine elections which shall be by universal and equal suffrage and shall be held by secret vote or by equivalent free voting procedures."[9] The minimum basis of global norms and standards in the conduct of elections was thereby established, namely, that voting must be free (i.e., by universal suffrage that is free of intimidation), fair (i.e., by secret ballot that allows equal opportunity to all candidates and voters), and fairly frequent (i.e., so that the people can exercise their choice and participation periodically).

Later, in 1966, the International Covenant on Civil and Political Rights was adopted. Article 25, Section B of the Convention supports the concept contained in the UN Declaration of Human Rights by stating that every citizen has the right "to vote and to be elected at genuine periodic elections which shall be by universal and equal suffrage and shall be held by secret ballot, guaranteeing the free expression of the will of the electors."[10] Other significant endorsements of the election-specific clauses above are to be found in the European Convention on Human Rights (1950); the Conference on Security and Cooperation in Europe's Copenhagen Meeting (1990); and the American Convention on Human Rights, San José Pact (1969). Of course, the United Nations Charter itself also supports these norms and standards of elections through its endorsement of the principle of self-determination, and its declaration that the promotion and protection of human rights constitute one of the organization's central purposes.

Chief among the other international actors developing electoral norms and standards are donor governments and regional organizations that give assistance to new and emerging democracies to improve the conduct of their elections. The US Agency for International Development (USAID) and the Canadian International Development Agency (CIDA) are two of the leading bilateral government entities working in the field of elections. Also providing significant election assistance are the Swedish International Development Cooperation Agency (SIDA), the Norwegian Agency for Development Cooperation (NORAD) and the Danish International Development Agency (DANIDA). On a multilateral level are organizations such as the European Union, the Organisation for Security and Co-Operation in Europe (OSCE), the Organization of American States (OAS), the Commonwealth Observer Group and the Francophonie.

There are also international, regional, and national nongovernmental organizations and political party institutes that have long worked in the area of electoral assistance. These organizations have used and built upon the body of international norms and standards in the conduct of elections. For example, on the international side, the International Institute for Democracy and Electoral Assistance (IIDEA) and the International Foundation for Election Systems (IFES) have approached elections from both the theoretical side by building a solid body of experience and lessons learned in the field, and from the very practical side by supplying technical expertise and election materials to election authorities. There are also political party institutes such as the US-based National Democratic Institute for International Affairs (NDI) and International Republican Institute (IRI) that have provided technical expertise to political parties, election officials, and elected representatives and have also observed elections with a view to providing constructive suggestions on how the process can be improved. There are also the German *Stiftungs* (e.g., Friedrich Ebert and Konrad Adenauer), which are the main providers of assistance to political parties in much of the developing world. This assistance ultimately impacts upon how the assisted parties contest elections and govern if they win. On a regional level, organizations such as the West Africa–based Study and Research Group on Democracy and Economic and Social Development in Africa (GERDDES-Afrique) have made a name for themselves as independent and impartial observers of both elections and the democratization process in the region. Finally, on a national level, groups such as National Citizens Movement for Free Elections (NAMFREL) in the Philippines were groundbreakers in the concept of domestic groups observing—often in conjunction with international groups such as NDI—and commenting on the conduct of elections.

In offering electoral assistance, all of the international actors discussed above act upon a request from the country conducting the election. Some require a formal written request from the government or electoral authority. In such cases, the observer group would normally issue a statement at the end of the election commenting on its administrative and other aspects. Some organizations, however, in the absence of a formal request, may unofficially "monitor" the polling and refrain from issuing a statement at the end. Others work exclusively with domestic monitoring groups in a given election and only observe the balloting through the work of the national observers. Over the past 10 years or so, international election monitoring has grown in popularity and impact. The tools at the disposal of election monitors have also grown more sophisticated, as such things as Parallel Vote Tabulation (PVT), "quick counts," and improvements in computer and information technology have made election fraud more difficult. International and national organizations have also built up a practice of issuing statements that are progressively moving away from the "free and fair" declarations in favor of a more detailed and constructive statement of the positives and negatives of the election.

THE PRACTICE—CASE STUDIES

Election is both a process and an event. Over the past decade, several elections that took place in developing countries indicate their complexities and country peculiarities. At the same time, there are a number of issues faced in electoral process that are common to democracies. This section describes five of the elections in the past few years which have drawn a great deal of interest on the part of the international community. Based on these and other examples, the last section of the chapter identifies specific issues and policy and program responses to deal with them.

South Africa (1994)—Transition to Post-apartheid Era

The April 27, 1994, general election in South Africa was a truly inspiring display of democracy in the making.[11] Nineteen political parties contested the election, which ended in the formation of a multiparty legislature tasked with selecting the head of a government of national unity (Nelson Mandela, leader of the ANC party) and with approving the final draft of an interim constitution. The election was also remarkable for its role in the conflict resolution and reconciliation processes in post-apartheid South Africa. Many observers attribute these positive developments to the relatively slow pace of the transition process and to South Africa's selection of proportional representation as an electoral system, which was all the more remarkable given the long history of first-past-the-post, single-member district elections.

The electoral system put in place during the transition process was one of proportional representation and lists, with half the National Assembly (200 members) being chosen from nine provincial lists and the other half being elected from a single national list. The selection of proportional representation was the result of a long and relatively slow negotiation process between three of the main political actors—the African National Congress (ANC), the National Party (NP), and the Inkatha Freedom Party (IFP)—that began in 1990. The proportional representation allowed these three main parties each to win something significant in the poll. The ANC won a strong majority in the National Assembly and majorities in seven of nine provinces, and the NP and IFP won legislative majorities in their provincial strongholds. Moreover, all three of these parties were represented in an initial government of national unity, which contributed to the stability of the South African transition. After the 1994 elections, a Government of National Unity (GNU) came into being to shepherd what remained of the transition process. The GNU was to last for the first five years of the new South Africa (1994–1999) and be made up of all the parties that gained a minimum of five percent of the seats in the National Assembly.

As for the technical aspects of the election, the electoral law established a fully autonomous Independent Electoral Commission (IEC) composed of 16 high-profile individuals (11 from South Africa and five from abroad) who were appointed as commissioners. The IEC that administered the 1994 elections was ad hoc in nature and did not become a permanent institution until 1996. The IEC had autonomy to appoint its own polling officers and to establish IECs at the provincial and district levels. IEC did an excellent job of training poll workers and sensitizing citizens about the importance and procedures of voting. Polling stations were manned by more than 200,000 local officials and volunteers, and at least 100,000 police officers, soldiers, and reservists. There were approximately 22 million eligible voters in South Africa, of whom 19 million voted. This made the voter participation rate a high 86 percent.

The 1994 election in South Africa was remarkable for many things, one of which was the rare decision not to use an electoral register. Voters were allowed to cast their ballots at any polling station, provided that they showed an identification card demonstrating their proof of South African citizenship. As a control measure, electoral officials stamped voters' hands and identification documents when the voters received a ballot. This system thus combined into one task what are normally two separate functions: verifying voter eligibility and controlling the legitimacy of the voting process.

South Africa used a single, or "unique," ballot that listed all of the 19 parties on it, complete with their symbols and a picture of the party leader. Voters simply had to manage one slip of paper and indicate their choice on it. As for cost, the 1994 election cost an estimated US$11 per voter, extremely expensive compared to most other elections but not unusual for such a transitional event.

There were, however, a number of administrative problems in the 1994 election. These included poor organization of the vote in some areas, with some polling stations not opening at all or some not receiving adequate quantities of ballot papers, and long lines nearly everywhere, causing some voters to return multiple times before being able to cast their votes.

The electoral law allowed political party voting agents to observe the polls. Parties played a key role in the vote verification process. The mass media also played a key role in the election. During the preelection period, the written press, the radio, and the televised press, and even the mass marketing and advertising campaigns, contributed to the ideological liberalization of the society. Public media, especially television time, was allocated on an equitable basis and, by all accounts, television coverage during the election was quite fair.

The watershed 1994 election in South Africa worked because it was the result of a lengthy and comprehensive negotiation process between the key stakeholders. All of these parties were able to reach a consensus on the rules of the game and to accept the people's verdict. As a result, the system of governance put in place had solid foundations and broad-based acceptance and support among the people and the various political leaders. This was evident in the latest South African national elections, held in 2004, which by all accounts were considered fair and transparent.

Ghana (1996)—Institutionalizing the Credibility of Elections

As in many other developing countries, the results of the 1992 elections in Ghana were widely disputed, leading to the mistrust of the electoral process by the opposition groups. One of the challenges after the 1992 elections was to institutionalize the credibility of the electoral process in the country. To achieve this objective, several measures were undertaken by the new Electoral Commission, established in 1993. The Commission dealt with the legitimate concerns of political parties about the compilation of a new voter register, a new voter education program, training for election officials, and advance planning of electoral events. The Commission replaced the old voters' register with the new one in 1995, with active involvement of political parties in planning and implementation of the registration process including the registration form, the structure and content of the register, and related matters. Twenty centers were set up for the purpose of registration. Provision was made for the party agents to challenge a person's application for registration if it did not meet the requirements. After a two-week period of public scrutiny, the provisional register was compiled. Objections raised during the public scrutiny period were resolved by district judicial officials, with the appeals going to the High Court.

Concerning the training of election officials and party agents, the Election Commission identified procedures to be followed during the election. This was followed by practical training for different categories of officials. The Commission launched the public education program to provide basic information to the voters about the election process including mechanisms for voting. The program activities were carried out through the electronic and print media, posters, pamphlets, and discussions with groups such as those of women and young voters. Nongovernmental organizations and religious groups were also involved to disseminate information related to the electoral process. In order to enhance the credibility of the election and to improve people's perception about the fairness of the election, the Commission introduced transparent ballot boxes to avoid the common perception in the 1992 elections of stuffed ballot boxes. Another mechanism to improve the trust of the voters was the establishment of the Inter-Party Advisory Committee, which brought together representatives of the political parties and the Election Commission in regular meetings.

The credibility of the 1996 elections was also enhanced by active involvement of national-level independent observers. Representatives of civil society played an important role in the process. These included the Christian Council of Churches and the Ghana Legal Literacy Resource Foundation. The two organizations which were directly involved in the election process were the Network of Domestic Election Observers (NEDEO) and Ghana Alert. The NEDEO consisted of 23 national organizations including Christian Council, Federation of Muslim Councils, Trade Union Congress, Ghana Journalists' Association, and Bar Association. Ghana Alert and NEDEO together trained more than 4,000 personnel in the country and sent them to all of the 200 constituencies and 3,100 polling stations. The monitoring of elections by these domestic organizations had many advantages—better knowledge of the local environment by the monitors; the ability to observe and report on the situation before, during, and after the elections; the ability to establish a rudimentary parallel vote count to check the cases of fraud; and the Election Commission's enhanced integrity and its independence from the ruling party.

The results of the reform measures introduced by the Election Commission were clear during the 1996 elections—creation of conditions for competitive elections, 78 percent voter turnout, evaluation of the election as fair and transparent by international and domestic observers, and the absence of large-scale post-election violence. The Election Commission showed its independence by deciding that all voters in major cities would be issued photo IDs and that those in rural areas were to get thumbprint IDs. It also resisted pressures to deny accreditation to domestic election observers.

Despite the above achievements, some weaknesses of the electoral reform were observed in the 1996 election—a relatively high level of expenditure for a second transition election, irregularities in the registration process, extensive use of state resources including print and electronic media by the incumbent president, and persistent doubts among the opposition groups about the impartiality of the Election Commission. Most of the funds for the election were provided by the donor community, raising issues about the future independence of the Commission when it is forced to charge the expenditures to the Consolidated Fund.[12]

Indonesia (1999)—Sea Change in the Electoral Process of an Authoritarian Polity

In May 1998, Indonesian President Suharto resigned after 32 years in power. Amid economic, social, and political upheaval, the successor government pledged a more democratic form of government and initiated the transitional process by calling for elections. Legislative elections were scheduled for June 7, 1999.

The June 7, 1999, elections were remarkable for several reasons. They were the first competitive elections held in Indonesia since 1955; they featured fairly good electoral organization of a large geographic area (3,000 miles worth) and population in a short amount of time; and they were marked by a high level of participation on the part of both the electorate and domestic civil society organizations. Voter turnout among Indonesia's more than 112 million eligible voters was also extremely high—estimated at 92 percent—particularly among women. There were no political party boycotts and there was minimal violence, despite a seven-week delay in announcing the results.

The June 7 elections were also noteworthy in that they were organized under a new legal framework that, while complicated, represented an improvement over the previous electoral legislation. The legal framework set up following the resignation of former President Suharto comprised three new laws on: the electoral system, political parties, and the legislative assembly.

The law on the electoral system created an independent election commission (KPU) that established a presence in each region and district. The KPU comprised 48 representatives of political parties running in the election and five representatives of the government. The KPU established the National Election Committee (PPI), which was tasked with completing the voter registration process within one month (April to May 1999). Unfortunately, the KPU's effectiveness was compromised by the fact that it was not a completely independent entity, administratively or financially, from the government. The government appointees controlled 50 percent of the vote in the KPU, the supporting Secretariat reported both to the KPU itself and to the Ministry of Home Affairs, and the KPU did not have control over its own budget.

Another important innovation of the June 1999 election was the involvement of political parties in its organization. Under the new law, political parties were allowed to organize and receive legal recognition; 48 of them did so and presented candidates for the elections. Even more importantly, political parties and candidates accepted the legal framework as the basis for electoral competition. Political parties were represented on electoral bodies at all levels, their agents monitored the voting process at polling stations, and copies of the tally sheets from the vote counts were given to party agents at most precincts.

The law allowed, and the Election Commission accredited, domestic nonpartisan election monitors. An estimated 300,000 Indonesians, mobilized by numerous efforts, including the United Nations, observed the polls as nonpartisan election monitors. Equally significant was the conduct by one of these groups of a parallel vote tabulation (PVT)[13] to verify independently the accuracy of the tabulation of official results. These groups made an enormous contribution to public confidence in the election by organizing and implementing programs to educate voters and mobilize election monitors. These efforts energized broad civic involvement in the political process. More than three million Indonesians served as polling officials, political party agents, and domestic nonpartisan election monitors in over 300,000 polling stations. This effort was all the more impressive given the short time frame for organizing the elections and given the enormous size of Indonesia. Also remarkable was the freedom of the press to cover the campaign period and elections without government interference. This freedom of the press encouraged public confidence in the process and enthusiasm to participate.

International observers also participated in the poll. The National Democratic Institute for International Affairs (NDI) and the Carter Center, working in collaboration and with funding from USAID, sent 100 observers from 23 countries to observe the polls. NDI and the Carter Center maintained close coordination and cooperation throughout the election period, with other international monitoring organizations including the European Union, the National Citizens Movement for Free Elections (NAMFREL), and the Asian Network for Free Elections (ANFREL). NDI and the Carter Center also worked with other international organizations that assisted the electoral process, including UNDP, the International Republican Institute (IRI), the International Foundation for Election Systems (IFES), the Asia Foundation, and the Australian Electoral Commission. In addition, NDI and UNDP operated a joint facilitation center for other international observer groups.

The 1999 elections in Indonesia represented a sea change in governance in that country. They were remarkable for the progress Indonesians were able to make in a brief period of time. These elections cemented Indonesia's transition to democracy and helped build civic participation and confidence in domestic political processes. This was evident in the elections for the National Parliament held in 2004, which by all accounts were considered free and fair and were accepted by parties as legitimate.[14]

Mexico (2000)—Transforming the Electoral Process

The July 2, 2000, general elections marked a democratic watershed in Mexico that was decades in the making. For the first time, the reins of national government changed hands democratically between two political parties, and electoral

institutions that had been discredited through past state manipulation were rehabilitated and, through their performance, Mexico experienced a reinvigoration of
the democratic process.

The success of the 2000 elections rested in large part on the 1996 push to
reform legislative provisions establishing the electoral and political frameworks,
as well as the complete reform of the Instituto Federal Electoral (IFE). The IFE
is the public entity responsible for organizing federal elections in Mexico. It was
created in 1990 pursuant to new electoral legislation and is a permanent, independent, and autonomous entity that is constituted by the legislative branch. The
IFE has responsibility for, among other things, training and civic education; electoral geography; rights and prerogatives of political parties and political groups;
the electoral roll and voters lists; design, printing, and distribution of electoral
materials; preparations for election day; tallying results; declaring valid and issuing certificates for deputies' and senators' elections; and regulating both electoral
observation and opinion polls. The IFE has worked hard since its inception to
develop and sustain its institutional memory. One way in which IFE has done
this is through the creation of the Professional Electoral Service (SPE), a career
system for specialized employees that aims to provide qualified personnel to meet
the needs of the electoral service.

While overwhelmingly positive in their conduct and results, the 2000 elections in Mexico proved the most expensive ever to be organized in Latin America. The cost of the 2000 election was approximately US$850 million, of which
$350 million went to political parties and $500 million to organizing the election.
Among the most important of these activities in this second category were voter
education, neutral media reporting, and training for pollworkers.

The 1994 electoral reform also created a Special Prosecutor for Electoral
Crimes (FEPADE) to address violations of electoral law. The FEPADE's performance during the 2000 elections was disappointing, however, as it failed to
prosecute many violations of vote-buying and voter coercion. As a result of this
deficiency, the Mexican Chamber of Deputies formed its own "watchdog" commission to oversee public spending during the 2000 election year.

Mexico is one of several countries that provides subsidies to candidates and
parties both for routine organizational costs and for election campaigns. On the
other hand, the electoral law also imposes spending limits on candidates that are
dependent upon the size of their district and the office they seek. Mexico is one
of relatively few countries that allow foreign donations for candidates and parties.

The voter turnout rate in the 2000 election was 65 percent of the 59 million
registered voters. In addition, hundreds of thousands of Mexican citizens volun-

teered as polling officials, political party pollwatchers, and nonpartisan election observers. Civil society organizations and political parties played a significant role in ensuring that the 2000 elections were free, fair, and as participatory as possible. Mexican election observer groups, such as Civic Alliance, a nationwide coalition of civic organizations that has monitored national and state elections, Confederación Patronal de la República Mexicana (COPARMEX), and the Mexican Academy of Human Rights, helped to bolster public confidence in the elections through domestic observer efforts and the performance of "quick counts" to verify election results. Political parties trained and deployed their cadres of party pollwatchers who were stationed in thousands of polling sites to watch the voting and counting processes. The 2000 elections also drew hundreds of foreign observers to help monitor the voting process, virtually all of whom were resoundingly positive about the conduct of the election. The 2003 Parliamentary Elections cemented the progress made by Mexico in ensuring the transparency and legitimacy of the electoral process in the country.[15]

Kyrgyzstan (2000)—Election in a Transitional Economy

Kyrgyzstan became independent from the Soviet Union in 1991 and began a transition to democracy and a market economy. Since then, the Central Asian republic has made significant progress in its transition with the aid of a well-educated population, a democratic constitution, reform-minded authorities at the highest national levels, a free press, and a growth of civil society organizations. The country, however, has also confronted numerous obstacles to its democratic process, including the dissolution of the parliament in 1995 and the flawed conduct of the October 1998 referendum, the October 1999 local elections, and the February and March 2000 parliamentary elections. Further, the country lacks strong judicial, legislative, and anticorruption institutions, features an overly strong executive branch, and is struggling with corruption.

Adding to these obstacles were the extremely problematic presidential elections Kyrgyzstan held on October 29, 2000. Indeed, most observers declared that serious flaws in the preelection period and on election day translated into an overall electoral process that fell short of international standards. The elections also failed to comply with the OSCE commitments to which the Kyrgyz government voluntarily agreed. Despite what was considered an adequate electoral framework and competent administrative preparedness, patterns of state-led interference and political harassment appeared to point to weak political will on the part of the government to ensure that Kyrgyz citizens enjoyed the opportunity to participate in free and fair elections.

Askar Akayev was elected president of the newly independent Kyrgyzstan in 1991, was reelected in 1995, and declared his candidacy for the October 29 election despite some constitutional confusion as to whether this was allowed. The constitutional court had ruled in 1998 that Mr. Akayev was eligible to run; again in 2000 because the current constitution was adopted after his first election, however, many remained convinced that the prohibition against more than two terms should have applied to Mr. Akayev. The electoral framework put in place prior to the presidential elections featured many questionable provisions that seemed designed to eliminate candidates rather than regulate the process. For example, the election law provided for a Kyrgyz language test to be administered to potential candidates by the Central Election Commission. Although the constitution requires the president to have a command of the state language, neither the constitution nor the election law specifies how this competency should be measured. Seven of 19 potential candidates failed the examination, which was administered in a subjective manner that was neither public nor uniform.

The Central Election Commission, which established a presence at the district and town levels, established a total of 2,090 polling stations throughout the country. The electoral code in Kyrgyzstan provides for a high level of transparency for the tabulation of results, allowing observers and candidates the possibility to audit the aggregation of results at all levels. Unfortunately, it appears that this high level of transparency for the tabulation of results was compromised by serious violations before the results were entered into the computerized system.

During the period prior to the presidential election in Kyrgyzstan, several independent media outlets were confronted with judicial proceedings or harassment from officials in response to election-related articles. Some journalists reported receiving pressure from government authorities to pursue or avoid specific election-related topics. In addition, civil society groups were limited in their access to the polls. The Central Electoral Commission refused to register the main coalition of NGOs so that its members could monitor the October 29 presidential election, saying that the coalition had not been formally registered by the Ministry of Justice. Parliament became involved in this affair and on October 21 the chairmen of three Kyrgyz parliamentary committees issued a joint statement calling on the Central Electoral Commission to allow the coalition to observe the polls, but to no avail.

In the end Askar Akayev was reelected for a third five-year term as president of Kyrgyzstan, defeating five rival candidates and officially winning approximately

75 percent of the vote. Voter turnout was estimated at 64 percent. The OSCE declared that the poll failed to comply with OSCE commitments, and the National Democratic Institute for International Affairs (NDI) issued a critical report citing as problems the exclusion from the ballot of prominent opposition candidates, pressure on voters to cast their ballot for the incumbent, interference by local authorities in the election process, and propaganda on behalf of the incumbent by most media outlets.[16]

KEY ISSUES IN ELECTIONS

A number of ingredients go into making elections free, fair, and regular, and determine how conducive elections ultimately are to the democratic process. The aforementioned elections in five developing economies and other recent elections highlight the significance of the following issues in ensuring free and fair elections—and the subsequent deepening of democracy.

Legislative Framework

Perhaps the most important factor in determining the quality of elections is the package of laws—comprising the constitution, electoral legislation, administrative regulations, and codes of conduct—that determine the rules of the electoral game. These rules can be neither too stringent nor too flexible—they must be "coherent, complete, systematic and fully applicable,"[17] so as to lend the utmost credibility to the system. Moreover, the legislative framework should be sustainable over the long term and therefore reflect the "institutional, economic and administrative level of the country."[18] To varying degrees, each of the above case studies of elections shows the significance of electoral legislation, administration regulation, and code of conduct. It is the legislative framework that determines the type of regime—presidential, parliamentarian, mixed, etc.—and the electoral system—majority-plurality, semi-proportional, proportional representation, or a combination thereof. In its transition to democracy after decades of authoritarian regime, Indonesia, for example, has been struggling with the legislative framework that can lead to a transparent and stable electoral process. It has found it easier to delineate a package of electoral laws but extremely difficult to make it work in practice. The 2004 parliamentary elections, however, show progress in the quality of electoral process. For South Africa, the legislative framework reflected a transformation of the political system. Cambodia is an example of a country in a post-crisis situation.

Most constitutions outline only the broad strokes of an electoral system and leave the specifics to the electoral law and decrees. When deriving an electoral system, the important determinants include the selection of electoral formula, the delineation of constituencies, the choice of voting system, and the administration of responsibility for elections.

In many democratic transitions, Krygyzstan for example, it is reform of the legislative framework that becomes the galvanizing issue. In some West African countries in the early 1990s, where Ministries of the Interior traditionally organized elections, opposition forces seized upon revisions to the legislative framework—through the creation of independent election commissions—as a means to achieve more profound democratic changes. Today there persists strong debate over the legislative framework and, more specifically, the electoral laws in countries such as Côte d'Ivoire, Cameroon, and Togo.

The legislative framework also delineates two other important elements of elections—namely, the voting method used and the frequency with which elections take place. The constitution will usually contain reference to the terms of executive and legislative officials, thereby establishing the electoral timetable. In some parliamentary systems (e.g., Canada, United Kingdom), however, general elections can be called by the Prime Minister at any point during his or her leadership. In this instance, the electoral body is given a set timetable during which to organize elections. It is the electoral law and other decrees that explain the precise voting method to be used—for example, the type of ballots used, how they are cast and counted, how the itinerant, illiterate, and other citizens are to vote and what kind of assurances are in place to prevent fraud. As the case studies in this chapter show, voting methods were key issues in South Africa, Ghana, and Indonesia.

Voter Rolls and Registration

Prior to an election there are few more contentious issues than the composition of the voter rolls and the system put in place to correct outdated rolls and register new voters. Indeed, "free and fair elections are not generally considered possible without a means of verifying legitimate voters."[19] The case studies of Benin and Peru show how verification of legitimate voters is crucial to enhance the legitimacy of an election. Mexico presents a good practice of the process of voter role and registration due to the active involvement of different groups including the civil society and political parties. There are a variety of methods used to compose and maintain voter rolls and to register new voters. Among these are maintaining a periodic list (that is reproduced at each election), establishing a permanent list (that is maintained and updated perpetually), and using a civil registry (from which a voters' list will be culled in times of elections). Each system has its advantages and disadvantages. For example, maintaining a periodic list can be a useful and galvanizing voter education tool but it requires considerable resources and efficiency. On the other hand, establishing a permanent list implies quicker readiness but it relies heavily on the initiative of citizens to update their own; information. Use of a civil registry is cheaper than the other two alternatives, however, it renders the electoral authority dependent upon the government for information.

Role of Political Parties

Political parties—and their candidates—are at the very heart of elections. Parties, embodied by their leaders and candidates, vie for political power, shape issues, and represent voters' interests. Political parties play different roles depending upon the legislative framework. For example, in Uganda, where political parties were officially outlawed, de facto parties have instead sprung up in the form of issue-based parliamentary coalitions. Also, how a party selects its candidates is quite significant to the choice voters ultimately have. Many countries employ a list system where parties internally derive a list of candidates that is then submitted to the voters. In other countries, political parties hold primary elections—sometimes open only to registered members of the party and sometimes open—to winnow down the candidates that are ultimately submitted to the full electorate. And, in most systems there is the phenomenon of independent candidates who run outside of the political party system. The legislative framework is also important in terms of defining the role political parties play in organizing elections (i.e., political party composition of the election commission, role and conduct of party poll watchers, etc.), and in defining whether party-based electoral provisions are centralized or decentralized.

In emerging democracies, there are often acute inequalities—in terms of resources, name recognition, and platform development—between ruling and opposition political parties (Benin, Mali, Peru, Mexico). These inequalities often manifest themselves most acutely in the mobilization and allocation of resources and in access to state media. In developing countries that have been dominated by the presence of one party, there is the need to "level the playing field" with respect to other parties. This leveling would include providing all parties with access to state media and resources on an equitable basis. New parties also need assistance, which is sometimes provided through international organizations, in developing campaign strategies, election calendars, and resource mobilization methods. Campaign finance itself is a sensitive issue in emerging and consolidated democracies alike. This makes the legislative framework governing how a political party raises and reports resources extremely important to the transparency and legitimacy of the electoral process.

The involvement of a range of political parties and their acceptance of electoral results are extremely important to the legitimacy of new democracies. Non-ruling parties have been instrumental in pushing for liberalizing reforms in Eastern Europe, Latin America, Asia, and Africa. However, it is important to remember that opposition parties unwilling to operate within the system can derail elections that are free and fair. For example, in 1997 the opposition parties boycotted the Mali presidential elections due to lingering disputes over the electoral lists. Thus, despite his strong belief in democratic principles and desire to conduct an inclusive process, President Alpha Konaré was reelected in a landslide vote that was free and fair but tainted by the absence of the opposition.

One reason for the unwillingness of many political parties in Africa to play by the rules of democratic process is that most countries with a multiparty system went through a long period of one-party systems or authoritarian regimes. One study, for example, identifies five variants of modal regimes in the Sub-Saharan Africa from independence to 1989. Out of 45 countries, 13 were "plebiscitary one-party systems"; eleven were "military oligarchies"; thirteen were "competitive one-party systems"; two were "settler oligarchies"; and only five were "multi-party systems."[20] It takes a while for the culture of political tolerance to emerge with such legacies of one party and authoritarian regimes over a long period after independence. It is not uncommon to find that those who are defeated at the polls refuse to accept the results leading to political instability and, in some cases, military takeover.

Voter Education

Voter education is essential to the full and knowing participation of the electorate in the democratic process. This was one of the key activities in the electoral process in Indonesia, South Africa, Ghana, and Cambodia. If voting is truly the means through which the people exercise their will, then voter education is the process that informs that will. Voter education is undertaken by a variety of actors in a democratic society, including the electoral authority, political parties, the state, and civil society. Its central purpose is to inform citizens of who may vote and how and to sensitize them as to the importance of voting in a democracy. Voter education is delivered to the electorate in a number of ways, such as through the media (e.g., television, radio, and newspapers); printed materials such as posters and flyers; arts and culture; commercial advertising; and face-to-face methods.

The type of voter education method used most effectively depends upon the characteristics of the electorate. For example, in a highly literate and computerized population, Internet-based voter education information can be made available, along with public information television and radio spots. In a less literate and highly mobile population, however, traveling skits, visual aides, and radio programs in a variety of local languages have proven highly effective at mobilizing voters. Voter education initiatives are often targeted at women, the poor, and youth.

Role of Civil Society Organizations and the Media

Civil society organizations (CSOs) play a special role in getting out the vote and in mobilizing candidates to run for office. They also represent special interests that candidates seek to embrace in the hope of obtaining the organizations' endorsement. Depending upon their resources and national representation, civil society organizations can be quite powerful in determining who is elected, particularly in countries with lax laws on campaign finance. Women's groups in particular can be quite effective in encouraging women to stand for office or to play a larger role in party politics. In consolidated democracies, leagues of women voters often emerged from suffragist movements in the late nineteenth and early twentieth centuries. More recently, there has been a trend towards direct campaign finance to support women candidates. Many women's organizations in the developing world are undertaking initiatives to support the candidacies of women through training and sometimes financial assistance, and to build women's capacities to lead once in office.

In addition to civil society organizations, the media also plays an important role in voter education, in campaigning, and in circulating the results and reporting on any electoral disputes. In some countries, there are gag orders on the media to prevent them from publishing exit polls or results predictions until the polls have closed everywhere in the country. The case studies of Indonesia, Ghana, and Mexico show how the perceived legitimacy of an election is influenced by the freedom of media to evenhandedly report on the position of various parties and candidates.

Voting Operations

Voting operations represent a somewhat mundane but crucial element of the electoral process, in that they ensure access to the vote. Voting operations are the processes through which adequate voting materials are delivered to polling stations on time, the vote is undertaken in accordance with the electoral law, and the tabulation and transmission of results are conducted fairly and efficiently. Voting operations also refer to those arrangements by which absentee, immobile, blind, or other eligible but challenged voters cast their ballots. This is also the process through which polling sites are selected, something that very much affects the accessibility of the vote, particularly in rural areas. It is often problems in voting operations that form the largest and most intractable electoral disputes on the part of political parties. This is so in consolidated and emerging democracies alike, as proved by the highly contested voting operations in Florida during the 2000 US presidential election.

The organization of elections presents enormous financial and logistical challenges to those countries with large and diverse landmasses. In some countries such as India and Russia, voting takes place across a number of time zones and in extremely remote locations, necessitating advance distribution of voting materials and in some cases an advanced voting timetable to ensure that results are received in line with the rest of the country. In Sahelian countries, such as Mali and Niger, itinerant voting booths are sent out by camel days in advance of the polls to catch nomadic populations as they move through the desert. In Indonesia, dispersal of the population to many islands leads to logistic problems in the conduct of elections. In those developing countries that hold first-time elections, the election infrastructure and material do not exist and therefore need to be purchased. Also, the pressure to conduct free, fair, and state-of-the-art elections expediently often results in last-minute spending on big-ticket items such as specially designed ballot boxes and photo voter identification cards. In countries that do not have permanent electoral management bodies, the high cost of elections—and the need to reinvent the materiel wheel every few years—can render election administration unsustainable save through donor support.

Information Technology and Cost

Advances in information technology in the past decade have changed how elections are conducted in many parts of the world. Internet voting is now an option in some countries, as are optical scanners and touch-screen voting machines. Advances in information technology have also resulted in the production of more accurate voting lists and the more rapid tabulation and transmission of results and, in turn, their more rapid dissemination to the public. Yet advances in information technology do not necessarily translate into more efficient or more cost-effective voting systems. Indeed, depending upon the type of electoral system and the infrastructure in place in a country, simple voting techniques such as marking a paper ballot can prove just as effective in reflecting the will of the voter as more sophisticated techniques such as optical scanners. Over the long term, however, advances in technology do promise more cost-effective and sustainable elections that reduce the administrative burden. Where advances in information technology have recently proven very useful is in the more rapid manipulation of voting data. For example, new software programs and high-speed telecommunications can make highly accurate election results publicly available over the Internet almost immediately, thereby increasing public confidence that the results are genuine.

There are wide variations among different regions and among countries within the same regions concerning the per elector cost of elections. In Africa, for example, the cost per elector has ranged from US$22.00 in Angola and $11.00 in South Africa to $0.60 in Ethiopia and $1.60 in Benin. In most cases the cost is between one and four dollars. In Asia and the Pacific, the cost was $1.00 in India, $0.50 in Pakistan and $0.17 in Bangladesh. The cost of the Cambodia 1998 election was $45.50 because of the post-crisis setting in which the elections were organized under the supervision of the international community. In Latin America, the cost ranges from $11.60 in Nicaragua, $6.50 in Dominican Republic, $6.20 in Panama to less than $3.00 each in Brazil, Costa Rica, Chile, and Guatemala.[21]

Role of International Observers

The role of international observers in national elections has grown tremendously during the past 10 years. International observers played an important role in South Africa, Cambodia, Indonesia, and Peru. As the frequency of international observation has grown, so too has the body of international practice with respect to election observation. For example, it is generally agreed that credible international election observation missions cannot "parachute" into a country immediately before an election and leave immediately after; rather, they need to study the entire electoral and political framework. It is also generally agreed that such missions need to be large enough to ensure adequate coverage of the country and that the observers must be free to go wherever and speak to whomever necessary. Electoral authorities have therefore also liberalized considerably during the past 10 years in terms of the access and freedom they afford to international observers.

The role of international election observation is multifaceted and includes some or all of the following, depending upon the country in question: legitimizing genuine election processes; building public confidence and participation in democratic elections; identifying significant irregularities and electoral fraud and/or deterring such developments; contributing to conflict management by encouraging peaceful resolution of disputes; catalyzing the democratic reform process by making recommendations for improving election and political processes; and informing the international community of human rights conditions—particularly concerning civil and political rights that surround election processes.[22]

Electoral Management Bodies

In addition to the ingredients listed above, one factor is so important to democratic governance that it deserves a longer discussion. This is the type of Electoral Management Body (EMB) in place in a given country. The role of EMBs is to organize an election. Depending upon the system, this can include revision of the voter lists; registration of new voters and voter identification; dissemination and collection of voting materials; training of poll workers; voter and civic education; announcement of the results; and so on. The management of the electoral process influences the way in which the rest of the world views a country's commitment to democracy and, more importantly, the extent to which a country's voters accord legitimacy to their government.[23] The case studies of Mexico, Ghana, and Indonesia show the significance of electoral management bodies in enhancing the legitimacy of election as an event and that of the electoral process.

EMBs come in a variety of models, including a temporary or a permanent body; a partisan, partially partisan, or nonpartisan body; a centralized or decentralized body; a specialized judicial body or government ministry; or even a mixture of several of these types that is not easily categorized.[24] One thing fairly common in all EMBs is the requirement to act as both an administrative and a supervisory body. One or both of these functions can be compromised depending upon the model used. For example, excessively large EMBs can be unwieldy and slow to make and implement decisions. EMBs dominated by political parties can wind up stalemated in partisan battles. And EMBs not fully independent of the government can find their actions subject to charges of manipulation and fraud. A growing consensus is emerging that EMBs need to be three things in order to fulfill their mandate in today's democracies: independent,[25] nonpartisan, and professional.

On the surface, temporary or quasi-governmental bodies might appear to be more cost effective in the short term, but research has shown that permanent and independent EMBs are the most cost-effective alternative.[26] This is because such EMBs develop experience and expertise in basic planning and cost-effective techniques. Permanent, independent, and multiparty EMBs also tend to encourage greater credibility in the electoral process. Indeed, the perception of neutrality and impartiality is critical in order for EMBs to successfully function as institutions of governance. As Lopez-Pintor states, "although independence and permanence in themselves are not sufficient conditions to guarantee free and fair elections, they provide significant opportunities for enhancing transparency and public confidence and hence for safeguarding the franchise in the early stages of democratization and well beyond."[27]

A recent survey of electoral management bodies shows that elections are organized by independent election commissions in 53 percent of democracies, government under the supervision of an autonomous electoral authority in 27 percent of democracies, and directly by the executive branch in 20 percent of democracies.[28] With the global trend towards democratization, many developing countries are creating permanent commissions that are independent of the executive branch, include representatives of various political parties, and are staffed by professional civil servants. In most of the Latin American democracies and some in Africa and Asia, the status of the electoral management bodies is included in the Constitution to ensure that the executive branch does not interfere in open and transparent process of elections. The practice also shows that—despite differences between the common law systems of the Anglo-Saxon world and Continental Europe—some degree of deconcentration of electoral administration is required to facilitate voter registration, voter education, and related tasks.

There are regional variations concerning the type of institution. In North America and Western Europe, 86 percent of the governments run the elections either directly or by government under supervisory authority. In Latin America, 70 percent of the countries have independent electoral commissions. In Asia and the Pacific, 63 percent have independent electoral commissions and 30 percent are government run. In Africa 53 percent of the elections are run by independent electoral commissions and 39 percent by the government under supervisory authority.

The case studies in this chapter (especially Indonesia) show positive roles by the international community—including bilateral donors and multilateral organizations—in strengthening the capacity of electoral management bodies and holding fair and free elections. The role of the international community, including international observers, was particularly important in Indonesia, Cambodia, and Peru. With the creation of independent electoral management bodies at the national level, the number of regional and international associations has increased.

To varying degrees, each of the case studies presented in this chapter shows significant contribution of electoral management bodies to the strengthening of democratic governance and the rule of law. In the case of Peru, poorly managed election has a negative effect on the democratic system. The experiences in other countries show that the most effective EMBs are independent, permanent, multiparty, not too large, and composed of a mixture of types of appointees (e.g., judges, political party representatives, civil society representatives, etc.). Such EMBs improve the institutional framework surrounding elections, thereby building confidence in the system and trust between its actors.

CONCLUSION

Free, transparent, and regular elections provide a necessary basis to promote and sustain democracy. The quality of electoral process is more important than election as an event. Improving the quality of electoral process, however, requires a legislative framework accepted by political groups, active engagement of political parties and civil society organizations, independence of media, and, in some cases, monitoring by international observers. As the case studies presented in this chapter highlight, the quality of electoral process is also significantly affected by the role of electoral management bodies in facilitating the performance of such tasks in electoral process as voter education, voter rolls and registration, and the use of modern information technology. Elections, thus, are means to sustain and consolidate democracy—not ends in themselves.

ENDNOTES

1. James D. Fearon, "Electoral Accountability and the Control of Politicians: Selecting Good Types Versus Sanctioning Poor Performance," ed. Adam Przeworski, Susan C. Stokes and Bernard Manin, *Democracy, Accountability and Representation* (Cambridge University Press, 1999).

2. Samuel Huntington, *The Third Wave: Democratization in the Late Twentieth Century* (Norman, OK: University of Oklahoma Press, 1991), 7.

3. Huntington, *Third Wave*, 7.

4. Fareed Zakaria, *Future of Freedom: Illiberal Democracy at Home and Abroad* (New York: Norton, 2000).

5. Huntington, *Third Wave*, 190.

6. Michael Bratton and Nicolas Van de Walle, *Democratic Experiments in Africa* (Cambridge: Cambridge University Press, 1998), 194–220.

7. Thomas Carothers, *Aiding Democracy Abroad* (Washington, DC: Carnegie Endowment for International Peace, 1999), 20.

8. Huntington, *Third Wave,* 185.

9. United Nations Universal Declaration of Human Rights, art. 21, sec. 3, http://www.un.org/overview/rights.html.

10. International Covenant on Civil and Political Rights, art. 25, sec. B, www.ohchr.org/english/law/ccpr.htm.

11. Sources: Andrew Reynolds, ed. *Election '94 South Africa: The Campaigns, Results and Future Prospects* (New York: St. Martin's Press, 1994); National Democratic Institute for International Affairs, *The Politics of South Africa on Election Day,* April 1994 (Washington, DC, 1994; International Republican Institute Web site (www.iri.org).

12. Sources: E. Gyimah-Boadi, "Institutionalizing Credible Elections in Ghana" *The Self-Restraining State: Power and Accountability in New Democracies,* (Boulder: Lynne Rienner, 1999); NDI Observer Delegation Preliminary Statement on the December 7, 1996 Ghana Elections, Author: National Democratic Institute, Date: 12/10/1996; Ghana Pre-Election Assessment Statement, Author: National Democratic Institute, Date: 11/19/1996; The Web sites of the three major democracy assistance providers, NDI: www.ndi.org; IFES: www.ifes.org; USAID: www.usaid.gov/democracy/

13. PVTs are also referred to as "quick counts," and are calculated by compiling random statistical samples from a sufficiently large number of polling stations to provide a low margin of error. PVTs rely on good communication and centralization of information by those conducting the exercise.

14. Data sources: International Institute for Democracy and Electoral Assistance, *Democracy in Indonesia* (Stockholm: IDEA, 2000); UNDP, Elections in Indonesia (Jakarta: UNDP, 2000); *Electoral Law of Indonesia* (Jakarta: Government of Indonesia, 1999); Election Reports of NDI and IFES.

15. Data sources: National Democratic Institute (NDI) Statement of the International Delegation to Mexico's July 2, 2000, Elections, Mexico City, July 3, 2000 Author: NDI, Date: 7/3/2000; Statement of NDI Second Pre-election Delegation to Mexico, Mexico City, June 9, 2000 Author: NDI, Date: 6/9/2000; Statement of the NDI Pre-election Delegation to Mexico's July 2, 2000 Elections,

Mexico City, May 12, 2000 Author, NDI, Date: 5/12/2000; International Federation of Electoral Systems (IFE) Web site, Democratizing Mexico: Public Opinion and Electoral Choices by Jorge, I. Dominguez, James A. McCann.

16. Data sources: OSCE Office for Democratic Institutions and Human Rights, *Analysis and Recommendations Concerning the Election Code of the Kyrgyz Republic,* 26 May 2000; OSCE Report on the elections; National Democratic Institute (NDI) Web site.

17. Pablo Santolaya, and Diego Iñiguez, Administration and Coordination of Elections (ACE Project), Legislative Framework Section, www.unpan.org.

18. Ibid.

19. Keith Archer, ACE Project, www.unpan.org.

20. Bratton and van de Walle, *Democratic Experiments in Africa,* 77–79.

21. Rafael Lopez-Pintor, *Electoral Management Bodies as Institutions of Governance* (New York: UNDP, 2000), 21–29.

22. National Democratic Institute (NDI), *Lessons Learned and Challenges Facing International Election Monitoring,* Washington, DC: National Democratic Institute for International Affairs, 2001.

23. Andrew Scallan, "Management Considerations—An Introduction," ACE Project, www.unpan.org.

24. Robert F. Bisceglie, "Types of Electoral Management Bodies," ACE Project, www.unpan.org.

25. To the extent possible; legislatures in most countries determine funding to EMBs, which means that EMBs are not 100 percent independent.

26. Lopez-Pintor, *Electoral Management Bodies,* UNDP, 2000, 71–80.

27. Ibid.

28. Ibid., 119.

CHAPTER 3

INTEGRITY IN GOVERNANCE
COMBATING CORRUPTION

Accountability, transparency, and integrity are essential elements of democratic institutions and processes. They apply not only to public institutions but to private and civil society organizations as well. The accountability of public officials, the transparency of public decision-making, access to information, and the implementation of enforceable ethical standards and codes all have significant impacts on democratic institutions and poverty reduction strategies.

This chapter defines the concepts of integrity, ethics, and corruption. It discusses the forms, magnitude, and causes of corruption in developing countries and its impact on the quality of democratic institutions, economic development, and poverty reduction. It presents case studies of some good practices in combating corruption and analyzes core issues of policy reform.

ACCOUNTABILITY, TRANSPARENCY AND INTEGRITY

Accountability is the pillar of democracy and good governance that compels the state, the private sector, and civil society to focus on results, seek clear objectives, develop effective strategies, and monitor and report on performance. It implies holding individuals and organizations responsible for performance measured as objectively as possible. It has three dimensions. Financial accountability implies an obligation of the persons handling resources, public office, or any other position of trust to report on the intended and actual use of the resources. Political accountability means regular and open methods for sanctioning or rewarding those who hold positions of public trust through a system of checks and balances among the executive, legislative, and judicial branches. Administrative accountability implies systems of control internal to the government including civil service standards and incentives, ethics codes, and administrative reviews.

Transparency promotes openness of the democratic process through reporting and feedback, clear processes and procedures, and the conduct and actions of those holding decision-making authority. It makes understandable information and clear standards accessible to citizens. Integrity completes the continuum of accountability and transparency.[1] It is synonymous with incorruptibility or honesty. It requires that holders of public office should not place themselves under financial or other obligations to outside individuals or organizations that may influence them in the performance of their official duties.

FORMS OF CORRUPTION

Corruption has many facets and nuances in different cultures and societies. It is universally recognized as the behavior of public officials that deviates from accepted norms in order to serve private ends, and behavior in the private sector that breaches the public interest to gain special personal advantages. Corruption can be viewed from at least five perspectives:

1. The "moralist-normative perspective" defines corruption as inherently bad, as a lack of moral commitment and integrity among officials, and focuses on the negative effects of corruption on public morality, institutional discipline, and public trust of officials.

2. The "functional perspective" views corruption in the context of unique circumstances of every society. Thus the concept of corruption differs in accordance with cultural heritage, political and institutional structures, level of socio-economic development, political culture, and the period of transition.[2] In transitional periods, for example, political and bureaucratic institutions that are unable to cope with increased demands made upon them by entrepreneurs, businessmen, foreign investors, and others may allow corruption.

3. The "public office–legalistic perspective" stresses the importance of creating legal institutions and making laws. Corrupt behavior is thus based on deviation from rules against the exercise of authority for personal gain. One of the limitations of this approach in developing countries is the inability to enforce laws against the abuse of authority by those in power.

4. The "public interest–institutionalist perspective" seeks to explain how institutions shape individual officials and how collective and nonpecuniary goals are as much part of corruption as interest maximizing pecuniary corruption for personal gain.

Thus, the prospects of corruption by the individual official are limited by the norms, structures, and capacity of the institution to which the individual belongs and, therefore, the individual acts corruptly because of the fixed norms and conduct within the institution.

5. The "market-centered" perspective views every official as self maximizing and entirely bent on personal gains. Self-interest drives officials to avoid their responsibilities and to use the rules to serve their own ends. The individual officeholder converts political resources into goods necessary to initiate and maintain corrupt relationships with those outside the formal political decision-making process. This perspective, however, ignores the collective pressure on an institution and other limits of action and behavior by institutional norms and structure.

Political corruption has often been defined as a "transaction between the private and public sectors such that collective goods are illegitimately converted into private-regarding payoffs."[3] The most common forms of political corruption concern campaign finance, the awarding of government contracts on the basis of political support or affiliation, donations to political campaigns with the expectations of later benefits in the form of political appointments, the use of political position to leverage kickbacks or illicit payments, and appointment to high office on the basis of patronage. Large-scale bureaucratic corruption is more likely to take place in the privatization of public enterprises, distribution of land, implementation of public works projects, or awarding of major government contracts. It can take many forms—to obtain contracts or assets, to gain access to benefits, to avoid paying taxes, duties, or levies, to obtain permits and licenses, to influence legal and administrative outcomes, or to speed up or slow down government processes. It can also involve outright theft, as when government revenues and resources are simply stolen, salaries are charged for work not performed, and legitimate taxes are collected but not passed on to the government.

Some of the recent cases of corruption in high places that made the headlines in the national and international news media show the complexity of the political and economic interests, as is described below with respect to Thailand, India, the Philippines, and Indonesia.

Prime Minister Thaksin Shiniwatra of Thailand won the biggest electoral mandate in about 70 years of electoral politics in Thailand. Before being elected, he was indicted by the Anti-corruption Commission of Thailand for concealing millions of dollars in assets while he was serving as Deputy Prime Minister in 1997. He was also accused of stock manipulation and tax evasion. He is alleged to have transferred a large number of shares back and forth to his servants, babysitters, drivers, and security guards. The paradox was that his conviction could have damaged the political party he represents but would, on the other hand, have been a major advance for the rule of law in the country where governance is traditionally influenced by patronage, payoffs, and power blocks.[4] As soon as the case opened, the stock prices slumped and the value of baht, the national currency, went sharply down. In the end, the highest court acquitted him of any charges, thereby allowing him to continue in power and, despite some lingering doubts, contributed to strengthening the rule of law and increasing awareness of the need to combat corruption in high places.

In India, dot-com journalists conducted a sting operation on the country's army brass and political leaders. The President of Bharatiya Janata, the governing party, admitted after seeing the hidden camera shots, to taking cash from a journalist posing as a businessman who wanted help to get a defense contract. The scandal led to the resignation of the President of the ruling party and the country's defense minister. Political parties in India often raise cash from businessmen, sometimes through black money, which is not reported to the income tax authorities.

The former president of the Philippines, Joseph Estrada, was arraigned on July 10, 2001, on the charge of "plundering" the country while in office. He was accused of stealing or misusing $76 million during his two-and-a-half-year presidency. Similar accusations had led to impeachment proceedings against him in 2000. When it appeared that he might survive impeachment, large-scale public demonstrations took place against him leading to the Supreme Court decision that he had lost his legitimacy, after which the military escorted him from the presidential palace.[5]

In Indonesia, the world's most populous Muslim country, President Abdurrahman Wahid was stripped of the presidency by People's Consultative Assembly for his failure to account for corruption charges against him and his attempts to dissolve the Parliament. It is ironic that he was the first democratically elected president of Indonesia after over three decades of authoritarian rule by former President Suharto, who was earlier deposed because of nationwide popular protests against him prompted largely because of corruption and nepotism charges against his family.

In many cases, bureaucratic and political corruption coexist and reinforce each other. In societies characterized by a concentration of economic and political powers in a few hands, political and private sector elite are closely linked. In such circumstances, it becomes extremely difficult to ensure accountability of the ruling groups even though the country might have a democratic structure.

CORRUPTION AND THE QUALITY OF DEMOCRATIC PROCESS

Systemic corruption is very much a political issue because it affects the relationships between the state and society and because it affects political processes and outcomes.

On the one hand, corruption significantly influences politics because most forms of corruption lead to misuse of political influence. It results in bypassing due process, weakening civil rights, and "blocking off legitimate channels of political access and accountability while opening up (and concealing) illicit new ones."[6] It can also lead to the weakening of political institutions and the loss of the people's trust in the political system. In many cases, military regimes use a high level of corruption in society to justify the overthrow of governments. Corruption has adverse effects on the quality of political process because it ignores three key elements of the democratic process—representation, debate, and choice.

On the other hand, politics affect the types and magnitude of corruption in many ways. Corruption can be used in contentious and politicized ways that sometimes make it difficult to differentiate corruption from partisan scandals. Political opponents who are discouraged from criticizing the existing government might find corruption a useful way to challenge the government without threatening its claim to political power.[7] In democratic regimes, parties in power also consider public perceptions about the extent of corruption. In new and old democracies alike there is a general sense of alienation of people from politicians because of the expanding role of money in politics and their increased awareness about transparency in governance.

Corruption appears as several "syndromes." Johnston has identified four of these. In the "interest group bidding" syndrome, the elite are more accessible than autonomous and there are more economic opportunities than political ones. Interest groups resort to their economic resources such as campaign contributions to influence political decisions. This is typical of liberal democracies such as the United States, the United Kingdom, and Germany. In the "elite hegemony" syndrome, an "entrenched political elite facing little political competition and few meaningful demands for accountability dominates and exploits economic opportunities, manipulating political access (a scarce and valuable commodity) in return for further economic gains." Examples include China, Nigeria under military regimes, and South Korea. In the "fragmented patronage and extended factionalism" syndrome, the elites are accessible but need to seek power in the situation of intense political competition and scarcity of resources leading to fragmented politics. The elites are politically insecure and usually not able to sufficiently reward their followers through patronage. Examples include Russia and pre-Fujimori Peru. Because countries in such situations tend to be politically unstable, there are much greater chances of extreme corruption. Under the "patronage machine" syndrome, the elite manage to control political competition by manipulating scarce economic rewards through systematic use of patronage. This leads to the concentration of political power in a few hands.

Patronage is used to keep control, with corruption inherent in such circumstances. Examples of this type include Mexico and Indonesia before the democratic reforms in the two countries.[8]

Quantifying the impact of corruption on political change is difficult because of a lack of data. Corruption can lead to systemic political change or breakdown of the political process or to major shifts in political power (such as in Liberia, Niger, Nigeria, the Philippines, the former Soviet Union, and Sudan). Or it can lead to regime change and "realignment of political competition" (such as in Argentina, Bangladesh, Indonesia, Mexico, Pakistan, South Korea, and Thailand).[9]

Even though corrupt politicians can be voted out of power in a democratically elected government, democracy—especially during early stages—is not necessarily a cure for corrupt practices. In many developing economies, corruption at high levels of government coexists with democratic reforms. As developing countries pass through a transition period, consensus-building and legitimacy remain problematic. One important aspect of political legitimacy is the use of power of the state by officials in accordance with prearranged and agreed-upon rules. Where civil servants exercise considerable power, as in most of the new nations, they may themselves take the initiative in seeking legislative authorization for what they wish to do. When such legislation is adopted, it does not represent political control over bureaucracy.

The prevalence of corruption in a country may indicate the extent to which civil servants are able and willing to violate laws or permit their violation. Bribes may be given to induce officials to perform their duties—as in granting licenses and permits— or to overlook nonperformance. A constitution is expected to provide the foundation for effective rule. When laws cannot be enforced, however, public apathy and disillusionment turn against the institutions. When the constitution rests upon a precarious base of support, the system is discredited and overthrown easily. Consensus fails to develop and legitimacy crisis persists, opening the system to corrupt practices.

In countries where political corruption is pervasive, its corrosive effects undermine the functioning electoral bodies, parliaments, the judiciary, and other government institutions. It creates a negative political environment less hospitable to the institutionalization of democratic processes and practices. The parliaments in developing countries are much less powerful than other organs of government, particularly the executive branch. Government agencies are subject to weak accounting controls and do not face serious scrutiny by the legislature or legal institutions. In some cases, the judiciary is perceived as incapable of taking action on cases concerning government misuse of funds or abuse of power.

The need to make elections free and fair has been on the national agenda of many countries, but corrupt influences on the outcome of elections have become widespread. In many developing countries, elections are marked by violence, massive fraud, vote buying, and electioneering under government auspices. In Pakistan, for example, four elections were held in quick succession between 1988 and 1997 and each time the loser raised questions about the fairness and impartiality of that particular election. The allegation of rigging in the 1977 elections led to the military takeover. In Bangladesh, successive elections have led to serious disputes between the ruling and opposition parties about the outcome, leading to a constitutional amendment that provides for an interim government three months before a national election is held to ensure that the ruling party does not misuse its power during the election. Because modern political campaigns require more resources than old-style contexts and because many candidates in developing economies use their own funds in the absence of public funding, politicians assume a successful outcome will lead to financial returns either through corrupt practices or through legitimate political patronage.

Furthermore, elections in developing countries have become more expensive. Because money invested in elections has to be paid back and most candidates use their own funds, the incentives for corruption can be seen at two levels—to be elected and to remain in power. As the case of the Philippines shows, rising election campaign expenses result from massive spending on media, advertisements, transport, public relations, and a semisecret kitty to buy votes.[10] Elections, therefore, have been increasingly understood in terms of access to the "spoils system"—which in practice opens the way for elected representatives to tap into public money, in many cases without proper safeguards against the abuse.

In the absence of organized and disciplined political parties, legislatures in developing countries tend to be weak and unable to perform their constitutionally guaranteed powers. Parliaments in many countries do not provide an effective forum for public debate on policy issues of national importance. The executive branch of government, with the support of civil servants, monopolizes power and usurps the roles and functions of parliament and political parties. Excessive discretion and weak accountability of the executive branch leads to more corruption. In the absence of an adequate system of checks and balances, disincentives for the diversion of public funds are not enforced. Many political parties tend to become personal devices of politicians to gain power rather than vehicles for debate on national policies and programs. A common trend is to join the winning party after every election in the hope of getting favors. The involvement of legislators in the design and implementation of development projects is one of the mechanisms to get favors from the ruling party. In 1990, for example, the Eighth Congress of the Philippines created a countryside development fund for infrastructure projects. In Pakistan, the legislators were provided development funds worth five million rupees each in 1986.[11] The executive branch sometimes uses special budgetary funds and political patronage to purchase the votes of legislators to gain a vote of confidence in the parliament.

An independent and well-functioning judiciary is a central pillar of the rule of law. Corruption reduces public confidence in the rule of law. Corrupt officials strengthen the hold of criminal elements in society. Furthermore, the lack of public faith in the judiciary leads to the decline of ethical standards and dilutes public integrity. In many countries, the judiciary fails to take action on cases concerning government misuse of funds or against politicians of the incumbent government. Poorly paid and overworked judges and court officials are left vulnerable to offers of bribery or misuse of patronage as well as assaults or intimidation. In the case of the Ukraine, for example, judges largely remain dependent on local authorities for their housing, and those who rule against city officials appear to be susceptible to delays in getting houses.[12] Corruption in the judiciary allows the wealthy to buy justice directly by bribing judicial staff and indirectly through their access to the best lawyers. Bribes can be used to speed up court decisions in countries with serious delays and a backlog of cases.

Political corruption can be entrenched in democratic systems of both developing and developed countries. When the campaign finance rules are not enforced and the judiciary is too weak to hold corrupt politicians accountable, a group of politically well-connected middlemen collects bribes in return for the misuse of political patronage by those in power, and some serve as specialized "party cashiers" to collect money from sources such as the construction industry for the party coffers.

IMPACT ON ECONOMIC DEVELOPMENT AND POVERTY ERADICATION

Corruption lowers investments, decreases efficiency, and becomes an additional tax on business. Furthermore, it misallocates scarce resources by diverting them to private pockets and reduces expenditures for development projects and social safety nets. High levels of corruption lead to expansion of the "unofficial economy." Corruption renders government regulations ineffective by allowing evasion of public health and safety requirements, disregard for regulations, and avoidance of environmental pollution penalties.

Corrupt practices can distort the allocation of resources and weaken the performance of government. Though the "impact of corruption on a country's economic health will obviously depend on what bribery is buying," argues Susan

Rose-Ackerman, "cross-country research suggests that high corruption levels are harmful to economic growth."[13] Her review of the literature on relationships between economic growth, levels of corruption, and the efficiency of legal and government institutions points to several conclusions. The policy environment affects patterns of export and import substitution; ineffective public enterprises and regional development policies and programs have negative impacts on productivity; and public policies can have unanticipated consequences of creating incentives for illegal activities. Strong and stable government institutions including an independent judiciary and low levels of corruption have beneficial effects on economic growth; high levels of corruption are related to low levels of investment measured as a share of GDP. In brief, more competitive economies tend to be less corrupt.[14]

Studies of the impact of corruption on government procurement policies in several Asian countries reveal that these governments have paid from 20 percent to 100 percent more for goods and services than they would have otherwise.[15] The example of East Asia is often cited to show that high levels of corruption and impressive growth rates can take place at the same time and that the end-result of high levels of corruption is dependent on what the payoffs are used to purchase. However, as Wei argues, corruption works like a tax on foreign direct investment. Therefore, reducing corruption and inside dealings would have further improved the performance of the East Asian economies. The magnitude of the harmful effects of corruption on economic growth is unclear. "Because corruption is tied to other features of government structure," argues Rose-Ackerman, "reducing corruption without a more fundamental change in the behavior of public institutions is unlikely to be successful in promoting growth."[16] Another interesting aspect of the relationship between corruption and economic growth is that as long as the economy is expanding rapidly, corruption is more tolerable because everyone can benefit directly or indirectly. However, as Chhibber argues, a regime is vulnerable during economic downturn because it is not able to satisfy all groups who expect a share in the spoils.[17] The Front de Libération Nationale (FLN) in Algeria, he notes, lost power because a serious fiscal crisis led to a takeover by Front Islamique du Salut (FIS), a religious party. The FIS was strongly supported in the 1990 elections by the small business sector and public sector employees. These groups were negatively affected by downsizing and partial market opening that resulted from the end of the oil boom. To deal with the budget deficits, the government introduced reforms aimed at overturning the centralized, industry-based socialist programs. Political corruption increased in the 1980s, raising costs for the middle class and the public employees who were less politically powerful than the industrial class.

More specifically, the poor suffer from corruption in many ways.[18] First, because of their weak ability to pay, the poor suffer the most in an illegal price system, receiving a lower level of such social services as public housing, education, and health. Second, state officials prefer to design large-scale public sector projects that provide high levels of payoff and fewer chances of detection. Thus the infrastructure investments are biased against projects that provide direct benefits to the poor. Third, in countries with high levels of corruption, the poor face higher tax burdens or fewer services because of their inability to pay off tax collectors. Fourth, the poor suffer losses in selling their agricultural produce when corrupt officials create monopolies, such as agricultural marketing boards, to extract personal gains. Fifth, corruption in state regulatory and taxing apparatus severely impedes the growth of indigenous, small-scale enterprises in towns and cities. Finally, "petty corruption" is a source of income for lower-grade civil servants who, though not poor, must support their immediate and distant relatives. Thus while large-scale bribery by senior officials enriches the wealthy, the less wealthy civil servants also accept bribes. Grand corruption is usually not visible. However, petty corruption—such as a policeman asking for bribe for a legitimate service—is more visible and affects the day-to-day lives of the people.

MAGNITUDE OF CORRUPTION

It is difficult to measure the magnitude of corruption because of data scarcity and the varying economic, political, and social impacts it has on developing countries. Many studies have been done, however, on the magnitude of corruption in developing countries. A report by Asian Development Bank points to some staggering figures:[19]

- As much as $30 billion in aid for Africa has ended up in foreign bank accounts. This is twice the GDP of Ghana, Kenya, and Uganda combined.

- Over the last 20 years, one East Asian country is estimated to have lost $48 billion due to corruption, surpassing its entire foreign debt of $40.6 billion.

- In another Asian country, over the past decade, state assets have fallen by more than $50 billion, primarily because corrupt officials have been deliberately undervaluing them in trading off big property stakes to private interests or international investors in return for payoffs.

- Corruption can cost many governments as much as 50 percent of their tax revenues. When custom officials in a Latin American country were allowed to receive a percentage of what they collected, for example, there was a 60 percent increase in custom revenues within a year.

Although there are significant variations among countries concerning the magnitude of corruption, the problem is serious enough for governments in developing and developed countries, civil society organizations, the private sector, and bilateral and multilateral development partners to join forces in an international movement to combat corruption. Many governments in developing countries—Uganda and Nigeria, for example—and financial institutions including the World Bank and International Monetary Fund have initiated specific programs to combat corrupt practices.

CAUSES OF CORRUPTION

Fundamental causes of corruption are economic structures, institutional capacity to design and implement reform strategies, and the lack of political will. Economic reforms including liberalization and privatization and independent anticorruption bodies are necessary. However it is the lack of political will to combat corruption that further expands illegal practices, especially in transitional economies.

Corruption is a problem of poor governance. It is a symptom of something that has gone wrong in the management of the state. It also indicates that institutions designed to govern relationships between citizens and the state are used instead for personal enrichment of public officials and the provision of benefits to the corrupt.

The basic cause of corruption is monopoly and discretion without adequate accountability. This implies that the expanding role of government in development has placed the bureaucracy in a monopolistic position and has enhanced the opportunities for administrative discretion. Corruption results from excessive regulation, increased bureaucratic discretion, and lack of adequate accountability and transparency systems. The state intervenes in the economy to provide a framework for economic and social activities—the protection of personal and property rights, the provision of public goods not supplied by the market, the redistribution of income, and the provision of opportunities for education, health, and employment. State intervention, however, is also likely to expand the discretion of public officials to make decisions. It is the misuse of this discretion that is one of the primary causes of corruption.

The discretion of public officials, however, is needed to promote innovations and respond to specific problems. In the final analysis, effective accountability makes it possible to increase the discretion of public officials.

The causes of corruption are both economic and political. A recent study commissioned by the United Nations identifies five main causes.[20] First, payments are made for goods and services that are available below the market price. Examples include when producer goods were sold in China both at the state subsidized prices and on the free market, when prices of oil were set artificially low in Nigeria, when payoffs were needed to get credit in Russia and Eastern Europe, and when South Africa's twin currency system was a source of payoffs. When the service is scarce, those with the ability to pay the highest are able to get the service.

Second, bribes can serve as incentive payments for government officials to undertake their tasks effectively. Firms and individuals are willing to pay in order to avoid delays—for example when the government department does not pay its bill on time, when such services as telephone connection and driver's licenses are delayed, and when fees have to be paid for even routine services. Continuation of such practices, however, undermines the legitimacy of the state.

Third, bribes can reduce costs for the firms when governments impose regulations, levy taxes, and enforce criminal laws. Payoffs would reduce the "regulatory load." When a state has many inefficient regulations and imposes a high level of taxes on businesses, bribes to avoid regulations and taxes may raise the efficiency of the firm. Thus firms make an alliance with tax collectors or others responsible for enforcement of public regulation and enforcement to lower the cost for the firm, dividing the benefits between the firm or the taxpayer and the public official. While such practices result in savings for the firm, the revenue losses for the state are enormous, limiting its ability to perform its tasks effectively.

Fourth, payments to obtain major contracts, concessions, and privatization of state-owned enterprises are the main cause of "grand corruption" that can have significant impacts on government budgets. Illegal payments could be made by a firm to be included in the list of prequalified bidders, to gain inside information, to structure the bidding specification to favor the firm giving the bribe, to win the contract, or to avoid quality controls. Examples of grand corruption are found both in developing and developed countries—allegations of up to $7.1 million against senior ministers in Zimbabwe and a Swedish telecommunication company for the "circumvention" of local tender board procedures; allegation of bribes in an airplane deal between the Republic of Korea and several US companies, with the national security advisor to former President Roh Tae Woo acknowledging receiving money from businesses involved in the contract; bribes paid to win contracts to build Terminal 2 at the airport in Frankfurt leading to an increase in the prices of about 20–30 percent.[21] The privatization of state-owned enterprises increases opportunities for corruption in ways similar to large-scale infrastructure projects.

Fifth, bribes are also used to buy political influence and votes. Corrupt practices sometimes fund political parties, election campaigns, and vote purchasing by politicians. In some cases those in power also use state resources, patronage jobs, and other favors denying the legitimate recipients of these benefits. Business domination of the political process can lead to political parties losing their ideological focus, as the studies of political systems in France and Italy show.[22] In Japan, some businesses were asked to fund and elect selected candidates by the former Prime Minister Tanaka Kakuei.

Finally, the business climate is negatively affected when the judiciary is perceived to be corrupt and the legal and regulatory framework is not enforced. Businesses seek private arbitrators and use other mechanisms such as protection provided by organized crime in order to operate in the country.

There are other causes of domestic corruption, including loopholes in the laws defining it, conflict of interest on the part of those directly involved in making decisions, inadequate funding for the civil service, and weak systems of government auditing and monitoring. Domestic corruption is also likely to increase where the press is not free to expose misuse of authority and public resources, where civil society organizations are not actively engaged in holding those in power accountable for their actions through advocacy and public awareness, and where political opposition is too weak to expose corrupt practices through the use of parliamentary and other forums.

Political Will

Without political will, government promises to reform the civil service and promote transparency and accountability remain rhetoric. Governments often emphasize political will in their public policy statements to combat corruption and reinvent the relationship between government, the private sector, and civil society to bolster the image of political leaders. "The principal challenge in assessing political will," argues Kpundeh, "is the need to distinguish between reform approaches that are intentionally superficial and designed only to bolster the image of political leaders and substantive efforts that are based on strategies to create change."[23]

Six indicators demonstrate genuine political will: (1) the extent to which the causes and context of corruption have been rigorously examined and accurately understood; (2) the degree to which strategy design is participatory, incorporating and mobilizing the interests of many stakeholders; (3) a focus on strategic issues based on the assessment of costs and benefits of a particular reform to achieve the stated objective of the political leader; (4) positive incentives and sanctions to ensure compliance; (5) the creation of an objective process to monitor the impact of the reforms and incorporating those findings into the policy goals and objectives; and (6) the extent of structural competition in economic and political activities.[24]

Domestic and Cross-border Corruption

Corruption has emerged as a truly global political issue requiring a global response. The driving forces for this change include increasing levels of education and political awareness around the world, the availability of more information, and the proactive role of the media, all of which have forced political leaders to ensure greater accountability for their actions. The end of the Cold War and the wider democratization of developing countries have accelerated government responses to cross-border corruption. Globalization offers new development opportunities because of rapid movement of capital, people, information, and enterprises from place to place. The emergence of an integrated international economy has also contributed to the perception of corruption as an issue with global ramifications. Corruption among officials in Latin America, for example, is linked with drug-inspired crime in American cities. However, it is extremely difficult to obtain evidence of corrupt activities and to ensure accountability of the actors involved in cross-border corruption because of their ability to do business almost anywhere and because "governments of developing states and international organizations, with their finite resources and limited mandates, may be no match politically or economically for powerful interests, often working in secret, that hold the leverage underlying cross-border corruption."[25]

Domestic and cross-border corruption are closely related.[26] Economic policies can encourage cross-border corruption. This is particularly the case with "excessively" open economies and those economies going through rapid transition such as Russia and many other countries in Eastern Europe. Some economic policies such as multiple exchange rates and systems of price controls could "encourage the growth of unofficial markets and extensive corruption."[27] Countries that are dependent on foreign technology and expertise or on the export of natural resources in the global market are more vulnerable to the pressures of outside speculators and middlemen. Furthermore, where property rights and contracts are not guaranteed, foreign firms might sometimes pursue other, sometimes illicit, means to protect their interests.[28]

The responsibility for cross-border corruption is shared between local partners and multinational corporations, requiring reforms both domestically and internationally. Multinational firms have an obligation to refrain from bribing public officials in the developing world and thus to reduce illegal payoffs in international trade and investment because sometimes these firms have strong market power and leverage that can have serious negative impact on socioeconomic and political development in developing countries.

COMBATING CORRUPTION

The need to combat corruption is widely recognized by policymakers in developing countries and international organizations such as the UN agencies, the European Union, and the Organization for Economic Cooperation and Development (OECD). Financial institutions such as the World Bank and the International Monetary Fund and regional development banks also recognize corruption as a serious problem negatively affecting their work.

When corruption is endemic, piecemeal reforms are not likely to make a difference. Partial solutions can offer some help to countries with strong and relatively clean government traditions. Other countries need more comprehensive reforms.[29]

Case Studies

Some countries have enacted and implemented successful anticorruption policies and programs that contain lessons for other countries.

Corrupt Practices Investigation Bureau, Singapore

In Singapore, the People's Action Party (PAP) made anticorruption policy one of its priorities in 1959 when it came to power. The government strengthened the powers of the existing Corrupt Practices Investigations Bureau (CPIB) that has been reporting directly to the Prime Minister since 1970. The Bureau requires government ministries and departments to review their internal processes to reduce incentives for corrupt practices. The government has undertaken several steps to reduce incentives for corruption, including increasing wages of civil servants and improving their working conditions, rotating officials, and increasing supervision.[30]

The case of Singapore shows the significance of an independent Commission to combat corruption. In an authoritarian regime with weak rule of law, however, such a model could be used as an instrument to victimize political opponents. Both Independent Commission Against Corruption in Hong Kong (ICAC) and CPIB had sufficient resources, highly qualified staff, a supportive legal framework, independent judiciary, and a competent public administration system. These conditions do not exist in many of the developing economies—making the replication of the model more difficult

Directorate on Corruption and Economic Crime in Botswana

In 1994, Botswana established the Directorate on Corruption and Economic Crime (DCEC) based on the Hong Kong Model and staffed by the former members of the Hong Kong agency and by the local personnel. The DCEC is operationally independent, though officially overseen by the President. It can investigate and prosecute offenders, prepare strategies to combat corruption, and provide public education and training. With a high conviction rate and collection of fines in excess of its operating costs, DCEC is perceived in the region to be a good practice of combating corruption in a democratic country. Many factors account for Botswana's success in combating corruption. The operational independence and prosecution powers of the DCEC enabled it to get involved in the cases involving politically influential people. Focus on strong enforcement provided deterrence against future abuses. Financial independence and viability gave DCEC more operational independence to pursue its objectives. Botswana's success was also based on some structural factors— a favorable political climate, state capacity to govern, effective civil service reforms, macroeconomic stability, a strong resource base, and the record-keeping capacity of the government.[31]

The Integrity Pact in the Republic of Korea

In South Korea, the Seoul City Government adopted the Integrity Pact (IP), by which the city government and companies submitting bids agree neither to offer nor to accept bribes in public contracts.[32] All bidders for the city's construction projects, technical services, and procurement are required to sign the pact to fight corruption. During the bidding stage, the IP is explained to bidders and only those who agree with the "Bidders' Oath to fulfill the IP" are qualified to register their submissions. A related government official also submits "the Principal's Oath to the IP." During the contract's concluding and execution stage, both parties must sign a "special condition for contract." Provisions are made to protect and reward those reporting inside corruption. The violators of the pact may face termination of contracts and are banned from bidding for other contracts for six months to two years. The Integrity Pact is being implemented in two stages—the first stage for projects at the Head Office and Project Offices, and the second stage in the 25 autonomous District Offices in Seoul.

The IP Ombudsmen will monitor the process of implementation. Specific guidelines were issued for the bidders' submissions, employees of bidders, encouragement of the company code of conduct, and the Principal's Oath to fulfill the obligations of the IP. Guidelines were also issued concerning the termination of the contract for violation of IP, the three-stage public hearings on the contract process, and the bidding procedures. The IP Ombudsmen—a team of five persons appointed by the Mayor of Seoul with one of them being Chief—were appointed to monitor the process of implementation. The functions of the IP Ombudsmen were to review and inspect all documents for construction projects of US$4,200,000 or above, organize public hearings at different stages, ask for audit on specific issues and participate in the IP Operational Committee. The IP Ombudsmen were not allowed to hold a concurrent job at the National Assembly, a local assembly, a political party, or any company participating in the bids for public projects.

The Philippine Centre for Investigative Journalism

The Philippine Centre for Investigative Journalism (PCIJ) is an independent, nonprofit media agency specializing in investigative journalism. It was founded in 1989 by nine Filipino journalists who recognized the need for newspapers and broadcast agencies to go beyond day-to-day reporting. The PCIJ is founded on the belief that the media play a crucial role in scrutinizing and strengthening democratic institutions and should thus be a catalyst for social debate and consensus for public welfare because well-researched information communicated to citizens leads to informed public opinions and public decisions.

The PCIJ aims at providing training for investigative reporting to full-time reporters, freelance journalists, and academics. In addition to training, it uses information technology to optimize research and investigation as well as to systematize access to data. It has been conducting 10-day training seminars on "investigating corruption" at both the national and regional levels. Because the reports prepared by the Centre are well researched and well documented, they have contributed to a deeper understanding of issues and have thus had an impact. The reports have produced government actions dealing with corruption, public accountability, and environmental protection.

The factors that have led to the success of the PCIJ are the professional expertise available in the Centre, giving it recognition among its clients, and its focus on capacity building and training. Its self-sustaining operations and high quality outputs have attracted the attention of development partners nationally and regionally.

Corruption and the Institutional Revolutionary Party (PRI) in Mexico

During the past decade, political and economic developments in Mexico have resulted in some advances in the fight against corruption. In response to economic crisis and globalization, Mexico undertook economic reforms to eliminate state monopolies in such industries as banking, communication, and mining and reduced the discretionary powers of the public officials in exchange controls, tariffs, and pricing. Privatization and deregulation reduced official discretion and opportunities for corruption, even though the process was "marred" by fraud, nepotism, and influence peddling. However, a more independent media played an important role in increasing public awareness and anger about corruption that undermined PRI's legitimacy, weakened its patronage system and, ultimately, led to its defeat in the presidential election. Reforms dealing with financial disclosure, the audit system, and the judiciary have created mechanisms and processes that could, given political will, contribute to anticorruption efforts.

The above reforms did not succeed in achieving their objectives because corruption and misuse of the political patronage system were central to the PRI's system of control. The public officials, thus, made bold public proclamations about anticorruption legislation and revised government procedures but, given the political context, these could not be effectively implemented.

The newly elected government of President Fox gave priority to combating corruption. With the breakdown of the PRI's long stronghold on access to political and economic power, the stage was set for comprehensive reforms based on political will. Though progress has been made in combating corruption under the Fox administration, control of the Congress by the opposition parties has constrained many of its reform efforts. One of the lessons from Mexico's one decade of experience in designing and implementing anticorruption reforms is that political will and political context are key ingredients to make these efforts successful.

COMPONENTS OF REFORMS

Four components of reforms are essential for combating corruption: prevention, enforcement, public awareness and support, and institution building.

1. Prevention. Simplifying government programs and procedures and minimizing or eliminating discretion can prevent corruption. Prevention also requires civic education to raise public awareness of the people's rights and obligations, to compensate public service with decent wages, and to reward good performance. One of the most effective preventive measures is to end corrupt programs and to modify laws that have loopholes for corrupt practices. If subsidy programs and price controls are eliminated, the bribes that result from them will also disappear. If a corrupt parastatal organization is privatized, for example, the level of corruption should go down. Yet, it is not always possible or even desirable to end all government social programs and leave them entirely to the market. In such situations, it is essential to repeal or modify relevant laws to eliminate loopholes. While, in general, reforms that increase the competitiveness of the economy can help reduce corruption, privatization in developing countries can itself be a source of corruption and may require reforms that remove rent-seeking incentives after a state enterprise is privatized.

2. Enforcement. Many countries with high levels of corruption have formal statutes but these are not effectively enforced. It is essential to establish independent investigators, prosecutors, and adjudicators who will perform professional duties in an independent fashion. The provision of adequate powers of investigation and prosecution should be consistent with international human rights norms. Other elements of enforcement are the development of channels for effective complaint making or whistle blowing, and the imposition of powerful incentives for the would-be corrupt, including civil penalties and blacklisting.

3. Public Awareness and Support. It is extremely important to determine public perceptions in order to provide baseline information against which to measure the progress of anticorruption reforms. A free press, a dynamic civil society, and freedom of information laws are essential for increasing public awareness and support.

4. Institution Building. In implementing anticorruption policies, the first step should be to establish an independent commission against corruption with broad investigative, prosecutorial, and public education powers. The commission should have strong support from the top political leadership, operational independence in making decisions based on facts, and adequate resources. Public support is likely to be stronger when someone with a reputation for integrity heads the commission.

Establishing an independent commission is necessary but not sufficient; other institution building measures are essential, including:

- Strengthening oversight institutions such as the Office of the Auditor General and the Office of Ombudsman;

- Improving performance and quality of public service through civil service reforms aimed at improving wages and working conditions of civil servants; increasing competitive pressures within the government to lower the bargaining power of individual officials; public awareness of the payers; a merit-based, transparent system of selecting civil servants; and effective monitoring to ensure compliance with the regulations;

- Establishing an independent and impartial Election Commission to ensure legitimacy of the electoral process and redesign the electoral process to reduce incentives for giving voters personal benefits;

- Creating Public Accounts Committees;

- Strengthening the capacity of the police to function effectively as the frontline investigation agency and enabling the police to work closely with other oversight bodies;

- Improving access to justice and strengthening the capacity and independence of the judiciary; and

- Instituting a system of checks and balances including multiple "veto points" to ensure the consent of a series of institutions representing different constituencies, the ability of citizens and media to obtain information about the operations of the government, protection of the rights of the individual against the state, and the use of international organizations for leverage in promoting anticorruption strategies.

Experience suggests that an increase in salaries and wages of civil servants, the promotion of democracy and political liberty, and the enactment of economic reforms such as privatization and liberalization are not guarantees that corruption will be reduced. Equally important are the implementation of anticorruption programs and changes in the social and political environment in which they are carried out.[33]

CONCLUSION

Corruption negatively affects the quality of democratic process. It weakens institutions of governance including electoral management bodies, parliaments, political parties, and the judiciary. It negatively affects the poor. It takes many forms and is caused by economic, social, and political factors. Despite some recent successes as reflected in the case studies presented in this chapter, magnitude of corruption in developing economies is such that it calls for concerted local, national, and global actions to promote accountability, transparency, and integrity in the political process. Main components of the reforms at systemic level are prevention strategies, enforcement of existing regulations and norms, public awareness to elicit citizens' cooperation, and institution building.

ENDNOTES

1. United Nations Development Programme, *Country Assessment in Accountability and Transparency* (CONTACT) (New York: UNDP, 2001), 1–15.

2. R. Sandbrook, *The Politics of Africa's Economic Stagnation* (Cambridge: Cambridge University Press, 1985), 59.

3. Arnold J. Heidenheimer, Michael Johnston and Victor T. LeVine, eds. "Introduction" in *Political Corruption—A Handbook* (New Brunswick, NJ: Transaction Publishers, 1997), 6.

4. *New York Times,* April 10, 2001, A.9.

5. *New York Times,* July 11, 2001, A.3.

6. Michael Johnston, "Public Officials, Private Interests, and Sustainable Democracy: When Politics and Corruption Meet" in *Corruption and the Global Economy,* ed. Kimberly Ann Elliot, 83 (Washington, DC: Institute for International Economics, 1997).

7. Ibid., 64.

8. Ibid., 72.

9. Ibid., 67.

10. Isgani de Castro, "Campaign Kitty" in *Pork and Other Perks: Corruption and Governance in the Philippines,* ed. Sheila S. Coronel, 218 (Metro Manila: Philippine Centre for Investigative Journalism, 1988).

11. Mohammad Waseem, *The 1993 Elections in Pakistan* (Lahore: Vanguard Books, 1994), 85.

12. World Bank, *World Development Report 1997* (NY: Oxford University Press, 1997), 100.

13. Susan Rose-Ackerman, *Corruption and Good Governance* (New York: UNDP, 1997), 35–45.

14. Ibid.

15. Asian Development Bank, *Anti-Corruption Policy* (Manila, Asian Development Bank, 1998), 1–15.

16. Rose-Ackerman, *Corruption and Good Governance,* 40.

17. Pradeep Chhibber, "State Policy, Rent Seeking and the Electoral Success of a Religious Party in Algeria," *Journal of Politics* 58, no. 1 (1996): 126–48.

18. Rose-Ackerman, *Corruption and Good Governance,* 45–47

19. Asian Development Bank, *Anti-Corruption Policy.*

20. Rose-Ackerman, *Corruption and Good Governance,* 6–34.

21. Ibid., 24–25.

22. Yves Meny, "'Fin de Siecle' Corruption: Change, Crisis and Shifting Values," *International Social Science Journal* 149 (1997): 309–20; Donatella della Porta, "Actors

in Corruption: Business Politicians in Italy," *International Social Science Journal* 149 (1996): 349–64.

23. Sahr J. Kpundeh, "Political Will in Fighting Corruption" in *Corruption and Integrity Improvement Initiatives in Developing Countries* (New York: UNDP, 1998), 98.

24. Ibid., 90–100.

25. Michael Johnston, "Cross-Border Corruption: Points of Vulnerability and Challenges for Reform" in *Corruption and Integrity Improvement Initiatives in Developing Countries*, 13.

26. Johnston, "Cross-Border Corruption," 14.

27. Ibid., 19.

28. Ibid., 19.

29. This section builds on the work of Transparency International, especially *Transparency International Manual* (Berlin: TI, 2000).

30. Among others, see Rose-Ackerman, *Corruption and Good Governance;* and Phyllis Dininio with Sahr Kpundeh and Robert Leiken, *USAID Handbook for Fighting Corruption* (Washington, DC: Center for Democracy and Governance, U.S. Agency for International Development, 1998).

31. Among others, see Rose-Ackerman, *Corruption and Good Governance;* Alan Doig and Stephen Riley, "Corruption and Anti-Corruption Strategies: Issues and Case Studies from Developing Countries" in *Corruption and Integrity Improvement Initiatives in Developing Countries* (New York: UNDP, 1998).

32. Seoul Metropolitan Government, *Integrity Pact* (Seoul: Seoul Metropolitan Government, 2000); and Metropolitan Government, *Clean and Transpararent* (Seoul, 2001).

33. Doig and Riley, "Corruption and Anti-Corruption Strategies," 45–62.

CHAPTER 4

STRENGTHENING PARLIAMENTARY PROCESS

The legislative branch of government performs important functions—including law making, representation, and oversight—that are essential to promote and sustain democracy and good governance. As the principal representative branch of government, legislatures play a critical role in formulating development strategies, authorizing the use of resources for social and environmental priorities, and creating an enabling environment for civil society and private sector groups to play their respective roles in promoting growth and in ensuring the accountability and transparency of the governing institutions.

Some legislatures perform additional functions—serve as an electoral college to put the government into power in a parliamentary systems such as the one in India; use apportionment formulae recognizing ethnic, economic, and geographic differences for legislative representation such as in Ethiopia; play a role in executive removal through votes of no confidence, as in the case of parliamentary systems; and public education though public debates and discussions on national policy issues. Furthermore, legislatures provide a forum for the discussion of national policy issues and serve as a recruiting pool for other government positions.

Democratically elected legislatures represent a broad range of interests and areas and are more accessible to the people—thus providing a venue for the articulation of public complaints and demands and for the discussion of societal differences on national policies and programs. In addition to articulating the needs and preferences of the people, legislatures enact legislation and, subsequently, translate preferences of the majority into national policies.

This chapter examines the theory and practice of the role of parliaments in the developing countries of Asia, Africa, Latin America and the Caribbean, the Arab states, and Eastern Europe. After an overview of types of legislatures, four critical aspects of the role of parliaments are discussed: (1) the relationships between the parliamentarians and their constituencies, (2) relationship with the executive branch

including oversight functions, (3) the roles of political parties and parliamentary committees, and (4) mechanisms to ensure representation of all segments of the society.

TYPES OF LEGISLATURES AND THEIR CONSTRAINTS

In practice, the legislatures in different political systems perform functions ranging
from "rubber stamping" the decrees of the executive branch to those that represent
different interests and undertake a rigorous oversight and accountability of the executive branch. John Johnson and Robert Nakamura have identified four types of legislatures.[1] The "rubber stamp" legislatures—common in authoritarian countries and
in some cases in "guided" democracies—serve as tools of the executive branch
endorsing decisions already made. Legislatures in many of the countries in the Arab
region fall into this category.

"Emerging legislatures" are those in the process of significant change from one
type to another, reflecting changes in all aspects of the political system. Such legislatures are given more powers and responsibilities to play a larger role in the governance
of the society. Examples of these legislatures are Bolivia and other Latin American
states. With the introduction of democracy in the previously military-led governments—Nigeria for example—legislatures are expected to play a more active role in
lawmaking, oversight, and the representation of different interests in the governance of
the society. With the collapse of the former Soviet Union, legislatures in Central and
Eastern Europe are playing a more significant role in governance process.

"Arena legislatures" provide a venue to represent and articulate societal differences,
to discuss public policies from different perspectives, and to assess government actions
by different criteria. To achieve these objectives, they need a party leadership system
and a committee structure. They need enough internal capacity to serve as an informed
critic and a refiner of proposals shaped mainly by outside actors in the executive branch
or in the party system. The British House of Commons is an example.[2]

The "transformational legislatures" articulate and represent diverse societal preferences and demands as well as independently shape policies emerging from their
representation of diverse preferences. To achieve these twofold objectives, they need
internal structure that can channel conflict, reconcile differences, as well as initiate
policies. The presidential systems—such as the one in the United States—with separation of powers between the executive and legislative branches are more likely to
follow this model.

Parliaments in developing countries face many constraints that affect the performance of their functions—limited human resources, a lack of adequate information, a legacy of authoritarian regimes, a tendency on the part of the executive branch

to ignore the legislature, financial constraints, and weak infrastructural facilities.

In developing countries, the functioning of parliaments is determined by historical legacies. In much of Africa, for example, the sovereign authority was exercised by a largely hereditary king or vassals, supplemented by appointed administrators and consultative councils. With colonization, the colonial rulers began to exercise final authority over such matters as taxation and expenditure, lawmaking and enforcement, justice and the police. With such structures, the focus of decision-making shifted from their own chiefs to the new administrative hub with "official" or "modern" institutions and processes. With the passage of time, consultative bodies with legislative powers subject to the discretion of the Governor—executive head in many of the former colonies—were created leading during the pre-independence phase to elected African members of the legislature, some of whom were given ministerial responsibilities. After independence, the dominance of the executive branch and often the ruling political party continued. Even though parliaments had been granted independent authority by the constitutions of most newly independent states, their powers continued to be concentrated in the hand of the executive branch and the ruling political party. The democratization phase in Africa, especially in the 1990s, however, increased political pluralism and enhanced the role of parliaments in the political decision-making.[3]

Over the past few years, a number of countries in the Arab region have attempted to strengthen legislatures for a combination of reasons—among others, to enhance their legitimacy and popular base, to mobilize the support of the people for specific public policies, to respond to pressures from below for enhanced political participation and to lessen tensions, and to present a positive image to the outside world by creating a viable forum for dialogue so societal actors could discuss agreements on public policies with the opposition.[4] With the above in view, the constitutional prerequisites of parliaments have been increased. To varying degrees, parliaments in the region have become more active through such mechanisms as parliamentary debates, question and answer sessions, investigative committees, and assistance to their constituents to get services from the executive branch. They are increasingly involved in discussing such public policy issues as economic reform, electoral procedures, and governmental accountability. Over the past few years, they have begun to discuss some of the sensitive issues such as human rights and political prisoners (in Morocco) and the role of ruling family in managing overseas investments (in Kuwait). In 1996, a set of constitutional changes in the constitution of Morocco was introduced, leading to strengthening the role of parliament to promote reconciliation among different interest groups. The political representation of people has increased from 1.3 parliamentarians per 100,000 inhabitants in 1997 to 2.2 after the 1998 elections. Similarly, the establishment of the second chamber of parliament has increased the number of parliamentarians from 333 to 595.

Based on their review of countries in the Arab region, Baaklini, Denoeux, and Springborg have identified three categories of countries.[5] The first category consists of countries where institutional arrangements for parliament as the "principal arena for political competition" have been firmly established and government and the opposition parties have agreed on the constitutional framework. The examples of this category are Lebanon and Morocco. The second category consists of countries that have undertaken steps to provide an enhanced role to the parliament but lack a clear national consensus on the basic rules of the political game. Examples include Jordan and Yemen. The countries in the third category are in early stages of broad-based agreement on the institutional arrangements for political competition, with the legislature having only a limited role. Furthermore, the electoral laws make it difficult for opposition parties to gain a significant number of seats in the parliament. Most countries in the region fall in this broad category.

The influence of the Arab parliaments on policy formulation varies not only from one country to another but also from one public policy field to another. For example, the Arab parliaments almost always defer to the executive branch on issues dealing with security, foreign affairs, and defense. However, they are more active in debating and in some cases suggesting amendments to bills in such areas as taxation, spending on education and health care, agriculture, and public works.[6]

International development partners have increased their assistance—especially in new and restored democracies—to strengthen parliamentary systems and institutions. In Africa, for example, over half of the countries benefited from the externally funded parliamentary improvement programs. Most projects were funded through multilateral mechanisms—a recognition that developing countries are more likely to work with multilateral institutions instead of bilateral donors in politically sensitive areas such as support to parliaments. Types of assistance provided to parliaments included infrastructure development, improvement of parliamentary services and processes, awareness building, training of the Members of Parliament (MPs), and legislative content development.[7] Donor organizations supporting parliaments in Asia, Africa, Latin America, and Eastern Europe include the European Union (EU), the United Nations Development Programme (UNDP), Inter-Parliamentarian Union (IPU), Organization of American States (OAS), and bilateral donors such as the United States, the United Kingdom, and Belgium. Their assistance has facilitated making rules of procedure, improving mechanisms to draft laws, establishing procedures to ensure the independence of parliament from the executive, and organizing training programs and policy workshops. They have also provided funding to procure equipment and supported the introduction of new information technologies.

THE PARLIAMENT AND CONSTITUENCY RELATIONS

Democracy and good governance provide mechanisms for consultation, interaction, and exchange between the government and the people to ensure that the views and aspirations of the people are incorporated into the government decisions affecting the lives of the people.[8] This is particularly the case with regard to parliamentarians. Even though elections provide an opportunity for citizens to express their preferences, they, nevertheless, take place sometimes at long intervals. Where elected representatives interact with citizens on an ongoing basis, they are more likely to act on their behalf. Effective parliamentarian-constituent interaction and relationships strengthen the people's connection to the government, and provide an assessment of how the government policies and programs are working. Consultation and exchange between a parliamentarian and citizens are mutually beneficial. Legislatures with proactive and ongoing ties to their constituency increase their chances of being reelected. The immediate benefit to the constituents is that their views and preferences are considered and their interests protected in the process of enacting legislation and formulating policies. Because parliamentarians are expected to represent diverse interests and because at least part of their business is undertaken in public, it is easier for the constituents to learn about what their representatives are doing. Parliamentarian-constituent relations can affect the primary functions of a legislator representation, law-making, and oversight of the executive branch—by "shaping member motivation and incentives, by providing local content and human context to decisions, and by providing a way for constituents to measure performance of legislators and to assess government actions.[9]

Parliamentarians in developing countries face serious challenges in their interactions with the constituents.[10] The most time-consuming is the expectation from the constituents that the legislator can provide them direct assistance in dealing with their individual problems and needs. These could include finding a job for them in the government, helping them get access to some of the government services such as allocation of land for housing and loans from the government-controlled banks, and location of government-initiated services in their areas. While in the developed countries, legislators have qualified staff to respond to the constituents and meet their legitimate grievances vis-à-vis government agencies and departments, in most developing countries the parliamentarians have to spend so much of their time dealing directly with the constituents that they are not able to perform many of their legislative tasks.

One consequence of these patron-client politics is a tendency on the part of legislators in developing countries to seek financial allocations from the executive branch for each member of the parliament for local-level development projects—school and hospital buildings, feeder roads to villages, appointment of additional teachers and health care workers in the existing government facilities, for example. In effect, this requires that the parliamentarians perform functions that usually are performed by local government councilors. There are two points of view on this practice. One is that the national legislators have to be directly involved in identifying and implementing local development projects because local government systems are weak and because in patron-client politics this is the only way to get reelected. The second is that by spending too much of their time in managing local development projects, parliamentarians are not able to pay sufficient attention to their primary tasks of national legislation, debate on national policy issues, and oversight of the executive branch.

A second challenge faced by the parliamentarians in their relationships with the constituents concerns competing demands of the constituents and loyalties to the party and leaders. Breaking with the party can sometimes help the constituents but might lead to stricter oversight and criticism of the executive branch. The parliamentarians have to constantly strike a balance between the two in the case of a conflict. Some electoral systems indirectly discourage stronger ties with the constituents such as some restrictions on reelection in Mexico and electoral mechanisms—party list systems for example—that limit the development of strong ties with the constituents. In multimember districts, interaction and identification between legislators and constituents usually is not as strong as in single-member district systems.

The third challenge faced by parliamentarians in developing countries in their relationships with the constituents is the resource constraint. While the executive branch dominates and controls resources, the legislatures have inadequate information systems and limited staff—in some cases none—to assist them to liaise with the government agencies on behalf of their constituents, and to examine how different legislation affects the constituents.

Developing countries have adopted many approaches to improve parliamentarian-constituency relations. Some countries have reformed the electoral system to effectively link legislators and constituents. For example, in the mid-1990s Bolivia devolved high levels of political and financial authority and resources to over 300 municipalities. This led to fear among the members of Bolivia's National Congress that the powers of their institution had been reduced because government funds were going to municipalities directly, unlike the old system in which the national legislators were constantly in the spotlight—negotiating with the executive branch to obtain more funds for their areas.

Members of the National Assembly in South Africa are popularly elected—from a nationwide party list—under a system of proportional representation. They, thus, do not have a specific district as their own. The Assembly, however, has developed a mechanism to improve legislator-constituent relationships and interaction. Each party in the Assembly is granted an allocation of funds in proportion to its relative size for the use of constituent services. Each of the parties has developed its own mechanism for constituent outreach. In the case of the African National Congress (ANC), for example, the party whip assigns a geographic area—usually surrounding a member's hometown—to each of the ANC members along with a portion of party constituency budget. Each member is accountable to the ANC for funds through period reports which, in turn, reports to the National Assembly Administration.

Other measures for constituency outreach include opening the legislature to the public, providing legislators with physical space to interact with constituents, and using specific tools for communication. Parts of parliamentarian debates are broadcast or televised in some countries such as Bangladesh, and there are public galleries to observe parliamentary proceedings. To effectively perform their representative roles, parliamentarians require communication and easy access to their constituents—including opening constituency offices in the legislature, constituency offices in the districts, legislative staff, and resources for members to travel to their districts when meeting with the constituents. In some countries such as Kenya, Tanzania, and Uganda, parliamentarians receive allowances for them to visit their constituents at frequent intervals. Parliaments use many communication tools to interact with their constituents and representatives of civil society—publication and broadcast of legislative proceedings, committee deliberations and hearing deliberations (such as in India, Mexico, and Brazil), independent journalistic coverage (Chile), parliamentary newsletters (Mozambique), legislative Web sites (Peru), and legislative directories (Uganda, Bulgaria, Bolivia).

Public hearings—including formal ones held in the legislature and informal town-hall meetings held in the district—provide an opportunity for parliamentarians to hear the view of citizens and experts on important public policy issues. The National Assembly in Mozambique, for instance, has held hearings on many issues including on the ratification of a new constitution.

Legislator-constituent outreach is also facilitated by civic education programs aimed at informing the public about the structure, functions, and roles of the government. Parliaments need to ensure that the constituents understand the important role they play in the democratic process. Otherwise, the perceptions of the public about their parliamentarians continue to be negative. Costa Rica and Chile have active civic education programs including publications describing different branches of government.

Mass media plays an important role in improving the public image of the parliamentarians' performance. In countries such as Gambia and Ghana, "the risk of being charged with criminal libel for reporting events in and around parliament and facing either imprisonment or crippling fines, may significantly inhibit the free relay of information to the public."[11] In many African countries, however, it is a fairly common practice for the parliamentary committees to hold public hearings, sometimes outside the capital, and to invite petitions from the general public.

Finally, civil society organizations play an important role in lobbying legislators for policy reform or to represent the needs and demands of the constituents. They also observe the performance of MPs, draft proposals for MPs, provide alternative sources of information, and undertake legislative advocacy dealing with specific legislation. One area of common concern to civil society groups and MPs is the legislation for freedom of information. Where NGOs at the country level are not strong enough to undertake legislative advocacy, they can depend upon the regional and global-level NGOs as their sources of information and best practices.

THE RELATIONSHIP WITH THE EXECUTIVE

Parliamentarians interact with the executive branch in the process of performing their lawmaking, representation, and oversight functions. Where the executive branch is dominating, usually through a political party, the parliaments are not able to effectively check abuses of the executive. On the other hand, a confrontational legislature leads to the breakdown of effective legislation and good governance. To promote their complementary roles, the executive branch needs to recognize the parliament as one of the pillars of democracy, and the parliament needs to work on a bipartisan basis to achieve societal goals.

The relationship between the executive and legislative branches depends upon two models of the demarcation of functions between the two—the presidential system in which the chief executive is elected by the people and members of the parliament are elected by different geographic or other units, or the parliamentary system under which the executive is usually the head of the majority party in the parliament. The separation of powers is particularly important in the case of the presidential system because in such situations the executive usually has more powers than the parliament.

In practice, countries have followed different models based on country-specific situations. The 1996 constitutions of Guinea-Bissau, for example, combined the characteristics of presidential and parliamentary systems, providing for both president and prime minister to be directly elected in a multiparty system. As head of the government, the prime minister had to resign if asked by a majority of the members of the People's National Assembly. The Assembly was empowered to approve the national budgets and development plans and relations with other states. Such a structure was considered essential to "redress" the authoritarian nature of the previous military rule.[12]

In Mozambique, the Parliament has the power to approve, alter or reject legislation submitted by the president. However, the government has encroached upon the parliamentary responsibilities because of the Parliament's weak technical and human resource capacity. One indicator of this is that the number of laws based on drafts submitted by the parliamentarians is still very small. Most of the legislation is submitted by the president, who can withdraw these bills at any time.[13] Even when a bill is passed by the Parliament, the president can send it back for modification. He can also ask that the bill be approved by a two-thirds majority. Furthermore, the funding for the parliamentary oversight of economic and social plans and the state budget has largely been financed through external sources, which further limits the negotiation powers of the Parliament.

The case of Chad shows the same trend. Even though the 1996 Constitution emphasized decentralization to regions as a mechanism to reduce the powers of the executive at the center, the president and the prime minister, usually both from the same party, were, in practice, in a better position to take leadership in public policy and lawmaking than the new National Assembly, which lacked the technical and human resource capacity necessary to provide leadership. Even though the National Assembly had the power to approve the budget, it did not have the means to scrutinize its use. "This was particularly unfortunate because much existing law in Chad remained colonial, with heavy bias towards concentrating power in the executive and the capital."[14]

Many parliaments tend to play a passive role in lawmaking. In the case of Lesotho, for example, most bills originate from the executive branch because it has relatively more technical capacity to do this. The legislature is expected to "pass" bills. Because Lesotho was, in the year 2000, virtually a one-party parliament, the laws were not based on adequate inputs from different segments of the society.[15]

The constitutional context is key to the relationship between the executive and the legislative branch. In the case of Malawi, for example, the 1964 Constitution was based on the Westminster model of parliamentary democracy. In 1966, however, a new constitution made the president both the head of state and of the government and created a one-party state. Thus no one could be elected to the National Assembly unless the person was a member of the Malawi Congress Party. In May 1993, the people voted for a multiparty system of government. The present constitution came into force in May 1995. It has created a strong doctrine of separation of powers between the executive, legislative, and judicial branches. Furthermore, it states that all legislative powers of the republic shall be vested in parliament. The new constitution, thus, provides a framework for parliamentarians to assert their role vis-à-vis the executive.

OVERSIGHT FUNCTION

Oversight by the legislature is aimed at ensuring the executive's accountability for its actions including the money it spends. To perform this function effectively, legislators need adequate constitutional authority, sufficient staff resources to scrutinize programs, and the political will to force the executive to make changes in programs.

The oversight function of the parliament is essential for checks and balances and for the effective functioning of democracy. While in the presidential system the executive signs the bills passed by the parliament—and thus checks the legislative branch—parliaments in developing countries find it difficult to check the activities of the executive, usually because of the dominance of one party and the legacy of a weak legislative branch. Oversight powers and functions of an effective parliament include the ability to remove the executive, to obtain required information from the executive, and to control the budget. Also important is the committee system to monitor and assess the government activities. Parliaments in many developing countries, however, are too weak to effectively exercise their powers of oversight. In the case of many African countries, for example, "often the parliamentary functions and powers spelled out by the Constitution bear little resemblance to the legislature's actual role. This stems from the legacy of the colonial system, the one-party system and/or the military dictatorship, all of which concentrated powers in the executive, leaving parliament marginalized."[16] In addition, parliaments in Africa do not have adequate information about government activities and the "capacity to process that information, the will to act, and the power to back up its demand for improvement, access or response."[17]

Oversight of government income and expenditure policies—"the power of the purse"—is the primary tool for parliamentary oversight. It leads the executive branch to get parliament involved in general spending policy even before the formulation of a budget. To effectively perform its function of oversight of government income and expenditure, parliament should have (1) the powers to approve the budget and to review its implementation, (2) access to advance information and analysis about the budget, and (3) mechanisms for parliamentarian committees to hold public hearings.

The experience in the Arab region shows that the contribution of the parliaments to the compilation, review, and approval of the budget is "minimal." Because the budget presented to the parliament usually provides general principles instead of specific appropriations, the government officials are in effect able to use extensive discretion. Even though parliaments have the power to reject the budget, they rarely exercise this power and directly challenge the executive because of their fear that the parliament might be dissolved.[18] The parliamentarians use several techniques to perform their often very limited oversight functions. These include the request for information, the question and answer period, the deliberation of parliamentary committees, the general parliamentary debates, and special investigation committees.

Parliamentarians in developing countries use several oversight instruments. MPs can put questions to the ministers to inform the public about executive decisions and activities. This is a common practice in Mali, Uganda, Bangladesh, and Zambia. A motion enables the parliament to challenge or modify the government action. Though used extensively in many countries, the experience in Africa shows that parliamentarians lack an adequate research capacity to support their arguments, leading in many cases to the defeat of such motions. Another oversight instrument is the impeachment or censure of the president or ministers based on procedures specified in the constitution. In the case of Uganda, for example, several ministers have been removed due to censure motions. Finally, parliamentarians can raise questions during the debates on bills or departmental budgets.

The performance of the oversight function is particularly difficult in countries, such as Lesotho, that are characterized by political instability and the absence of effective opposition. In Lesotho, all 65 constituencies were won by one party. In 1998, the ruling party won 79 out of 80 parliamentary seats. Even though Lesotho is a multiparty state, the dominance of one party in effect leads to inadequate scrutiny of the executive branch.

Watchdog institutions responsible to parliament—auditor-general, ombudsman, human rights institutions, parliamentary committees—play a central role in the system of checks and balances. The office of the auditor-general should be empowered by the constitution to audit and check proper utilization of funds authorized by the parliament to different ministries and departments. In African countries, however, the auditors-general have inadequate funds and staff to effectively perform their tasks. Furthermore, the executive branch tends to in many cases ignore the decisions of the legislature's Public Accounts Committee. "Consequently, the many cases of misappropriation and mismanagement of public funds, the innumerable cases of fraud, irregular expenditure, and procurement malpractices exposed by the Auditor-General are not remedied by the government."[19]

While the report of the auditor-general is an important tool for the legislature to ensure accountability and transparency, the effectiveness of this tool depends upon many factors—the timely receipt of the independently audited report of the government accounts, and prompt presentation of the unbudgeted spending such as for emergencies to the legislature, the ability of the legislature to elicit the views of experts in public hearings, the role of the public accounts committee in the legislature, and the ability of the legislature to take actions to correct misappropriation of funds.[20]

The case of Chad shows the limitations of the auditor-general as an instrument of oversight of the executive by the legislature. Even though the 1996 Constitution had given sufficient powers to the Office of the Auditor-General to perform its tasks, up to the year 2000 the office had not yet fully developed its relationships with the government ministries and departments and local authorities that would enable it to receive adequate information to share with the Assembly's Finance, Budget and Accountability Committee or other Permanent Parliamentary Committees. Thus, in practice the government continues to be accountable to the president instead of the assembly. The assembly has not used its powers to censure and to vote no confidence. Nor has it been able to force the president to keep it regularly informed concerning foreign affairs and defense issues such as sending troops to the Democratic Republic of Congo. The same trend is discernible in the case of Burkina Faso, where the "decade old parliamentary system tended to suffer not only from the traditional African view of the Head of the State as the guarantor of social order, but from inadequate human, material and financial resources; lack of experience and training among MPs; the marginalization of the opposition and of women; and insufficient implementation of parliamentary procedures to date."[21]

Oversight of the executive by the parliament is largely exercised through committees that should include all political parties. Parliamentary committees usually have the powers to investigate and question ministers and public officials, ask for relevant information, and summon public officials. They consider bills, make amendments to them, and approve or reject them, and they also review policies and examine budgets.

POLITICAL PARTIES AND THE PARLIAMENT

Political parties play an important role in strengthening parliaments to hold the executive accountable. They serve as instruments to identify and present competing policy options and approaches to the electorate. Once a party comes to power, the parliamentarians from the ruling political parties can count on the support of the senior party leadership. Yet, the same senior party leadership usually holds executive positions and tends to listen more to the political party functionaries—whose support they need to get reelected—than to the parliament as an institution.

Political parties are one of the important mechanisms to organize the work of the parliament and to develop and review public policies. In both presidential and parliamentary systems, party caucuses and/or parliamentary party groups are organized to ensure that the party's policies are reflected in the legislation, to elect legislative leaders including committee chairs, and to develop strategies and approaches to pass legislation. In many countries, party factions are formed by members who share specific concerns and work together to influence the party's response to bills or issues.

One of the critical issues in influencing the parliament-political parties' interface is the electoral design—i.e., the way the chief executive and legislators are elected in two or multiparty systems. There are three categories of electoral design. "Plurality-Majority" implies that elections are held in single-member districts—such as in Uganda—with one candidate for each party in a geographic area. This method facilitates better linkages between the legislator and, subsequently, better constituency services. "Proportional Representation" usually requires that the parties present a list of candidates ranked in order, and that the citizens vote for a party. The parliamentary seats for each party are then determined in proportion to the votes won by each party. A "Semi-Proportional" system combines aspects of the above. In a bicameral legislature, for example, the lower house might be chosen by the plurality-majority and the upper house on the basis of proportional representation. Some of the countries using variations of this system are Bolivia, Lithuania, and Mexico.

In one-party systems, parliament's role in providing a forum to discuss alternative points of view and in holding the executive branch accountable is severely limited. Most one-party systems in Eastern Europe during the Soviet Union era discouraged the development of political institutions associated with liberal democracy including competitive political parties and strong civil society. In Uganda, the National Resistance Movement led by President Museveni started a one-party state (or movement) to deal with such issues as ethnic violence and constitutional crisis. He took power in 1986 as the leader of an armed movement and later led to democratic transition, i.e., a new constitution in 1995 and presidential and parliamentary elections in 1996. The constitution provided for an elected president and unicameral parliament consisting of 214 directly elected members from geographical constituencies and a specified number of indirectly elected seats for representatives of women, youth, the disabled, labor, and the army. In the referendum, held in June

2000, over 90 percent of the voters chose to continue the nonparty system established by the National Resistance Movement and about 10 percent preferred the multiparty governance system.

In many developing countries of Asia, Africa, Latin America, and Eastern Europe, political parties are not able to effectively perform their traditional functions of political education, mobilization, and the representation of different segments of the society. In many countries, opposition parties become inactive between elections while the ruling parties act like in the single-party system. Party funding is too dependent upon wealthy individuals. Because of a "winner take all" orientation and patronage from the ruling parties, politicians frequently switch party affiliations. In too many cases, the organizational structures of parties are not transparent. Without "internal democracy," parties are driven by loyalty to a charismatic leader instead of by commitment to a party platform and policy preferences.[22] The result is authoritarian party leadership, a weak party system, and one-party dominant parliaments.[23]

One of the main constraints on effective functioning of parliaments in Africa is the weakness of political parties. Though there has been an impressive increase in the number of multiparty democracies in the 1990s, in most cases this has not led to liberal and democratic societies where the judiciary protects the rule of law, where human rights of all citizens including minorities are protected, and where the powers of the executive branch are checked to guard against abuse of power.[24] The culture of power-sharing is typically lacking when the attitude is commonly one of "winner takes all." With the force of state apparatus and instruments of control at their disposal, the ruling elite who hold power are likely to prevent other legitimate political contenders from winning an election—which is obvious from the frequent abuses of power and vote rigging. They use their almost exclusive access to state-controlled resources to buy loyalties of potential political rivals, leading to political patronage of frightening proportions and "grand corruption" involving leadership of the ruling political parties. With the vast majority of the poor concerned with "bread and butter" issues including means of livelihoods and access to basic social services, the discussion of alternative policy options is usually left to the small group of the elite. In most cases, therefore, the political parties do not substantively and ideologically differ from each other. Democracy, including elections as events, is perceived to be a mechanism for the "legitimization of power" and the gaining of access to scarce resources.

There are other characteristics of the political parties in Africa that affect the political process in general and the functioning of the parliaments in particular. The political parties and their structures are not given adequate attention by the executive branch after the election has been held. Many of their leaders at different levels concentrate on improving the access of the party followers to the government facilities and programs. Usually a very small group of party leaders at the central government level make major policy decisions and allocate important jobs. The international community is an important source for skills training, financial resources, access to international NGOs and foreign correspondents, support for international observers and special programs for youth wings, women's associations, local government councilors, and state-level legislators. Despite many weaknesses of political parties in Africa, their most positive achievement "is less a change in political culture and practices but the fact that multiparty democracies offer more space to individuals, organizations, the press and civil society in general to put corrupt, brutal or inept rulers under pressure and create some degree of transparency and public debate."[25]

The role of political parties in the parliamentary process can be examined from at least three interrelated perspectives: the macro level of the political party system including interparty competition and the interaction of parties in the electoral and parliamentary process; the meso level including internal structures and the governance processes of parties; and the micro level including the identification of citizens with political parties and the extent of their participation in the electoral process. As the above discussion shows, in Africa the macro level interaction between the political parties and the parliament is determined by the political culture and the nature of politics among most of the countries—including tendencies to use the state's access to resources to support the loyalty of members of the ruling party and to keep the members of the opposition from benefiting from government-initiated programs. The state of the art with regard to the micro level is shown by a recent survey in eleven new democracies in Africa. It shows that most Africans do not identify with political parties; they participate in elections through political parties, but "may not vigorously defend multi-party elections"; their trust in political parties is low; and (in the case of Uganda and Tanzania) they have negative views about the capacity of political parties to represent all citizens.[26] Despite the above, the survey also showed that on the average 75 percent of the respondents considered party competition either "essential" or "important" to the concept of democracy, with 89 percent in Nigeria, 82 percent in Botswana and Zimbabwe, and 49 percent in Lesotho.

As compared to other regions, political parties in the Arab region are much less developed. In most cases they lack the capacity for policy analysis and for the articulation of consistent political programs. Opposition political parties are especially weak because they do not have access to political patronage. Weaknesses of mainstream opposition political parties slow down the democratization process and limit the role of the parliament in its relationship with the executive.

PARLIAMENTARY COMMITTEES

Parliamentary committees are units within the legislative branch that allow parliamentarians to review policy issues and bills more rigorously than is possible by the entire parliament. Their roles depend upon the governing system of the country.

In most countries, a bill is usually presented to a committee before it is adopted. Other roles might include initiating and amending bills, investigations, and budgetary reviews. The effectiveness of the committee system in shaping legislative outcomes depends upon many factors—the extent of expertise of the committee in a given policy area through stable membership, the ability of the committee to represent diversity and reconcile differences to identify concrete recommendations, the significance of the area of responsibility of the committee, and the degree of interest of other legislators and the people to influence the legislative outcomes of the committee.

The case for strong committees has been made on several grounds.[27] Because of increasing demand on parliamentarians, the committees serve as a useful mechanism for division of labor. Committees provide a forum to informally discuss different issues and reach agreements. The committee members and their staff provide institutional memory and expertise in the area of their concern. Furthermore, the committees can hold public meetings to disseminate information to the media and the public, to allow civil society and their leaders to present their views, and to provide an opportunity for the opposition members to influence the policymaking process. The criticism of strong committees is that they might reduce the distinction between political parties that are more directly responsible to voters, that an extensive committee system might be redundant or a threat to the constitutional powers of the executive, and that they focus on narrow areas of interest.[28]

The number and size of the committees differs from country to country and may not be in proportion to the size of the legislature. For example, the Senegal National Assembly has 120 members and 11 permanent committees while the French National Assembly has 577 members and six permanent committees. The US House of Representatives has 435 members and 19 permanent committees. The membership of the committees is usually allocated in proportion to each party's representation in the legislature. Most countries limit the number of committees for an individual member. There are, however, exceptions to this including India, Hungary, Argentina, and Namibia.

In most countries, the committee chairs are chosen from the majority party. In others, such as Romania, members from the opposition or minority parties may also chair committees. In Brazil and most other Latin American countries, committee chairs rotate on an equal basis. The role of the committee chairs in the parliamentary process depends upon the governing system. In a presidential system, the committee chairs lead the floor debate on a bill, while in a parliamentary system, a cabinet minister and the opposition leader lead the floor debate.

Despite their weak technical and human resource capacity, parliamentary committees in several African countries are playing an increasingly important role in promoting accountability of the executive to the legislature.[29] After the introduction in 1994 of the multiparty democracy in Malawi, two of the powerful committees—the Public Accounts, Budget and Finance Committee and the Public Appointment Committee—were chaired by the opposition. The president and the government ministers had been asked questions. Government officials had been summoned and they appeared before the two committees. In Uganda, the Parliament's Standing, Sessional, and Ad-hoc Committees reviewed bills and ministerial budget estimates as well as the implementation of the government programs. In Burkina Faso, the Parliamentary Committees undertook enquiries into the privatization of parastatals, though they were not able to force the President to take action on their recommendations.

ENHANCED REPRESENTATION

One of the challenges of legislatures in developing economies is to more effectively represent citizens. The ability of legislatures to effectively represent citizens is constrained by many factors—electoral systems that reward loyalty to the party over service to constituents, institutional weaknesses and inadequate technical capabilities, lack of democracy within the structures of political parties, inadequate media reporting on the legislature, and inadequate interaction between legislators and the constituents.[30]

The need to ensure adequate representation of all segments of the society in parliaments is widely recognized. For example, 76 countries and 159 political parties around the world are adopting quota systems to improve the representation of women and minority groups in parliament.[31] The practice of democratic transition in many developing economies, however, shows that in most cases landlords, urban entrepreneurs, former senior civil servants, and traditional "political families" get elected. This is a reflection of the egalitarian nature of the ownership of assets in a society, which blocks adequate representation of rural and urban poor, women, and other groups in the legislature. While money plays a major role in electoral process in developing and developed countries alike, the fundamental difference is that in developing economies most politicians spend their own personal wealth to get elected because the system of campaign contributions is limited in scope—if not nonexistent in some countries. In some countries, such as India, private businesses have begun to make major contributions to mainstream political parties. In Uzbekistan, about half of all deputies are nominated by the local bodies. Only 3.5 percent of the parliamentarians in the Arab countries and 11 percent in Sub-Saharan Africa are women.[32]

Developing countries recognize the need to ensure that different groups are represented in the legislature through special mechanisms. In the case of the Indian Parliament, for example, seats are reserved for scheduled castes. In many countries, seats are reserved for women. In the case of Uganda, parliamentary seats are reserved for workers, disabled, the army, youth, and women. In Namibia, women hold over 20 percent of seats in the Parliament. Countries such as South Africa, Tanzania, and Kenya are also undertaking steps to ensure adequate representation of women in the political parties—usually a springboard for being elected to the legislature and, eventually, positions in the parliamentary committees and the government.

In Lesotho, only two of 80 members of the National Assembly were women in 2000. The situation in Africa is summed up by the Report of the Fourth Africa Governance Forum: in many countries in Africa "political parties still tended to function as 'old boys' clubs,' financed by powerful men and meting out responsibilities and rewards to a small, select male group, often within social settings, such as bars and social clubs, that were not accessible to women or not conducive to active female participation."[33]

Despite legal equality of men and women in terms of political rights, women in developing countries are underrepresented in parliaments. For example, only 3.5 percent of all seats in parliaments in the Arab countries are occupied by women, as compared to 8.4 percent in Sub-Saharan Africa, 12.7 percent in Southeast Asia and the Pacific, 12.9 percent in Latin America and the Caribbean countries, and 22.2 percent in East Asia (including China).[34]

One of the reasons for the inability of parliaments to effectively represent different groups in society is that they do not always have the capacity to introduce legislation. In the case of the Arab region, for example, the predominant practice is that legislation originates from the executive branch and is usually vague, thus giving the government officials flexibility in the process of implementation. Furthermore, executive decrees are frequently issued which are not subject to approval by the legislature.

BUILDING THE POLITICAL CULTURE OF TOLERANCE

As developing economies go through the process of transition from authoritarian political system to democratization, building the political culture of tolerance in interactions and exchange between the executive and the legislative branches remains the most daunting challenge. Years of control without adequate opportunities to express ethnic, religious, and geographical priorities and aspirations has led in many cases to extreme forms of mistrust and unwillingness to accommodate alternative points of view. It is, for example, not uncommon for a democratically elected president or prime minister to disdain the elected parliament as an institution. Similarly, various committees have the tendency to scorn the executive and fail to engage in constructive dialogue with him. The lack of trust is most visible among the parliamentary groups of various political parties. The "winner take all" attitude of the ruling political parties in their actions in various parliamentary committees, and the obstructionist approach of the opposition groups in the parliament impede a bipartisan approach—a hallmark of effective work by parliamentary committee, and by the legislature in its interaction with and its oversight of the executive.

In many African countries, building the political culture of tolerance and pluralism is one of the most critical issues in the process of consolidation of democracy.[35] In Central African Republic, for example, political fragmentations among groups in the legislature constrain effective legislative initiatives in the National Assembly. In Chad, political parties inside and outside the legislature represent regional and ethnic positions to the extent that they usually do not find common ground. One positive trend is the recent Accord for Consensual and Participatory Democracy between the majority party and five of the eleven opposition parties to identify common ground on key issues. In Benin, many of the political parties have "narrow interest bases" making it difficult to build broad working coalitions to draft new legislation. Between 1991 and 1996, the parliamentarians introduced only 28 bills as compared to 234 by the government. Increased consultations among the parliamentary groups, however, is facilitating inputs from civil society in the process of drafting legislation.

Many measures are being undertaken by African countries to enhance political pluralism in the parliament. Even though ten political parties are represented in Kenya's parliament, additional members are appointed, in consultation with the opposition parties, to represent special interests. In Burkina Faso, some recent steps in this direction have been the statute on rights, and duties of opposition and public financing of political parties have the potential to promote democratic governance practice. Though the national referendum in Uganda held in 2000 endorsed the nonpartisan system established by the National Resistance Movement, the advocates of the movement maintain that in the context of Uganda it promotes the culture of political pluralism by its recognition of alternative ideological positions, its multi-tiered structure of decision-making, and its encouragement of civil society groups in the process of governance. As a result of a quarter century of civil war and political instability, Ethiopia too is in early stages of a culture of openness and transparency. In Nigeria, long years of military rule led to the election of legislators with extremely limited experience—in many cases none—in law-making.

CONCLUSION

One of the challenges of sustaining and deepening democracy in many parts of the developing world is strengthening parliaments as primary institutions of democratic governance. Progress has been made concerning representation of minorities and women in the parliaments, new constitutions and procedures for the legislative over-sight of the executive, and the emergence of the multiparty system. Yet, effectiveness of parliaments—especially in new and restored democracies—continues to be con-strained by the low level of interface between parliamentarians and the constituents, their weak internal capacity and resource base, the historical legacy of executive con-trol on the legislative branch, and weak oversight institutions. Other challenges include the inability of political parties to perform the functions of political mobi-lization and representation of various groups, weak parliamentary committees, and the absence of a culture of political tolerance. Future challenges to transform the role of parliaments in the democratic process include strengthening their oversight capacity through increased budget authority and oversight committees, increasing capacity building support to subnational legislatures, enhancing in-house parlia-mentary policy analysis and research services, and promoting regional networks of parliamentarians to promote good practices and to share experiences.

ENDNOTES

1. John K. Johnson and Robert Nakamura, A Concept Paper on Legislatures and Good Governance (New York: UNDP, 1999), www.undp.magnet.org 1–15; also see Inter-Parliamentarian Union, *Parliaments of the World* (Geneva: IPU, 2001); George Thomas Kurian, *World Encyclopedia of Parliaments and Legislatures,* vol. 2 (Washington, DC: Congressional Quarterly, 1998); and David M. Olson, *Democratic Legislative Institutions: A Comparative View* (Armonk, NY: M.E. Sharpe, 1994).

2. Ibid., 13.

3. UNDP, "The Contribution of the Parliamentary Process in Strengthening Good Governance in Africa," *Report of the Fourth Africa Governance Forum,* 2000 (New York: UNDP, 2000), 1–8.

4. Abdo Baaklini, Guilain Denoeux and Robert Springborg, *Legislative Politics in the Arab World—The Resurgence of Democratic Institutions* (Boulder, CO: Lynne Rienner , 1999), 3–4.

5. Ibid., 66–69.

6. Ibid., 52–53.

7. Inter-Parliamentary Union, *Ten Years of Strengthening Parliaments in Africa, 1991–2000* (Geneva: Inter-Parliamentary Union, 2003), 1–15.

8. UNDP, *The Legislature and Constituency Relations* (New York: UNDP, 2000), www.undp.magnet.org, 1–11.

9. Ibid., 1.

10. Ibid., 2–50.

11. UNDP, *The Contribution of the Parliamentary Process*, 18.

12. UNDP, *Fourth Africa Governance Reform*, Final Report-New York, 2000, 7.

13. Ibid., 9.

14. Ibid., 8.

15. Pontso Seketle, K. Lekhcsa and J. Akokpari, "A Final Report on the Workshop on the Contribution of the Parliamentary Process in Strengthening Governance in Lesotho," Lesotho (August 2001), 9.

16. UNDP, *The Contribution of the Parliamentary Process*, 19–21.

17. Ibid., 22.

18. Baaklini, Denoeux, and Springborg, *Legislative Politics in the Arab World*, 52–53

19. UNDP, *The Contribution of the Parliamentary Process*, 25.

20. Ibid., 25.

21. Ibid., 9.

22. UNDP, *Deepening Democracy in a Fragmented World* (New York: Oxford University Press, 2002), 70.

23. Patrick Molutsi and Anita Inder Singh, "Strengthening Representative Democracy: Parliamentary and Electoral Systems and Institutions" (paper presented, Fifth International Conference of New and Restored Democracies, Ulaanbaatar, June 2003), 4.

24. Rainer Erkens, "Some Observations on the Role of Political Parties in the Democratisation Process on the African Continent" (paper presented, Conference on Enhancing the Role of Political Parties, The Hague: April 24–25, 2001), 2–3.

25. Ibid., 3.

26. Michael Bratton, "African Views of Political Parties: Some Cross-National Survey Evidence" (paper presented, Conference on Network Democracy: Enhancing the Role of Political Parties, The Hague: April 24–25, 2001), 5.

27. UNDP, *Legislative Committee System* (New York: 2000), www.undp.magnet. org, 6. Also see Lawrence D. Longley and Roger H. Davidson, eds., "The New Roles of Parliamentary Committees," *The Journal of Legislative Studies,* Frank Cass, 1, no. 4 (1998); and National Democratic Institute, *Committees in Legislatures: A Division of Labor,* Legislative Research Series #2, (Washington, DC: National Democratic Institute, 1996).

28. Ibid.

29. UNDP, *Fourth Africa Governance Forum,* 9–10.

30. John Johnson, *Best Practices from the International Conference on Legislative Strengthening,* (Washington, DC: US Agency for International Development, 1997), 3.

31. See www.quotaproject.idea.

32. Patrick Molutsi and Anita Inder Kaul, "Strengthening Representative Democracy: Parliamentarian and Electoral Systems and Institutions" (paper prepared, Fifth International Conference of New and Restored Democracies, Ulaanbaatar, June 2003), 10.

33. UNDP, *Fourth Africa Governance Forum,* 13.

34. Ibid., 108.

35. Ibid., 10–12.

CHAPTER 5

PROMOTING HUMAN RIGHTS THROUGH INCLUSIVE DEMOCRACY

Civil, political, and economic rights are an integral part of democratic governance. In order to fully utilize their capabilities, citizens must have certain inalienable rights—freedom from discrimination, injustice, fear, and want. They must be able to participate in the political process. Democracy promotes and protects human rights through the rule of law, fair and transparent elections, representative government, and the protection of the rights of minorities.

After introducing the global framework for human rights, this chapter examines the relationship between democracy and human rights—focusing on the rights of minorities, the right of participation and freedom of expression, women's rights, and human rights violations in crisis situations. This is followed by a discussion on the role of human rights institutions, the "rights-based approach" to development, and the impact of globalization on human rights.

GLOBAL FRAMEWORK FOR HUMAN RIGHTS

Over the past 50 years, the world community through the United Nations has developed a large number of human rights instruments including treaties, conventions, declarations, and principles.[1] These are global agreements with defined obligations of states who have signed and ratified these, and clear legal framework for action at national and international levels. The core human rights instruments are included in six treaties: (1) The Covenant on Economic, Social and Cultural Rights establishes the rights, among others, to work; to an adequate standard of living including right to food, clothing and housing; to health; and to education. (2) The Covenant on Civil and Political Rights sets out, among others, the right to life, freedom from torture and slavery, liberty and security, equal protection of law, freedom of expression, equality and freedom from discrimination, and freedom of assembly and association. (3) The Covenant on

95

Elimination of Racial Discrimination is aimed at protection against discrimination in the enjoyment of economic, cultural, social, civil, and political rights. (4) The Convention on Elimination of All Forms of Discrimination Against Women (1979) is aimed at promoting the rights of women to participate in political, economic, and social life and to protect them against discrimination and exclusion. (5) The Convention on the Right of the Child (1989) seeks children's rights to life, identity, and nationality; protection against violence, abuse, and neglect; and freedom from exploitation. (6) The Convention against Torture (1984) protects against torture and other cruel and degrading treatment or punishment.

Treaty bodies or committees have been established for each of the above in order to monitor the compliance by the signatory states. These committees examine the states' reports on their obligations under the treaties. Serious violations are thus brought to the attention of the world community. However, the global enforcement machinery is either weak or lacking, with international pressure as the most viable mechanism to persuade the signatory states.

The promotion and implementation of the human rights standards are undertaken by relevant UN agencies such as International Labour Organization (ILO), World Health Organization (WHO), and United Nations Children's Fund (UNICEF). The Commission on Human Rights, its subcommissions, and various treaty bodies monitor the implementation. The Commission on Human Rights is a political body while the treaty bodies include specialized, technical expertise providing an integrated approach to human rights. Special Rapporteurs and Special Representatives work on specific themes or countries. The Office of the High Commissioner for Human Rights provides support for monitoring, technical assistance, and advisory services. The High Commissioner for Human Rights reports directly to the Secretary General and the General Assembly. The High Commissioner is responsible for promoting universal human rights and UN system-wide coordination related to human rights.

In order to comply with the international human rights framework, many countries have launched National Human Rights Action Plans or Programs. These programs have many components: human rights definitions and standard setting, promotion of awareness regarding such standards, public education about human rights and entitlements, activities dealing with such issues as maternal health care, monitoring of violations, progress in the realization of standards, and enforcement of standards.

There are two competing approaches to the realization of human rights. The "violation approach" emphasizes close monitoring and dissemination of human rights abuses—usually civil and political rights—and holding states accountable for upholding the law and fulfilling their international commitments. Organizations such as Amnesty International and Human Rights Watch play a visible role in this process. Within the UN system, the Office of the High Commissioner for Human Rights supports the work of various human rights committees and treaty bodies. The second approach, which complements the first one, takes a more comprehensive view of human rights emphasizing the protection and promotion of civil and political rights as well as the right to an adequate standard of living. This approach takes a holistic view of human rights emphasizing the realignment of national legislation with the standards and norms of global treaties ratified by states, enhancing the capacity of human rights institutions in the government to ensure enforcement of national legislation about human rights, and empowering civil society to promote and protect human rights.[2] The United Nations Development Programme, UNICEF, and many bilateral donors support this approach.

RELATIONSHIP BETWEEN DEMOCRACY AND HUMAN RIGHTS

Historically, human rights and democracy have been treated as distinct phenomena. Democracy has been associated with organization of government including institutional arrangements such as elections, party system, and separation of powers. Human rights have been focusing on individual rights and their protection. Furthermore, the organization of government and constitutional arrangements have been considered as an internal matter of the state reflecting sovereignty while human rights have been regarded as universal in scope and subject to international norms and regulations. Finally, academic division of labor between political science—focused on studying democracy—and law and jurisprudence—focused on studying human rights—has magnified these distinctions.[3]

Separation between democracy and human rights, however, is not tenable, because human rights "constitute an intrinsic part of democracy" and the guarantee of basic freedoms is essential for people's voice to be effective in public affairs.[4] On the other hand, one of the basic principles of democracy is popular control over collective affairs, ensuring the right of all citizens to a voice in public affairs. To be effective, this requires appropriate institutional arrangements such as electoral competition between political parties, representative legislature, and independent judiciary through which civil and political rights can be exercised.

The "defining features" of democracy are based on the principles of human rights.[5] The first defining feature—free and fair elections—contributes to political participation and nondiscrimination. Voter education and training, and the exercise of the right to vote increase political legitimacy of the government. The exercise of "people power" through free and fair elections has resulted in new democratic regimes such as in the Philippines, Nigeria, and Malawi. This has strengthened people's right to political participation and nondiscrimination in public affairs.

Second, an elected legislature enhances opportunities for the right to participation and nondiscrimination. As explained in chapter 4, through legislator-constituent interaction, the people have an opportunity to influence the process of lawmaking concerning their civil and political rights as well as enforcement of these laws. The Indian Parliament, for example, has been the most critical forum to raise the issue of discrimination based on language, ethnicity, religion, and regional affiliation. Effectively functioning parliaments also are a mechanism to hold the executive branch accountable for violation of human rights.

Third, independent media promotes the right to the freedom of expression. As discussed in chapter 10, media provides a mechanism for the people to express their grievances against the inability or unwillingness of the government machinery to enforce national legislation concerning civil and political rights. In many developing countries, independent and free media plays an important role in making people aware of corrupt practices in the government and exposing the exploitation of vulnerable groups such as children.

Fourth, the separation of powers among different branches of government protects citizens from abuses of their civil and political rights. Where the judiciary is independent, the executive branch is under obligation to provide every citizen due process of law. Similarly, a democratically elected legislature can check the arbitrary exercise of power by the executive. In democratic regimes, the executive branch keeps its professional independence in implementing laws. Thus, the separation of powers provides for a system of checks and balances—protecting the rights of individuals on the one hand and ensuring their fulfillment of obligation on the other.

Fifth, active civil society and a multiparty system—two important features of democracy—promote the right to peaceful assembly and association and thereby ensure accountability of the government. At the national and local levels, civil society organizations and political parties serve as intermediaries to articulate people's aspirations and to hold the institutions of the state accountable to their obligations. Organizations of slum dwellers in the cities of many developing countries have played an important role in changing government policies concerning land regularization and the provision of basic services.[6] International NGOs such as Amnesty International and Human Rights Watch speak against human rights violations throughout the world. The human rights NGOs use the "power of shame" to encourage state institutions to change their policies and responses; in Brazil, a petition filed by NGOs with the Inter-American Committee on Human Rights resulted in payment of compensation to prisoners' families and new guidelines on the treatment of prisoners based on the UN framework.[7]

Finally, devolution of political authority and resources to local governments provides more opportunities to local citizens to participate in local decision-making process. Where field offices of central government ministries and departments are under direct supervision and control of local governments, elected representatives of the people have an opportunity to take action against abuse of power.

The democratic governance practice in developing economies shows that social injustices—including discrimination against slum dwellers, squatters, migrants, ethnic minorities, and women—are widespread in both democratic and authoritarian regimes. The irony in democratic regimes is that "political incentives to respond to the needs of ordinary people may be offset by incentives to respond to the demands of the powerful or the wealthy."[8] Systematic biases against the poor exist in both types of regimes concerning access to such services as health, education, and shelter. Mali, for example, has made more progress than Togo in strengthening democratic structures but not in elementary education, infant mortality, and literacy.[9] Disparities in income, social advantages, and power exist in both types of regimes. For example, Brazil and the Russian Federation—two of the largest democracies in the world—have some of the widest income disparities, while Indonesia and the Republic of Korea (when under authoritarian rule) achieved significant economic growth but also reduced income disparities.

Democracy and Economic, Social and Cultural Rights

In many ways, the consolidation and deepening of democracy requires a guarantee of fundamental economic and social rights. The denial of such rights could lead to the inability of those affected to fully exercise their civil and political rights and thus, indirectly, affect the viability of democratic political institutions.[10] The granting of civil and political rights, some argue, might be formalistic for that segment of the population which is characterized by illiteracy, poverty, lack of communication facilities, and dependence upon local landowning groups in rural areas. In such situations, the concerned citizens are not able to exercise their right

Table 1: The Link Between Features of Democracy and Human Rights Categories

Defining Features of Democracy	Examples of Relevant Human Rights
Free and fair electoral processes and systems	Right to political participation Right to self-determination Right to freedom of expression Right to take part in the conduct of public affairs Right to vote and be elected
Elected parliaments with proactive constituent-legislator relations	Right to take part in the conduct of public affairs Right to equality Right to freedom from discrimination Right to vote and be elected
Independent judiciary and access to justice	Right to freedom from discrimination Right to freedom from torture and slavery Right to liberty and security of person Right to equal protection of laws Convention on elimination of racial discrimination
Separation of powers among branches of government	Right to life Right to equal protection of laws Right to freedom of thought and religion Right to form trade unions and strike
Free and independent media	Right to freedom of expression Right to social security and social insurance Right to an adequate standard of living Right to work

Table 1: Continued

Defining Features of Democracy	Examples of Relevant Human Rights
Multiparty system and active engagement of civil society organizations	Right to take part in the conduct of public affairs Right to freedom of expression and thought Convention on all forms of discrimination against women and on racial discrimination Right to freedom of assembly and association
Accountability and transparency in government decision-making process with enforcement of anticorruption strategies	Right to work Right to development Right to social security and social insurance Right to adequate standard of living including food, shelter, education, and health care
Devolution of political authority and financial resources to subnational and local governments	Right to take part in the conduct of public affairs Right to take part in cultural life Right of self-determination Right to freedom of assembly and association Right to an adequate standard of living including adequate food, shelter, and clothing

Source: Compiled from the UNDP and Office of the High Commissioner for Human Rights, *Human Rights Manual* (New York: UNDP, 2000).

to hold government officials accountable, even though they might have the right to due process; to have adequate access to justice, even though they have the right to freedom of expression; and to fight against police brutalities, even though there are explicit procedures against such actions.[11]

Two conclusions can be drawn from this. One is that the realization of political and civil rights does not require absolute economic equality among groups; the influence of the wealthy can still be curtailed through such measures as laws that prevent the concentration of media ownership, limit the amount which can be spent on election campaigns, and require sources of the party funding. The second is that all citizens need to have adequate means of livelihoods and income, education, and access to shelter and services such as water, sanitation, and primary health care in order for them to realize their political and social rights.[12] There are, in addition, long-term and indirect consequences of deprivation of basic economic and social rights—the weakening or even breakdown of democratic institutions, urban violence, the displacement of the rural poor and their migration to urban slums and squatter settlements, and eventually the use of excessive force by the state apparatus to deal with political instability.

Democracies must pay attention to the protection of economic and social rights for two major reasons: first, because investment in education, health, and fundamental economic and social rights is the best investment a country can make in its future, and second, because the institutions of a free market economy are vital for the civil society organizations that are central to the sustainability of democracy.[13]

Exclusion, Rights of Minorities and Inequalities

In democracies, competition for political power and access to power is based in principle on the number of persons supporting a party or individual. The contested issues are usually resolved through the principle of majoritarianism with the assumption that a minority group can be a part of the majority. The rights of minorities are particularly vulnerable where political parties and alliances, and subsequently the outcome of political competition, are based on the ethnicity of regional affiliation. Mistrust among the majority and minority ethnic groups, however, makes such alliances difficult to sustain. Therefore, the rule of the majority has to be reconciled with protection of the fundamental civil, political, and socioeconomic and cultural rights of minorities. For this reason, inclusive democracies provide for the protection of minority groups through specific measures—granting regional autonomy to the minority group, thus making them a majority in their own region; employing a quota system in the composition of the parliament, local government bodies, and executive branch of the government; and instituting various forms of power sharing and affirmative action programs.[14]

In many countries, minorities have been excluded from political participation and their civil and political rights have been violated. Unless democracy is "inclusive," the tendency would be for the majority to increase its power in politics, to question the loyalty of minorities, especially during social stress and economic crisis, to marginalize the language and culture of minorities, and to promote its own interest at the expense of minorities.[15] Violence against minorities is a serious issue even in developed countries, as indicated by attacks, intimidation, and discrimination against immigrants and other minorities in Western Europe.[16]

Inequalities in access to political power and economic resources lead to marginalization and discrimination against minorities. Where leadership of the majority is enlightened, mechanisms are introduced to share economic and political power to ensure the inclusion of minorities. Authoritarian regimes are more likely to abuse the rights of minorities. However, democratic transition would improve the situation of the minorities only if there are specific public policy interventions to protect the rights of minorities. Many countries have recognized the need for special measures to protect and promote the rights of minorities and other disadvantaged groups.

Malaysia, for example, introduced the New Economic Policy (NEP) in 1970s to reduce interethnic disparities in income and assets in order to promote "national unity." The Indian constitution provides for the protection of the rights of lower castes even though serious gaps remain in their implementation. More recently, a new amendment to the constitution has provided for the reservation of one-third of all seats in the Panchayati Raj institutions for women, in order to promote their participation in political decision-making.

Brazil is promoting sustainable development for the indigenous communities in the Amazon region through the improvement of legal protection of their land and the preservation of their cultural heritage. Bolivia, with a large indigenous population, has been implementing a program on the promotion and protection of human rights focused on strengthening institutions, disseminating information, and training public officials engaged in the administration of justice.

Despite the aforementioned examples of the realization of human rights, many democracies in developing and, some would argue in developed countries, harm human rights. This can take many forms—excluding minorities from participation, relocating the minorities from resource rich areas, and failing to establish rule of law. During civil wars, the rights of minorities in democracies are very likely to be violated. Yugoslavia and Sri Lanka are examples. Arbitrary exercise of power in new and restored democracies, especially those with a legacy of military rule, reduces the chances of human rights. Recently, elected governments in Fiji, Sierra Leone, and Ecuador changed because of military and or other unconstitutional means.

Many elected governments in developing countries have not been able to provide universal access to basic services for their populations—the primary indicator of economic and social rights. While this does not justify authoritarian regimes, for example, India, the largest democracy in the world, has not been able to provide the basic service of universal primary education.

Countries with a legacy of authoritarian regimes have taken several measures to protect human rights in the future. Truth and reconciliation commissions have been established to openly discuss the past abuses of human rights, to build national consensus and reconciliation, and to punish the offenders in order to discourage such violations in the future. The National Commission on the Disappearance of Persons in Argentina, and truth and reconciliation commissions in Chile, South Africa, and Uganda are examples. After the end of the military rule, a similar commission was set up in Nigeria as well.

Right to Participation and Freedom of Expression

Deepening of democracy requires that the people have an opportunity to exercise their right to elect their representatives. Free and fair elections are dependent upon independent electoral management bodies, sound procedures for voter registration and education, active involvement of civil society, including disadvantaged groups, and elimination of vote tampering. Appropriate legal frameworks facilitate the protection of the right to vote. Civil society organizations and the media play an important role in monitoring violation of rights. The internal structures and decision-making processes of political parties should be open, transparent, and participatory to ensure that these parties do not become "individual or family fiefdoms."[17] In addition, political parties can play an important role in the political culture of a country by demonstrating tolerant behavior and following a code of conduct that recognizes the right of all parties to campaign and disseminate their views on national policy issues, that bars corrupt practices and intimidation of voters, and that accepts the outcome of election results.[18]

Many developing countries of Asia, Africa, Latin America, and the Middle East have initiated measures to promote and protect the people's right to participation and freedom of expression. In India, the Federal Government through the Panchayati Raj Act of 1993 reserved 33 percent of seats in the three-tiered local governments for women. This had a positive effect on women's right to partici-pation in the local decision-making processes. The Center for Legislative Devel-opment in the Philippines provides elected women representatives at the national and local levels with training on such issues as legislative agenda setting and on the preparation of legislative proposals.

The African National Congress in South Africa adopted a quota for women in the parliament. The country ranks ninth in the world with 119 women in its 399-member National Assembly. In 1994, the newly elected government of South Africa in partnership with civil society organizations highlighted an alarm-ing rate of domestic violence against women. The government, civil society, and donor agencies launched the National Network of Violence Against Women that has placed UN volunteers to develop educational programs and training to reduce the incidences of violence.

The National Action Charter of Bahrain, approved by a 98.4 percent majority, provides for state guarantees of fundamental human rights—including personal freedom and equality, freedom of belief, freedom of expression and publication, and freedom to form civil, scientific, cultural, and professional associations.[19] A number of Arab countries have not adopted some of the most important international instru-ments—including the International Covenant on Civil and Political Rights—designed at the global level to protect and safeguard human rights and freedoms.[20]

Separation of Powers and Protection Against Human Rights Violations

In many fragile democracies, serious violations of human rights take place through elected representatives of the people. This does not imply that authori-tarian regimes are better than these "imperfect" democracies. The reasons for con-tinued violation of human rights include legacy of an authoritarian regime where old styles of governing continue even though persons in power have been elected. Where a major portion of the electorate is illiterate and the local power structure is inegalitarian, civilian leaders are likely to continue behaving like the old author-itarian rulers in their exercise of power, usually leading to "one-person democracy." In such circumstances, a coalition of independent media, civil society organiza-tions, opposition parties, and international human rights organizations can put pressure on the ruling elite to create a culture of accountability.

Separation of powers among the executive, judicial, and legislative branches of government is an important ingredient of an "inclusive" democracy because it provides for a system of checks and balances. Most violations of human rights take place because of arbitrary use of power by the state including police brutalities and violence against women. Media throughout the world expose cases of violence against women, rape, extrajudicial killings, torture, and other human rights violations by security forces.

The cases of El Salvador and Honduras show some of the steps that the countries can undertake to ensure that those responsible for protecting and promoting human rights do not abuse their authority. A comprehensive judicial reform was introduced in El Salvador with active partnership of the government, civil society, and international agencies. Two of the key elements of the reform have been the retraining of police and prosecutors and the implementation of public awareness campaigns to improve access to justice. In Honduras, police reforms led to the creation of a new Ministry of Security to create awareness of human rights by the police force.

Human Rights Violations During Civil War and other Crisis Situations

In most civil wars, humanitarian emergencies, and other crisis situations, there are serious violations of human rights, especially of minorities, the poor, and other disadvantaged groups. The atrocities committed in places such as Yugoslavia, Algeria, Angola, Burundi, Liberia, Rwanda, Sierra Leone, and Somalia have attracted the attention of the global community. As discussed in chapter 9, these crises lead to large-scale internal displacement, destroy economic infrastructure and environment, and weaken democratic governance institutions including public administration. In order to protect and promote fundamental human rights, it is necessary to develop programs that deal with the social and economic rights of combatants, displaced persons, and refugees, to build trust among the fractured communities, to establish new institutions in public administration, as well as in the judicial and security sectors, and to set up human rights institutions.

In Cambodia, human rights guarantees emerged as an important issue soon after the announcement of the Paris Peace Accord. There were calls, especially from the international NGOs and the press, for the trial of the leaders of Khmer Rouge to hold them accountable for human rights abuses committed by them. Concerns were also expressed about abuses in prisons during the transition and about the treatment of minority groups.

Over the past few years, Truth Commissions have been established to investigate human rights violations and extrajudicial killings in many countries including South Africa, Chad, Chile, Uganda, and the Philippines. Though the outcome of these commissions has been mixed, several factors contribute to their success—strong government that creates confidence among the parties concerned, the impartiality of the process, sufficient time to deal with the long process of such commissions, adequate legal and support capacity to manage the process effectively, and the strength of democratic institutions.[21]

The protection and promotion of human rights are particularly difficult in countries where there is no internally and/or externally recognized government over a long period of time or where the basic institutions of the state providing primary services have disintegrated. In Afghanistan, Iraq, and Somalia, armed conflict and the breakdown of institutions of state worsened the situation with regard to human rights.

Mozambique is a good example of a country that has made significant strides after recovering from a civil war. This has been attributed to durability of the peace process, the introduction of a multiparty system, and "political will on the part of the government in relation to increasing the freedoms of association, political participation, expression and the press, which create a favorable environment for pluralism and tolerance."[22]

HUMAN RIGHTS INSTITUTIONS

The implementation of international human rights standards is ultimately a national issue. In addition to an accountable executive branch and an independent judiciary, national human rights institutions play a pivotal role in translating the international human rights instruments into reality for the people. The scope of the work of national human rights institutions varies from one country to another. In most cases, their jurisdiction includes the protection of civil and political rights and the prevention of discrimination. Their authority and functions are defined in the constitutional provisions, legislative acts, or decrees.[23] Usually there are four types of functions performed by these institutions.

1. **To investigate alleged violations of human rights.** These institutions are usually not empowered to impose legally binding decisions on the parties concerned; rather, they rely on conciliation and arbitration. In some cases, these institutions are able to refer the cases to superior courts for a legally binding decision.

2. **To conduct public enquiries.** Such enquiries, especially those dealing with human rights violations of vulnerable and disadvantaged groups, generate a great deal of media interest and are a useful mechanism for educating the public.

3. **To provide advice and assistance to governments.** Functions of most national institutions under this category include bringing human rights violations to the attention of the national legislature and the executive branch, and making specific proposals to protect human rights. These institutions also play a role in monitoring the implementation of human rights standards.

4. **To promote human rights education.** Educating citizens about their rights and informing government and the private sector about their obligations is important to promote and protect human rights. Some of the activities in this regard are the training of police, prison staff, and security forces and the dissemination of information.

Analysis of recent experience by the Office of the High Commissioner for Human Rights shows that the effectiveness of human rights institutions in developing countries is influenced by six factors: (1) the independence of the institutions as reflected in control of their own finances and legal status; (2) a clearly defined mandate; (3) composition of the commission that reflects the diversity of population; (4) the accessibility of the human rights commission to the vulnerable groups; (5) the extent of civil society organizations' involvement in public awareness campaigns and their ability to serve as the watch-dog; and (6) the adequacy of resources allocated to the national human rights institution.[24]

Over the past decade, many developing countries have established institutions to promote and protect human rights. As a part of the national program for the promotion of human rights, the Government of Morocco established the Center for Documentation, Information and Training on Human Rights issues and introduced human rights in the curricula of schools and universities. The program also provides for the harmonization of national legislation with international human rights covenants and conventions, and for support to vulnerable groups including children, disabled prisoners, and migrant workers.

In Malawi, the National Assembly passed the National Plan of Action for Human Rights in 1995. A National Human Rights Commission has been established and an extensive nationwide process of public hearings and consultations has been undertaken.

South Africa's Human Rights Commission was created by the 1994 Constitution. One of the issues on which it has focused its attention is racism in the media. The Commission investigated the cases of racism brought to its attention by the Black Lawyers Association and the Association of Black Accountants of South Africa. Later, in its broader enquiry of racism in the media, the Commission clarified its understanding of racism, and consequently, promoted public discussion on the subject. The Commission forged collaborative and supportive relationships with the regular institutions of governance including the legislature and the judiciary, which improved its effectiveness.[25]

In many developing countries, civil society, too, has established national institutions to promote and protect human rights violations. In Pakistan, the

Human Rights Commission has been playing an important advocacy role in such issues as the protection of the rights of minorities, women, and children.

RIGHTS-BASED APPROACH TO DEVELOPMENT

Human rights and development are interdependent and mutually reinforcing. The right to education, shelter, work, physical security, and access to health care and other services is essential for the people to utilize their capabilities and enjoy life with human dignity. Denial of these rights would lead to a life of poverty and deprivation. Discrimination and inequalities further increase human deprivation. More specifically, child labor, forced prostitution, and the living conditions of street children show the abuse of the rights of children. In the case of women and minorities, discrimination and social marginalization further increase incidences of poverty among them. The denial of civil and political rights limits the potential of citizens to experience equality and freedom from exploitation. Many development policies over the past few decades have increased interregional and intergroup disparities. Today there is wide recognition, therefore, of the need for a holistic approach to development: without economic and social rights, citizens cannot fully realize their civil, political, and cultural rights. This should be considered in the process of policy formulation as well as in analyzing a problem, setting priorities, and allocating resources. The holistic approach emphasizes the needs of those groups and individuals who have been marginalized and excluded from benefits of development. Furthermore, it focuses on measures—rule of law, local organization, the accountability of public officials, etc.—that promote participation, equality, nondiscrimination, and opportunities for livelihoods.

A human rights approach to development is, thus, about "putting people first." As Hausermann states, "it is about ensuring that the impact of the policies are fully considered and that they are designed to put the interests of the people firmly at the top of the agenda."[26] Fundamental principles of the rights-based approach are as follows:

- universality, nondiscrimination, and equality;

- indivisibility and interdependence, implying that all rights are equally essential to the respect for the dignity and worth of every person;

- accountability, meaning duties and obligations of the state and the individual's participation, i.e., every person is entitled to participate in and enjoy civil, economic, social, cultural, and political rights;

- rule of law, meaning that rights must be protected by law with the disputes to be resolved through adjudication through independent processes;

- progressive realization, meaning that the states have to undertake steps to achieve progressive realization of all human rights within the limits of their available resources.

Over the past two decades, the international community has emphasized implementation of the right to development.[27] In 1978, the Commission on Human Rights recognized the right to development as a human right. In 1981, the Commission established the Working Group of 15 governmental experts to suggest specific proposals to implement the right to development and draft an international instrument on the subject. The right to development was reaffirmed by the Commission on Human Rights as an integral part of human rights and was proclaimed by the United Nations General Assembly in 1986, with the United States casting the only negative vote and eight other countries abstaining. It recognizes links between various categories of human rights and "enables the integration of the body of rights from the perspective of the individual's participation in sustainable development."[28]

It is obvious that there are cost implications for full realization of right-based development. The countries with stagnant economies do not have the financial capacity to be able to meet the basic human rights needs of all people. However, the obligation of the states is to ensure realization of the right to development in proportion to the resources of the society. The issue is about allocating resources, considering fundamental human rights in policy and program design, and ensuring fair sharing of benefits. In practical terms, this implies that the social sector is a high priority and military expenditure is a lower one. Economic, social, and cultural rights, thus, are not "entitlements" that can be guaranteed by every state today—but it is the obligation of the states to take action for the progressive realization of these rights.

A rights-based approach to development is primarily the responsibility of the country concerned. Civil society organizations play an important role in pressuring the executive and legislative branches to protect human rights. In Thailand, civil society organizations advocated an emphasis on children's rights in the Seventh National Social and Economic Development Plan. Policymakers and development practitioners need to pay attention to infrastructure projects that lead to forced displacement of local communities; such displacement can have a negative effect on the sustainable livelihoods of the people and can undermine their cultural roots. Many international development partners, too, share part of the responsibility for insisting on large-scale programs that do not pay sufficient attention to the impact of these projects on the daily lives of local people. There is a need, therefore, to develop guidelines for assessing the human rights impact of development programs. Such assessment needs to be built into the design, implementation, and evaluation of the project.

South Africa has attempted to systematically integrate a "rights-based" approach to development. The South Africa Bill of Rights enshrines obligation to promote and fulfill all human rights. To achieve this, the government has developed the National Action Plan for Human Rights in partnership with civil society and government ministries and departments. The government's Reconstruction and Development Program focuses on two overarching goals: to support sustainable livelihoods and to consolidate good governance. The government's plan of action also includes policy and program interventions to improve access of the poor to housing and shelter, launch of the National Network on Violence Against Women, to support the national crime prevention strategy, and to help those living with HIV/AIDS. Other actions that have been undertaken to promote a rights-based approach to development include the adoption of a constitution with enforceable economic, social, and cultural rights; the establishment of constitutional bodies such as the South African Human Rights Commission, with constitutional powers to monitor and assess the realization of economic and social rights; and the adoption of the National Crime Prevention Strategy.[29]

In Cambodia, human rights have been one of the components of the national program aimed at reconciliation and reconstruction. In view of the country's history of violence and repression, political and socioeconomic rights are seen as essential building blocks for a peaceful society. The government program includes activities in support of the rights of the child; problems of domestic violence and girls' access to education at all levels; training judges, prosecutors, the military, and police personnel in human rights norms and legal procedures; and the protection of the rights of squatters and the homeless. Because 40 percent of Cambodians live below the poverty line, the government is committed to improving the lives of the poor and to resettle and integrate thousands of internally displaced persons and refugees. The antipoverty interventions are linked with improving the processes and institutions of democratic governance. The Cambodian Resettlement and Reintegration Program (CARERE) has received support from several international development organizations.

Women's Rights

Women's rights are a key element of the rights-based approach to development. Though gender equality was recognized in the Universal Declaration of

Human Rights, it was only during the preparatory process of the First United Nations Conference on Women held in Mexico City in 1979 that the world community took systematic stock of gender equality, leading in 1979 to the Convention on the Elimination of All Forms of Discrimination Against Women (CEDAW)—an international human rights instrument. This was followed by the UN Conferences on Women held in Nairobi and Beijing. In the Beijing Plan for Action, recommendations dealing with "women in power and decision making" included the following: a timetable to eliminate all types of legal discrimination against women, the establishment of a framework to promote legal equality, initiation of specific measures to acquire a short-term threshold of 30 percent for women in national decision-making, and mobilization of national and international efforts to facilitate women's access to economic and political opportunities. The strategic objectives of the Beijing Declaration and Platform for Action are to ensure women's equal access to and full participation in decision-making process and to increase women's capacity to participate in the leadership and decision-making.

Several trends in women's participation since the 1995 Beijing Conference are discernible.[30] In 1998, the world population of women in parliament was 12.7 percent, with the highest presence in the Nordic countries (36.7 percent). This was followed by the Americas (15.5 percent), Asia (13.4 percent), Sub-Saharan Africa (11.6 percent), the Pacific (8.3 percent), and the Arab states (3.3 percent). In 1996, the percentage of women in both ministerial and subministerial-level positions ranged from zero percent in 15 countries (eight of which were in the Arab region) to 30 percent in Sweden and the Bahamas. Women's participation at the local level generally surpasses national trends. The number of women in decision-making positions in the United Nations has increased, as heads of agencies as well as staff at lower levels.

Even though many governments have adopted affirmative policies to promote gender balance, the threshold of 30 percent advocated by the United Nations Human Development Report 1995 remains remote, especially in the Arab region. Women are increasingly seizing opportunities for political participation at the local level that enables them to balance their political activities with their household responsibilities. Some of the recent UN-sponsored case studies of women's participation in the political process to promote and protect their rights show progress being made at the country and regional levels.[31]

The South African Women's Budget Initiative is one innovative mechanism to promote gender equality. This initiative has three components. The first is gender-specific expenditures that consist of funds allocated for programs that are targeted on gender lines, such as the economic empowerment program for unemployed women with children under five, initiated by the South African Department of Welfare. The second component consists of expenditures that promote gender equity within the public services—equal representation in management and decision-making positions, in different occupations, and in conditions of service. The third component of the initiative—mainstream expenditures—is the largest and the most difficult category, requiring serious consideration of gender concerns in allocations. This initiative emanated from an alliance between parliamentarians, women in the civil service, and civil society organizations—serving as a "shadow" engendered national budget.

Campaign Against Gender Violence in Latin America and the Caribbean is an example of a regionwide effort to respond to one of the key issues in women's human rights. In 1997, various UN entities joined forces to assist national and local-level actors to combat gender violence and enforce public and private standards. The objective was to shift violence against women from a private to a public issue by encouraging governments and citizens groups to expose the magnitude of this issue and the need for effective policy and program responses. The campaign consisted of four components: (1) Focus on increasing general awareness of the problem. In Brazil, for example, the slogan "A Life Free of Violence: It's our Right" is written on more than one million checks to the employees of the federal government every month. In Ecuador, the slogan is on a postage stamp. Media events included TV documentaries and programs on community and commercial radio stations. (2) The second component was to sensitize and motivate governments to formulate and implement new policies and programs to prevent violence against women and girls. For example, the Venezuelan Parliament passed the Law on Violence Against Women and Family that included severe penalties against physical violence and sexual harassment. In Peru, relevant heads of the departments signed the Inter-Ministerial Agreement on Violence Against Women. (3) Training programs were initiated to reshape attitudes and practices of local security forces. In the Caribbean, for example, a police training manual was prepared, and a "protocol of cooperation" between women's crisis centers and the district level police was prepared. (4) Political alliances among the civil society institutions, government agencies, training and research institutions, and the private sector were forged to enforce both the existing regulations and to create increased awareness about this issue.

IMPACT OF GLOBALIZATION ON HUMAN RIGHTS

In a rapidly globalizing world, state obligations are necessary but not sufficient to promote economic and social rights. The economic crises in Asia and the former Soviet Union and economic stagnation in many of the countries in Africa show the direct and indirect impact of economic policies of the developed countries, capital flows, trade regimes, and operations of nonstate actors such as transnational corporations on human rights, especially on social and economic rights.[32] In Indonesia and Thailand, for example, the inability of the state after the Asian economic crisis to maintain past achievements in the right to work, the right to health and education, and the right to an adequate standard of living can, at least partially, be attributed to the actors and processes outside the state boundaries. Standard national economic policies within the global market—high rates of savings and investments, openness, and trade promotion, to name a few—have had a negative effect on "social cohesion and standard of living."[33]

The imbalances of globalization are reflected in the attitudes and policies of rich countries that wrote the rules of global trade. These countries—Japan, the United States, and European countries—have been dismantling barriers when it comes to industrial goods, in which they hold a comparative advantage. But they continue to provide high levels of agricultural subsidies at home.[34] Developed countries provide about $1 billion a day in subsidies to their farmers, which encourages production and drives down prices. The farm bill passed by the U.S. Congress in 2002 amounted to $180 billion. The impact of these subsidies on the right to development and the livelihood of poor farmers in many countries—Burkina Faso, the Philippines, Vietnam, and Senegal, for example—is direct and immediate. In addition to hardships on the poor farmers, such policies also create a great deal of resentment against the developed world. Ending these trade-distorting farm subsidies and tariffs "could expand global wealth by as much as a half trillion dollars and lift 150 million people out of poverty by 2015."[35]

While the global economic framework emphasizes maximizing output and efficiency, the human rights framework provides normative standards. These apparently conflicting frameworks can, of course, be complementary in situations where there is a clear understanding on the part of the actors on both sides to maximize profits and efficiency gains with due recognition of the impact of national economic policies on the people's standard of living and basic human rights.

There are many positive impacts of globalization on human rights. To begin with, concern for human rights worldwide has increased with globalization. International NGOs as well as those based in developing countries have targeted multilateral corporations to create greater awareness of human rights concerns. The Internet and other forms of communication provide opportunities for freedom of expression, networking, and access to information. Nongovernmental institutions such as Human Rights Watch and Amnesty International have been active in monitoring human rights violations including exploitation of labor. In the age of globalization, multilateral and bilateral donor agencies have been advocating democracy and the human rights agenda in their programs of assistance. The opening up of economies is generally accompanied by the increased opening up of political processes and structures, as the case of the People's Republic of China shows.

Globalization also has a negative impact on the human rights agenda. It puts limits on national sovereignty and choices that democratically elected leaders make. Structural adjustment programs, for example, negatively affect the poor and other vulnerable groups, even though such programs might be considered essential for long-term macroeconomic stability. In particular, these programs increase international crime, and trafficking of women and children.

Recognizing the need to "unite the power of markets with the authority of universal ideals," the United Nations Secretary General launched the "Global Compact—Corporate Leadership in the World Economy" at the World Economic Forum in Davos in 1999. Hundreds of companies—representing different industries and geographic regions—have already joined the global compact. The compact asks companies to "embrace, support and enact, within their sphere of influence, a set of core values in the areas of human rights, labor standards and the environment."[36] Two of the nine principles deal with human rights. The compact asks companies to support and respect the promotion of internationally proclaimed human rights and to ensure that they are not "complicit" in human rights abuses. A company engaged in the Global Compact is expected to issue a clear statement of support for the compact and to advocate its principles, among others, by informing employees, shareholders, consumers, and suppliers about its tenets and to integrate these principles into the company's development and training programs. The company is also asked to provide one concrete example or a lesson learned in implementing the principle.

CONCLUSION

Human rights and democracy reenforce each other. The defining characteristics of democracy—a free and fair electoral process, the independence of the judiciary, legislative oversight of the executive, freedom of the press—are closely linked to sets of human rights—those dealing with participation and freedom of expression, equality before the law, freedom of expression, social security, and protection against discrimination based on religion, ethnicity, or gender. The experience in developing economies shows that the relationship between human rights and democracy can be strengthened through a two-pronged approach: (1) by enhancing the enforcement capacity of government agencies and civil society organizations—especially human rights institutions—to make people aware of their rights, enforce existing national and international legislative frameworks, and protect against human rights violations and (2) by using the rights-based approach to development to ensure that implications of economic and social policies and programs on the vast majority of the people including minorities, women, and marginalized groups are fully taken into consideration. There are both positive and negative impacts of globalization on human rights. The challenge is to forge partnerships to promote corporate social responsibility.

ENDNOTES

1. These are included in the two volumes of UNDP, *Human Rights—A Compilation of International Instruments* (New York: UNDP, 2000).

2. UNDP, *Integrating Human Rights with Sustainable Human Development* (New York: UNDP, 1998), 2.

3. David Beetham, "Democracy and Human Rights: Civil, Political, Economic, Social and Cultural Rights" in *Human Rights: New Dimensions and Challenges,* Janusz Symonides, ed. (Brookfield: Ashgate, 1998).

4. Ibid., 74.

5. *Human Development Report, 2000,* 56–58; On the metapolitical impact of human rights groups in North Africa, see Susan Waltz, *Human Rights and Reform: Changing the Face of North African Politics* (Berkeley: University of California Press, 1995).

6. G. Shabbir Cheema, *Urban Shelter and Services: Public Policies and Management Approaches* (New York: Praeger, 1987).

7. *Human Development Report 2000,* 58–59.

8. UNDP, *Deepening Democracy in a Fragmented World* (New York: Oxford University Press, 2002), 59.

9. Ibid., 60.

10. Beetham, "Democracy and Human Rights," 77.

11. Ibid.

12. Ibid.

13. Ibid., 81.

14. Ibid., 91–92.

15. *Human Development Report 2000*, 59–60.

16. Ibid, 60.

17. Ibid., 65.

18. *Human Development Report*, 2000, 66.

19. UNDP, *Arab Human Development Report 2002* (New York: UNDP, 2002), 108.

20. UNDP, *Arab Human Development Report* (New York: UNDP, 2000), 114.

21. UNDP, *Deepening Democracy in a Fragmented World*.

22. UNDP, *Democratic Governance in Mozambique* (Maputo: UNDP, 2000), 47.

23. Brian Burdekin and Anne Gallagher, "The United Nations and Human Rights Institutions" (Geveva: Office of the High Commissioner for Human Rights, 2001), 1–2.

24. Ibid., 6–7.

25. Clarence J. Dias, "Democracy and Human Rights: The Challenge of Ethnicity and Inclusive Democracy" paper presented to the International Conference on New and Restored Democracies, Ulaambaatar, June, 2003), 29.

26. Julia Hausermann, *A Human Rights Approach to Development* (London: Rights and Humanity, 1998), 146.

27. For a review of the evolution of the right to development, see Office of the High Commissioner for Human Rights, "A Note on the Right to Development" (Geneva: OHCHR, 2000).

28. Ibid., 4.

29. Shirley Mabusela, "Human Rights and Sustainable Human Development: How Development is a Necessary Means to Promote and Protect Human Rights," in *Human Rights and Human Development: Report of the Oslo Symposium* (New York: UNDP, 2000), 54–55.

30. Azza Karam, "Beijing + 5: Women's Participation: Review of Strategies and Trends" in United Nations Development Program, *Women's Participation and Good Governance: 21st Century Challenges* (New York: UNDP, 2000), 15–26.

31. Ibid., 41–70.

32. UNDP, *Human Rights and Human Development: Report of the Oslo Symposium* (New York: UNDP, 2000), 11.

33. Ibid., 10–11.

34. *New York Times*, December 30, 2003, sec. A, 20.

35. Ibid.

36. United Nations, *The Global Compact: Corporate Leadership in the World Economy* (New York: United Nations, 1999).

CHAPTER 6

DEMOCRACY AT THE GRASS ROOTS THROUGH DECENTRALIZATION

Decentralization—including political devolution, deconcentration, delegation, and transfer to nongovernmental organizations—promotes democracy and good governance by providing an institutional framework to bring decision-making closer to the people, and building partnerships and synergies among actors and organizations at many levels to achieve economic and human development goals. Policymakers, politicians, and practitioners in developing countries have over the years been supporting decentralization policies and programs, driven by a variety of internal and external factors. The scope of decentralization has ranged from the deconcentration of some of the routine functions of government departments and ministries to their field offices to the devolution of political authority and resources to local governments. The results of these efforts have been mixed. Yet, decentralization continues to be one of the predominant approaches to strengthen democracy, especially at the grass roots, and to improve service delivery.

This chapter examines mechanisms through which decentralization deepens democracy. It discusses four forms of decentralization, and driving forces because of which governments in developing countries have been trying to decentralize decision-making authority and resources. It also presents some good examples of recent decentralization policies and programs, the factors that influence the choice and impacts of decentralization programs, and the emerging focus on partnerships of local actors in the age of globalization.

DECENTRALIZATION AND DEMOCRACY

The decentralization of authority and resources from the center to subnational and local levels of government and administration is a necessary condition for promoting pluralistic politics and deepening democracy. Advocates of decentralization have provided a variety of reasons for political, financial, and administrative decentralization.[1] Decentralization can promote values of democracy and good governance in several ways.

First, it provides an institutional framework through which groups and individuals at many levels can organize themselves and participate in making decisions affecting them. It helps the development of democratic values and skills among citizens. It allows for greater representation of various political, religious, social, and ethnic groups. This enhances the active participation of local citizens and, consequently, the political legitimacy of the government. Decentralization can promote national integration. In countries that are deeply divided along ethnic or geographic lines, decentralization can provide an institutional mechanism to bring opposition groups into a "formal and rule-bound bargaining process," which can promote national unity as it did in South Africa and Uganda.[2]

Second, decentralization is seen as a more effective means to ensure the accountability of political leaders and government officials and, consequently, to improve access of the people to government-initiated services and facilities. More direct interaction between local residents and elected leaders promotes the culture of accountability. In places where local governments have sufficient political and financial authority, and where community-based groups are active, people have greater access to such services as primary health care, agricultural extension services, education, and low-income housing. Proximity to the demand base for a service produces a more effective response and promotes a more rationalized use of resources. This proximity also allows for closer monitoring by the beneficiary population of projects intended to serve them.

Third, decentralization promotes the institutionalization of democratic culture by providing opportunities to groups and individuals to make political and financial decisions affecting their jurisdiction. It reduces red tape and rigid and uniform procedures of central governments, relying instead on the knowledge, expertise, and experience of local people. It strengthens the capacity of local governments and civil society organization(s) because they perform some functions previously undertaken by central governments. It facilitates the exchange of information about local needs. Close interaction and dialogue among groups and individuals about local priorities and concerns increase their "stakes" in maintaining the political system and create a culture of tolerance of different points of view—a necessary condition for the consolidation of democracy.

Fourth, decentralized decision-making can provide a better framework for poverty reduction. Devolution of decision-making enables different viewpoints to be heard and incorporated in the public allocation of resources.[3] Two factors determine whether decentralization becomes a positive force to alleviate poverty— "horizontal equity" and "within state equity."[4] The first implies the fiscal and administrative capacity of local governments to deliver services at the same level as the central government does. Tax bases of different local governments vary. "Within state equity" implies differences among individuals within the region/subnational unit. In such situations, the ability and willingness of local government to initiate redistribution policies is the critical factor.

Fifth, decentralization promotes checks and balances between the center and subnational/local units of government and administration—a key ingredient of democracy and good governance. In addition to serving as one of the key levers of pressure against an authoritarian rule at the central level, it provides opportunities to the people to actively participate in the process of making decisions. While the system of checks and balances is usually seen in the context of relationships between the executive, legislative, and judicial branches of government, an effective partnership among different units of government with the constitutional provisions for both the central authority and rights and obligations of state and local governments creates the political environment of accommodation and negotiation to reflect the interests of different groups.

Finally, the transfer of authority and resources to local units of government and administration to design and implement development programs provides opportunities to local citizens to play a more direct role in development process: as catalysts for development and local change agents, they can make decisions about the location of services and determine local priorities. Decentralization also facilitates the growth of civil society organizations and networks because it provides the greatest scope for the establishment of civil society organizations about local issues that impact directly the lives of the people.[5]

Decentralization is not a panacea, however, for developing democracy and good governance. Many dangers and pitfalls associated with decentralization can impede the design and implementation of elements of liberal democracy. In some cases, "a decentralized political system can create niches for authoritarian figures (or movements) to consolidate their fiefdoms, safe from interventions from central authorities."[6] In countries such as Colombia, members of the opposition parties are subjected to violence. In some democracies with a federal system of government such as Brazil, there are serious tensions between the policies of the federal government and state governments. Policies of some governments can lead to more intolerance and discrimination. For example, political decentralization in Estonia and Latvia led to the exclusion of Russians—almost 40 percent of the population in Estonia—in the language and citizenships laws. Other dangers of decentralization are that it may increase geographic inequalities due to the different resource base of the subnational units, it may lead to redundancy and inefficiency because of the lack of clear delineation of authority and responsibilities, and it may lead to more divisions within the society based on ethnicity.[7]

Decentralization and Devolution

Decentralization is a broad concept. It can be both a means—such as to improve the efficiency and effectiveness of public services—or an end in itself—such as to promote the values of pluralistic, participatory democracy. It implies transfer of political, financial, administrative, and legal authority from central government to regional/subnational and local governments. Different forms of decentralization can be distinguished based on the extent to which power and authority are being transferred and/or the type of authority being transferred or devolved.

Devolution is aimed at creating or strengthening independent units of government by devolving functions and authority. Its fundamental characteristics are the autonomous nature of local units of government, the legally recognized geographical boundaries within which they exercise their authority, and the power of local governments to mobilize resources to perform their tasks. This form of decentralization also implies that local governments are seen as "institutions" that provide services to local citizens who have control over them. Local governments are one part of many levels of the national political system, each with mutually beneficial and legally recognized roles and responsibilities.[8]

Other Forms of Decentralization

While devolution is the foundation of effective decentralization, other forms of decentralization also play an important and complementary role in promoting the values of decentralized decision-making and thereby the democratic culture in the society. Deconcentration is defined as the shifting of administrative responsibilities from central ministries and departments to regional and local levels of government. It could include the establishment of field offices of the national departments, and transfer of some decision-making to the field staff. Even though this form of decentralization provides a very limited transfer of authority to groups and individuals outside the central government, this is the first necessary step in moving the process of program planning and implementation closer to the people.

Another form of decentralization is delegation, defined as the shifting of management authority for specific functions to semiautonomous or parastatal organizations including public corporations, regional planning and area development authorities, and multipurpose and single-purpose authorities. Under this form, broad authority to plan and implement decisions concerning specific activities is transferred to these organizations. This form of decentralization brings decision-making about specific activities closer to the people who are affected, too, though it does not provide direct channels for local political control as in the case of devolution.

Decentralization can also take place through transfer from government to nongovernmental institutions. This often involves contracting out partial service provision, administration functions, and deregulation or full privatization. Public functions could be transferred to trade associations, professional organizations, farmers' cooperatives, and women's and youth associations. This form of decentralization also positively affects the promotion of democratic processes because it allows decisions to be made through processes that involve a large number of political interests.

Each of the above forms of decentralization affects the promotion and consolidation of democracy to varying degrees and in different ways. Political decentralization is the foundation for plural, competitive politics at the national and local levels. Deconcentration has an indirect effect because it can improve understanding by local citizens of what the government is trying to do. Delegation is aimed at the efficient and effective performance of specific functions. Both deconcentration and delegation dominated by civil servants can serve as instruments to mobilize the support of government's development programs and to gain cooperation from local political constituents without "risking the displacement of (central) development goals by local political aims."[9] Finally, transfer of authority to nongovernmental institutions "debureaucratizes" some of the public functions by involving a larger number of groups and political interests.

DRIVING FORCES FOR POLITICAL DEVOLUTION

Many driving forces at the global, national, and local levels have influenced recent trends toward greater political devolution and the transfer of financial authority from the center to regions and local areas.

The demise of the former Soviet Union and the end of the Cold War have led to greater recognition at the global level of the need for political pluralism and the devolution of political and financial authority. In the past, political leaders such as those in some Southeast Asian countries—including Indonesia and Malaysia—used the communist threat as a reason to centralize political power. With the collapse of leftist and authoritarian regimes in Latin America, weaknesses in political structures and economic outcomes in these countries were exposed to the people. Some African countries played one superpower against the other. In the post–Cold War period, there are greater internal pressures on policymakers in the United States and the Western countries to promote and protect democracy and human rights in developing countries—even though strategic and economic interests continue to be important factors in their assistance programs.

An increase in ethnic conflicts and a demand for greater recognition of cultural, religious, and regional traditions have focused the debate on political devolution in such countries as Sri Lanka, Nigeria, and Sudan. One point of view is that increased participation in local decision-making would enable local groups to have a "stake" in the political system and would provide local actors with opportunities to influence local decisions directly.

Bilateral donors, multilateral agencies, and nongovernmental organizations are focusing on the centrality of democratic governance including political and financial accountability and transparency in promoting people-centered development. In some cases, this resulted in conditionalities, nudging political regimes to devolve more political power to local and community-based institutions. The rationale of development assistance agencies to support decentralized governance included giving responsibility for the provision and management of services to the level of government authority closest to the people, and enhancing the capacity and legitimacy of these authorities.[10]

The most critical driving force for political devolution was the demand by groups and individuals within the country for greater control over local political processes, greater transparency, better access to services, and more openness in the political decision-making process. With political awakening, improved infrastructural facilities, and better access to information, "pressure from below" was exerted to which the political actors at the national level had to respond.

The impact of new or restored democracies on devolution to local government, however, has not been uniform. In Pakistan, for example, the military governments of Ayub Khan in the 1960s, Zia-ul-Haq in the 1970s, and more recently General Musharraf have all introduced major local government reforms to strengthen the power and resources of local governments and allowed local elections in order to enhance the political legitimacy of their respective regimes. On the other hand, the elected governments of Zulfiqar Bhutto, Nawaz Sharif, and Benazir Bhutto either delayed local elections for a long time or did not sufficiently empower local governments to play a catalytic role in local economic development.

The Local Government Plan 2000 introduced by the military-led government of Pakistan is one of the most comprehensive local government reforms in the country's history in terms of local government's control over local resources and financial autonomy, district and subdistrict planning system, and local level information and monitoring system. The Local Government Plan integrates rural and urban local governments as well as government departments at the local level into one coherent structure in which district administration and the police are accountable to the elected chief executive of the district.[11] Even though the role of local governments in the development process has been increased, genuine political devolution and participation cannot be sustained without elected central and provincial legislatures. Recognizing this, elections for the National Assembly and Provincial Legislatures were organized in October 2002, which led to the civilian government at the national and provincial levels.

South Africa's local councils elected in 1995 are an example of a genuine attempt at empowerment. These councils were aimed at extending the democratic processes to local areas, and at creating institutional mechanisms for the delivery of goods and services. Furthermore, the creation of these councils was considered to be an important instrument to create equitable distribution of resources, by merging white-dominated and prosperous localities with poorer, black-dominated areas, and by providing new positions to political activists who had struggled against the anti-apartheid policies of the past under the leadership of the African National Congress.

In addition to global and nation-specific reasons, there are also region-specific factors that led to the expanding role of local governments—the advent of multi-party political systems in Africa, the deepening of democracy in Latin America after the latest wave of democratization, the transition from a command to market economy in Eastern Europe and Central Asian Republics after the demise of the former Soviet Union, the need to decentralize service delivery in East and Southeast Asia, and the ethnic and geographical necessity in South Asia.

SOME RECENT CASE STUDIES OF DEVOLUTION

The global trends towards devolution of political and financial authority are visible in many recent country level decentralization initiatives.

In **India**—the largest democracy in the world—widening popular participation in political decision-making is creating new opportunities and challenges. With the adoption of two amendments to India's constitution in 1992, local governments have been strengthened. In 1999, about 238,000 local councils were elected across the country. They are made up of three million elected representatives, one-third of whom are women and 660,000 are from the hitherto marginalized scheduled castes. These reforms have the potential to bring about major systemic change in the structure of local government in rural areas.[12] For example, in some villages, people are conducting "social audits" of government funds to ensure accountability and transparency. Because one-third of local councilors are women, they are exerting their influence as local leaders—weakening well-entrenched vested interests. *Gram Sabha* (village assemblies) are more frequently contesting corrupt practices and the abuse of power. This experiment in greater democracy at the grass roots, however, is not without its challenges—resistance by local traditional elite, increase in local conflicts, and difficulties of coordination.

In **Ghana,** the restructuring of local governments has provided more authority and resources to local governments. Within the guidelines provided by the National Development Planning Commission, districts have considerable autonomy to decide development needs and priorities on their own and have more control over resources. They can raise some of their own resources and negotiate directly with donors for district-level projects. Five percent of the national budget is allocated to them—based partly on need—specifically for development purposes. The advantages of devolution to district councils are that communities have a greater level of participation in development activities in their districts and that the district plans are more responsive to their needs. Yet, in many cases, plans as completed documents are given to the communities for approval with limited commitment and democratic decision-making by the communities. Another constraint on effective devolution to local governments is the reluctance of qualified staff to work in poorer areas due to lack of education and health facilities, especially in the remote areas. In addition, those who are transferred to poorer areas have sufficient authority but lack the capacity to carry out the work.[13]

The government of **Nepal** has been actively carrying out decentralization since the early 1980s, but it was only in the 1990s that these efforts focused on building participatory institutions. The turning point was the early 1990s with the introduction of a multiparty system and the passage of new laws. As a result, local governments have gained increased authority and responsibility and have been empowered to collect more taxes and strengthen their administrative capacities. District Development Committees were created to lead planning process at the local level. Villagers were encouraged to join community organizations in order to identify their needs. A Participatory District Development Program has helped empower committees in 20 districts to undertake participatory planning processes and design District Development Plans that have dealt with pressing local needs such as job creation, women's empowerment, and environmental management.[14]

Yemen's experience with decentralized governance dates back to its Local Development Associations of the late 1960s. These groups were able to mobilize most of their resources from local communities to build schools and local health clinics. Regional Development Initiatives, piloted in five governorates, emphasize fostering community self-reliance in addition to providing micro-credit and technical assistance. The number of civil society organizations in Yemen has been growing rapidly.[15]

Uganda has one of the most comprehensive of all decentralization programs in Africa. The new constitution adopted in 1995 calls for the devolution of power to local governments. The Local Government Act of 1997 grants local councils the powers to raise revenues and initiate their own development programs. Local councilors were elected in 1998. Subcounties are allowed to retain about two-thirds of the revenue collected in their areas. Though the local councils provide an institutional framework for the participation of local citizens, many local leaders and their constituents are held back by illiteracy, lack of knowledge of government procedures, and lack of awareness of their rights.[16]

The new decentralization policy in **Malawi** owes its origin to the introduction of a multiparty electoral system, which led in 1998 to a new decentralization policy and a new Local Government Act passed by the parliament. The key features of the policy are the deconcentration of central administrative authority to the district level; the integration of government agencies at the district and local levels; transfer of implementation responsibilities to the districts, assigning powers, functions, and responsibilities to other levels of government; and the promotion of popular participation and developmental activities at the district level. The overall objective is to create democratic institutions at the local level. The Local Government System is composed of district, town, municipal, and city assemblies. The initial assessment of the policy implementation shows that the legal framework for the decentralization policy is in place. There is an increased awareness of the decentralization policy at the national, district, and local levels. Several constraints, however, continue to impede implementation of the policy, including a shortage of human and financial resources, a lack of appropriate training programs, as well as weak vertical and horizontal management communication lines, and inadequate prior assessment of local capacities.[17]

FACTORS INFLUENCING THE SUCCESS OF DECENTRALIZATION

Many factors determine the success of decentralization including the devolution of political and financial authority. At the macro level, one of the lessons from the experience in developing countries is that a clear and coherent set of rules delineating the powers, responsibilities, and resources of each level of government should replace the centralized, hierarchical governance system.[18] At the micro level, ten recently published original case studies examined the impact of different forms of decentralization on strengthening democratic governance.[19] The research, sponsored by United Nations Development Program, was undertaken by universities and research institutions in developing countries in collaboration with the Department of Urban and Regional Planning at Massachusetts Institute of Technology (MIT). The case studies attempted to determine the contribution of five factors to the success of different forms of decentralization in improving local governance and service delivery: appropriate government policies and institutional structures; partnerships among different actors at the local level; leadership of local actors; and local administrative capacity and adequate financial resources.[20]

The case studies of decentralization programs and country-level examples of some of the recent decentralization policies show the critical factors that affect the implementation of decentralization.

Political Environment and National Legal Framework

The political environment and the national legal framework shape the form and content of decentralization policies and programs. Where a national political system is authoritarian, political devolution to local governments is constrained. Also important are the characteristics of the local power structure and the extent to which the beneficiaries are organized. In many developing countries such as Pakistan, Brazil, and South Africa, highly unequal land ownerships in rural areas have in the past led to the dominance of local vested interests in the economic and political decision-making process. In such circumstances, local political and economic autonomy can turn to control—and in some cases tyranny—by the local elite, requiring central government safeguards to protect the interests of the poor. Equally important are constitutional and legislative frameworks.

The politics and progress of decentralization in India provides an interesting example of the role of the national sociopolitical environment on the substance of political devolution and the way implementation takes place.[21] The 72nd and 73rd Constitutional Amendment bills were passed in 1991 in the two houses of the Indian Parliament and received the assent of the president in 1993. The final act included several features which have laid the foundation of democracy at the grass roots and an effective multilevel governance system accountable to people—the establishment of village, intermediate, and district-level *panchayats* (councils);

the election of mayors and municipal chairmen, in some states; the representation of members of the parliament in the local councils; vesting the conduct of local elections in an independent and autonomous Election Commission; and the establishment of Finance Commissions in the states to improve their financial base.

Explicit policies accompanied by legal reform and focused on specific sectors such as health, housing, and education improve the chances of successful decentralization programs. For example, in Brazil, a broad national decentralization initiative embodied constitutional and legal reform at the central level, enabling the local government of Belo Horizonte to develop its own policies of transparent and inclusive partnerships at the local level. The Philippines has developed one of the most decentralized governance systems in Asia since the passage of the Local Government Code in 1991.

One of the issues in political devolution to local governments has been the low level of the representation by women. Reserving seats for women has been suggested as a mechanism to enhance gender equity in political representation. In India, for example, the provision of one-third representation was generally accepted during the parliamentarian debates. There was strong opposition to the reservation of seats for women in the national parliament, which could be attributed to the perception on the part of many Members of Parliament (MPs) that one-third representation at the local government level did not pose a threat to them.[22]

Experience suggests that there are continuous tensions between elected representatives for national parliaments and for provincial legislatures from a local government jurisdiction and elected representatives of local governments. In new and restored democracies as well as in stable democracies in developing countries, the tendency on the part of political representatives at the national level is to focus more on local development activities and patronage and less on analysis of national policy issues and on national legislation. By assuming the de facto role of local councilors, members of the national parliaments tend to undermine the role of local government leaders.

Effectively balancing political power between central and local interests is essential to sustain decentralization policies and programs.[23] Bicameral legislative systems usually give equal representation to regions strengthening regional interests, or they may be selected by the regional governments themselves as in the case of India and South Africa. Similarly, the executive in most presidential systems and the parliamentarian system with a large majority have a greater ability to withstand pressures from regional interests. It is because of this that no one model is replicable for every country. The success of decentralization would depend on the ability of political actors to identify and support the political power balance.

Functions and Resources of Subnational Governments

One of the principles in the division of functions and responsibilities between the central and subnational governments is their respective comparative advantages in providing a specific service. The services provided by the center should benefit all subregions and show economies of scale. Subnational government should be responsible for services at the local level. The trade-off is between the need to ensure that the services provided by the center meet the preferences and priorities of diverse regional interests and the need for central initiatives to ensure interregional equality through redistributive policies.[24]

Clear distribution of functions and responsibilities is necessary but not sufficient to create an effective partnership between the central and subnational governments. Local governments need resources in proportion to their responsibilities. Because of difficulties in collecting property tax and, in most cases, the political unacceptability of a capitation tax, many municipalities such as those in Brazil and Jordan rely on different forms of business taxation. Transfers are essential tools at the disposal of the central government to fund services provided by local governments on its behalf, to ensure that decentralization does not take place at the expense of equity due to differences in the resource base of subnational governments, and to influence sectoral patterns of local expenditures.[25]

The grant of sufficient powers is necessary to increase the influence of local governments within the political system. Yet, the devolution of powers without resources does not increase the influence of local actors over development activities. The influence of the local actors in identifying local priorities and protecting the interests of local groups continues to be minimal.

The World Bank's *World Development Report, 1999/2000* shows an expanding role of local governments both on the revenue and the expenditure side. In 28 percent of the countries examined, locally generated revenue between 1990 and 1997 was more than one-fifth of their resources.[26] However, most countries still rely heavily on intergovernmental transfers to finance local expenditure.

Sometimes centrally created decentralization programs are innovative but are not effectively linked to an established local government system or sources of local political support. Thus, these programs continue to function as bureaucratic instruments of the central government.

Most of the UN case studies described above used innovative mechanisms in financing that either brought new and additional resources from higher levels or cost sharing among various partners. Service-specific decentralization in Brazil and Jordan brought both new resources and cost sharing among partners. In Honduras and India, local resource mobilization was enhanced. The specialized agency for a squatter settlement in Pakistan was forced to raise revenue from its activities and become financially independent when resources provided by the central government were cut. The primary health care innovations in the Philippines have been financed from various sources including the municipality's share of the internal revenue, appropriations from the central department, contributions from neighborhood groups, and revenues from income generation activities. The Polish case involved significant local cost recovery and the mobilization of capital from the private sector.

Equally important is technical assistance and training from the central government. In the case of Brazil, for example, educational programs were developed to promote community participation in health services reforms. In Pakistan, the Orangi Pilot Project, an NGO, was actively involved in the training of local leaders to design and implement the squatter improvement program.

The decentralization of fiscal authority does not automatically increase the resource base of local authorities. To begin with, the local governments with new authority might lack the administrative capacity to increase their resource base because of their inability to evaluate property and improve collection from the existing tax base. Local politicians also tend to be reluctant either to levy new taxes, even though these have been authorized, or to enforce tax collection, due to their linkages with local groups who might be defaulting. This is in conflict with the perception by national policymakers that decentralization would increase the local resource base.

More importantly, some local jurisdictions have a stagnant local economy—especially in remote rural areas—that limits their capacity to increase locally generated revenue. This requires central government intervention to reduce the disparities in the resource base of local governments in different parts of the country.

Accountability of Local Governments and the Role of Political Parties

An important set of rules accounting for the success of decentralization concerns the relations between local government officials and their constituents—the degrees to which local leaders are accountable to their constituents through formal mechanisms. Local elections are necessary starting points for this purpose. Other measures are electoral rules that encourage local participation and representation, active involvement of civil society organizations in local political processes, and effective local administration to deliver services in their areas of responsibility.

The role of political parties is important to institutionalize the local government system.[27] Experience in developing countries in Latin America and Africa shows that democratic transformation over the past few years has taken place with the active involvement of trade unions, religious groups, grassroots movements, and other groups in the society. Once the regime change takes place, however, these groups are not able to sustain their pressures from below. It is the role of political parties to maintain a link between the civil society and the government.

The reality of the situation in developing countries is that even when political parties are banned from participating in local elections—as happened in the case of Pakistan during the recent local elections organized by the military-led government—political parties find ways to bypass the ban on indirect participation of political parties. The involvement of political parties yields many benefits: better linkages of local councils with representative structures at the central level, connections with senior national government officials through the political party structures, and the provision of responsibilities to local political leaders to enable them to learn political skills and eventually to move to higher level political positions. Indeed, regularly elected local governments provide a training ground for future political leaders, as experience in many old democracies suggests. The participation of political parties is particularly important in the case of devolution of authority to local governments: this facilitates the emergence of multiparty, pluralistic politics, one of the core principles of democratic governance.

Historical Legacies and Traditional Authority Structures

The way a local government system works also depends upon historical legacies and traditional authority structures. Colonial rulers in Africa and Asia introduced many new institutions and structures of government and administration at the local level, parallel to traditional authority structures. Over the years, political party structures and representative institutions have been added at many levels. One of the challenges is to ensure the mutually reinforcing role of each of these structures in order to promote participatory local development. Malawi is a case in point. Three types of structures exist at the local level—traditional authority, political structures, and administration structures. The Traditional Authorities

Structure (chiefs, subchiefs, village headman) existed before colonial rule. During colonial rule, administrative and judicial powers were devolved to chiefs who played and continue to play an important role in mobilizing people for developmental activities. The political parties structures—extending from the national to village level—focus on elections to National Assemblies and District Assemblies. Since the 1970s, some of the central ministries and departments have deconcentrated certain functions to district and community levels. Each of these structures has its strengths.[28]

Weak Capacity at the Central Level

In order for decentralization policies and programs to succeed, central and state governments need to provide policy guidelines and training support to local governments. Where the capacity at the central level is weak, too rapid decentralization to local government might not yield positive results. After independence, most states inherited weak capacities to perform such functions as the maintenance of law and order, the provision of social services, the creation of legal and judicial systems and processes, and the management of natural resources. Some of the central governments themselves lacked the capacity to provide technical support to local governments. Human resources were concentrated at the national level. Furthermore, centrifugal forces within many societies threatened the legitimacy of the central authority.

Administrative Capacity of Local Governments

Often governments in developing countries maintain decentralized planning, decision-making, and management functions in local governments without considering the administrative capacities of the local and regional governments to carry out their new functions. Many countries have devolved or delegated functions to all local governments throughout the country. While local governments in more prosperous parts of the country take full advantage of the new functions because of their existing capacities, those in poor areas of the country have different levels of administrative capacity. This leads to further widening of gaps between local governments in different parts of the country. Usually there are severe shortages of skilled personnel at the local level—particularly in remote rural areas—where there are inadequate education, health, housing, and other facilities and services.

The attitudes and values of central government officials play an important role in enabling local government officials to exercise their assigned authority. Paternalistic and authoritarian attitudes of central government bureaucracy discourage elected local government officials from carrying out their newly assigned duties.

The Role of Civil Society and Community-Based Groups

The role of civil society organizations and community-based groups is cited as one of the most critical factors in making decentralization work at the local level. Farmers' associations, youth clubs, local branches of political parties, and women's organizations can increase local support and legitimacy for government intervention. In addition, they can serve as guardians of the interests of local groups and citizens. The role of these organizations is particularly important in improving the people's access to basic services by identifying target groups, increasing awareness of these groups about the governmental and nongovernmental initiatives, and in some cases directly providing services to the poor. Organizations of small farmers, for example, could be used to deliver agricultural inputs such as credit and fertilizers. Civil society organizations and community-based groups also play an important role in creating political awareness among the people at the local level. They provide disadvantaged groups with a mechanism by which to organize themselves. For example, some NGOs encourage landless laborers to organize themselves for better wages, which they might be afraid to do individually.

In the Philippines, the Balilihan Country Action Program (BCAP) involved neighborhood associations in designing and implementing activities in health and sanitation, agricultural development, education, livelihood and environmental protection, and other sectors.[29] In the Honduras Program, all communities in the municipality of Sinuapa have organized neighborhood associations. The distribution of municipal resources is based on the annual plans of these associations, which are jointly discussed by the associations and the coordinating municipal-level body.[30]

Local Leadership

The devolution of power and resources and the enactment of new local government legislation provide a framework for the emergence of empowered local governments accountable to their constituents. Yet, it is local leadership—from government, civil society, and the private sector—that accounts for variations in the performance of different local governments in different parts of the country.

In Honduras, for example, the role of the mayor of Sinuapa as a consensus builder between communities and the local government and as a mediator for national departments and international assistance agencies has been an important factor in the success of this devolution effort. The mayor organizes regular open council meetings to consult with urban communities and rural villages in order to establish priorities for the council work plan. In India, an informal coalition of local actors, led by a local NGO, put pressure on the government's Department of Public Health and Engineering to improve the effectiveness of local projects.

In the Philippines, NGOs and community groups have taken the critical initiative to bring about successful reform in the provision of services. The primary health care service delivery in Surigao City was implemented through women's clubs. A midwife from the city's health office along with Barangay (local area) health workers organized mothers in neighborhoods and trained them in nutrition education and sanitation. This facilitated the delivery of primary health care services including immunization, family planning, and nutrition education. In Brazil, too, community leaders worked together to ensure that the new health committee system would work properly in Belo Horizonte City.

PARTNERSHIPS FOR LOCAL ACTION: LOCALISM IN THE AGE OF GLOBALIZATION

Equitable and mutually beneficial partnerships among local actors—government, civil society, the private sector, and community-based groups—are instrumental both in putting pressure "from below" for the devolution of power and resources and in implementing existing decentralization policies and programs. In large metropolitan areas—Bombay, Mexico City, and Karachi, for example—local government structures can be remote from the day-to-day needs of the people. However, representatives of the metropolitan government and municipal government employees can forge mutually beneficial partnerships with the representatives of civil society organizations, the private sector, and community-based organizations. This enables the municipal government to elicit the participation of local citizens in municipal government initiatives. In addition, it provides a mechanism by which the other local actors can hold municipal government functionaries accountable to the people. More important, such "local-local" partnerships and dialogue benefit from potential contributions from each partner and utilize a full complement of human energy in the city.

An interesting example of local partnerships in support of local initiatives is the Local Initiative Facility for the Urban Environment (LIFE program), which is supported by the United Nations Development Programme in 12 countries.[31]

The design of the LIFE program is based on a two-pronged approach: the first is the creation of mechanisms and structures for promoting dialogue among local actors at the community, municipal, and national levels. These include national and/or city consultation to map priorities and establish criteria for support, the Program Selection Committee to review local initiatives to promote learning, the National Program Coordinator to promote interaction among actors, and community-based groups to suggest local initiatives that have potential for learning and replication at the municipal and/or national level. Second, the program provides small grants to those community-based initiatives that attempt to respond to local environmental problems such as waste management, environmental education, water supply and sanitation, primary health care, and income generation activities. The program combines the process of making local decisions with solutions to concrete problems faced by local communities. It supports both the process of dialogue and interaction of local actors and the solution to concrete environmental problems that affect the local people directly and immediately. The program is being implemented in 12 countries with a number of dialogue workshops and participants, and a number of local projects.

There are three stages of program development in each of the selected countries: (1) upstream—catalyzing national dialogue, developing strategies, and gathering support; (2) downstream—ensuring effective and collaborative small projects; and (3) disseminating and exchanging information nationally and internationally.

The LIFE program promoted democracy at the grass roots in several ways. First, the approach of the program empowered local actors due to increased dialogue among them about their local problems and the sharing of responsibilities among them. The result in most cases was an increased level of local and community organization and the ability of local actors to build on their own local initiatives as well as benefit from national resources because of the strength of the local organization. Second, the LIFE program provided a mechanism to civil society organizations and community-based groups to interact with other local and municipal leaders and representatives of national government in the area. Through their networks created through the structure of the LIFE program, local and community-based leaders are more likely to influence the process of resource allocation at the municipal level. Third, the program provided an effective mechanism for the participation of people in the development process. In most of government-initiated programs the concept of participation tends to be limited to eliciting the involvement of beneficiaries. However, the LIFE program provided a decentralized structure through which decisions concerning local environmental problems could be made locally.

The case of the LIFE program shows the need for pro-poor local governance in which the civil society, urban government, the business sector, and the representatives of central government at the local level build partnerships to respond to problems that affect the poor—such as waste management, water supply and sanitation, primary health care, and education. The pillars of effective pro-poor local governance include elected and autonomous local government with adequate capacity and information base, strong developmentally oriented civil society organizations, a socially responsible business sector, and local partnerships of the government, the civil society, and the business sector.

CONCLUSION

Decentralization strengthens democracy at the grass roots—by providing opportunities for citizen participation in local decision-making, ensuring accountability of local political leaders and government officials, and promoting a system of checks and balances among various levels of government. Decentralization also promotes the institutionalization of democratic culture and improves the citizens' access to government-supported services. In view of this, many global forces and national factors have contributed to the recent trends towards decentralization—the end of the Cold War, increasing support from bilateral and multilateral development organizations, and pressures from within the countries due to improved access to information and demands for greater recognition of cultural and linguistic identities. Recent good practices of national-level decentralization policies and programs point to the potential to strengthen democratic governance at the local level. They also highlight key systemic constraints that are impeding the implementation of decentralization policies and programs—including limited financial and administrative capacities of local governments, weakness of national-level political and legal frameworks, and historical legacies and local power structures. Despite these systemic constraints, local-level partnerships among local actors—government functionaries, civil society organizations, the private sector—are paving the way in making decentralization work for the benefit of the people in this age of globalization.

ENDNOTES

1. Among others, see G. Shabbir Cheema and Dennis A. Rondinelli, eds. *Decentralization and Development: Policy Implementation in Developing Countries* (Beverly Hills: Sage, 1983); Jerry Silverman, *Public Sector Decentralization* (Washington, DC: The World Bank, 1990); John Cohen, *Administrative Decentralization for the 1990s and Beyond* (monograph prepared for the United Nations Department for Development Support and Management Services, New

York: 1995); Dennis A. Rondinelli, John Nellis and G. Shabbir Cheema, *Decentralization in Developing Countries* (working paper 581, World Bank Staff, Washington, DC, 1984); Harry Blair, *Assessing Democratic Decentralization* (Washington, DC: United States Agency for International Development, 1995).

2. World Bank, *World Development Report, 1999–2000* (Washington, DC: WB, 2000), 107–108.

3. UNDP, *Overcoming Human Poverty* (New York: UNDP, 2000), 55–62.

4. World Bank, *World Development Report 1999–2000*, 110.

5. Larry Diamond, *Developing Democracy: Toward Consolidation* (Baltimore: Johns Hopkins University Press, 1999), 123.

6. Ibid., 132–138.

7. Ibid., 133–138.

8. Cheema and Rondinelli, eds. *Decentralization and Development*, 22–24.

9. Harry J. Friedman, "Decentralized Development in Asia: Local Political Initiatives" in *Decentralization and Development*, 43.

10. Capital Development Fund, *Poverty Reduction, Participation and Local Governance: A Fund for Local and Community Development* (New York: Capital Development Fund, 1995).

11. Government of Pakistan, *Local Government Plan 2000* (Islamabad: National Reconstruction Bureau, 2000), 1.

12. K.C. Sivaramakrishnan, *Power to the People? The Politics and Progress of Decentralisation* (New Delhi: Konark Publishers, 2000), 3–22.

13. UNDP, *Overcoming Human Poverty* (New York: UNDP, 2000), 55–62.

14. Nepal Case Study in UNDP, *Overcoming Human Poverty*, 2000.

15. Yemen Case Study in *Overcoming Human Poverty*.

16. Uganda Case Study in *Overcoming Human Poverty*.

17. Department of Rural Development, University of Malawi, *Decentralized Governance in Malawi* Assessment Report (2000), 1–15.

18. World Bank, "Decentralization: Rethinking Government" in *World Development Report 1999–2000*, 112–113.

19. Nine case studies were published by UNDP, New York: Management Development and Governance Division, 2000. These were as follows:

1. *Universalising Health Care Access through Popular Participation in Brazil* by Mercés Somarriba, Edite Novais da Mata Machado, and Telma Maria Concalves Menicucci, Governance School of Minas Gerais, Belo Horizonte, Brazil.

2. *Decentralisation and Citizen Participation in Honduras* by Leticia Salomon and Oscar Avila, Centro de Documentacion de Honduras (CEDOH), Tegucigalpa, Honduras.

3. *Facilitating Local Participation through Rural Panchayats in India* by Chandan Datta, Society for Participatory Research in Asia, New Delhi, India.

4. *Extending Educational Access through Deconcentration of Services in Jordan* by the Jordan Institute of Public Administration (JPA), Amman, Jordan—Team leader: Dr. Zuhairal-Kayed; team members: Dr. Mohammed Ta'Amneh, Dr. Awni Halseh and Mutaz Assaf.

5. *Squatter Settlement Transformation through Decentralised Participation in Pakistan* by Aisha Ghaus-Pasha, Social Policy Development Center, Karachi.

6. *Expanding Basic Health Service Delivery through Partnership with the People in the Philippines* by Proserpina Domingo Tapales, University of the Philippines, Quezon City, Philippines.

7. *Releasing Local Private Enterprise through Municipal Strategies in Poland* by Grzegorz Gorzelak, Bohdan Jalowiecki, Richard Woodword, Wojciech Dziemianowicz, Wojciech Roszkowski and Thomas Zarcycki, Center for Social and Economic Research and University of Warsaw, Poland.

8. *What Makes Markets Tick? Local Service Delivery in Uganda* by Harriet Birungi, Betty Kwagala, Nansozi Muwanga, Tobias Onweng and Eirik Jarl Trondsen, Makerere Institute of Social Research, Kampala, Uganda.

9. *Decentralising Service Delivery through Participation in South Africa* by Steven Friedman, Richard Humphries, Paul Thulare and Tebogo Mafakoana, Center for Policy Studies, Johannesburg, South Africa.

20. G. Shabbir Cheema and Mounir Tabet, "Decentralized Governance for Human Development" in *New Millennium, New Perspectives—The United Nations, Security and Governance,* ed. Ramesh Thakur and Edward Newman (Tokyo: United Nations University Press, 2000), 261–295.

21. K. C. Sivaramakrishnan, *Power to the People? The Politics and Progress of Decentralization*, 3–22.

22. Ibid.

23. World Bank, *World Development Report 1999–2000*, 113–114.

24. Ibid., 115.

25. Ibid.

26. Ibid.

27. Ibid.

28. Department of Rural Development, University of Malawi, *Decentralized Governance in Malawi*.

29. Philippines case study—*Expanding Basic Health Service Delivery through Partnership with the People in the Philippines*.

30. Honduras case study—*Decentralisation and Citizen Participation in Honduras*.

31. UNDP, *Participatory Local Governance* (New York, UNDP), 1997.

CHAPTER 7

GLOBALIZATION AND PUBLIC SECTOR MANAGEMENT CAPACITY

Effective and efficient public sector management promotes and strengthens democracy and good governance. An effectively functioning civil service is essential in order to ensure that democratically elected leaders are able to protect the rights of citizens, and to mobilize resources through taxes and other sources in order to pay for police, judges, and services. A consolidated democracy requires the administrative capacity of the state to maintain law and order, and to promote and protect public goods such as the environment. Public confidence in the political system—and subsequently the political legitimacy of the government—is increased where the public service delivery system is effective, where the public officials are accessible to local citizens, and where government agencies and departments work together in well-coordinated, complementary ways. Equally important is the "capacity to govern"—to make important policy choices, to design and implement programs and actions to achieve policy objectives, and to anticipate emerging trends and challenges.[1] Public sector management capacity to perform the above and related tasks, however, requires qualified personnel recruited based on merit, human resource development strategies, motivated and committed civil servants, and transparent processes for policy formulation, budgeting, and implementation.

Over the past few decades, improving the public sector management capacity has been one of the most critical issues facing developing economies. With the rapid pace of globalization, the public sector is under even greater pressures to increase its capacity to deal with new challenges and opportunities presented by globalization—new information and communication technologies, the expansion of trade and investment, an increased focus on such public goods as the environment and human rights, and the proactive role of global institutions such as the World Trade Organization that affect development processes at the national level.

Globalization promotes democracy and global social awareness in many other ways as well. The use of modern communication devices including the Internet and the media has increased public awareness of human rights violations including child abuse, violence against women, and corruption among government officials. The advances in information and communication technologies and the reduction of transportation costs—two of the by-products of globalization—have enabled non-state actors at the national, regional, and global levels to form alliances against unde-mocratic policies and practices. The state and its institutions are under tremendous pressure from national and international actors to respond to development chal-lenges including increased accountability and transparency in economic and politi-cal decision-making. In view of the above, "a wide variety of values and systems of democracy, such as citizens exercising their basic political rights of electing their own governments, are increasingly becoming the global standards in the political arena."[2] The enforcement of these standards at the national level requires adequate manage-ment capacity at the national and local levels.

This chapter reviews key issues in public sector management capacity in devel-oping countries, the magnitude and impact of globalization on developing econ-omies, and the changing role of the state to meet new challenges. This is followed by case studies of public sector management innovations (in Malaysia, Singapore, and Uganda), as these relate to the issues of public sector management capacity and the changing role of the state.

CRITICAL ISSUES IN PUBLIC SECTOR MANAGEMENT CAPACITY

Developing countries have traditionally faced a set of critical issues in public sector management.

1. **Civil Service Reforms:** Many of the public sector management issues are usually discussed under civil service reform, which is defined either broadly as the major functions and responsibilities of government or, more narrowly, as issues of remu-neration, the number of employees, performance appraisal, personnel recruit-ment, selection, placement, promotion, and related issues. The market-based approaches to civil service reform are likely to focus on short-term cost contain-ment measures dealing primarily with payment and employment systems. The premise of such approaches usually is that structures, staffing levels, remunera-tion, job classification systems, and overall civil service costs are fundamental problems that need to be dealt with to ensure effective civil service reform.[3]

   There are many causes of civil service weaknesses in developing economies. First of all, governments are under tremendous pressure to provide employment, and this often results in the overstaffing of government departments and semi-autonomous organizations, especially in the unskilled and semi-skilled grades; in some cases the excessive staffing even leads to ghost workers who continue to be paid without working. A second cause stems from the favoritism in the recruitment process, because of which personnel with insufficient qualifications and experience are sometimes promoted to senior positions. Third, political and ethnic pressures make it difficult for the central civil service management agencies to take action against those performing at a sub par level. Fourth, the low salaries of the personnel lead to low morale, fewer incentives to work, and "moonlighting." In each of these situations, there is a breakdown in government performance.[4]

Over the past few decades, many developing countries also initiated institution-building programs aimed at such activities as enhancing the skills and knowledge of the personnel to improve their job performance, changing the structure and culture of the organization and the way it is managed, specifying the mission of the organization, and improving the quality and timeliness of the products and services of the organization.

2. **Leadership and Vision:** Good leadership and vision are essential if a government organization is to produce quality services. The "transformational" leaders are able to provide vision and direction to the organization, build consensus on strategy to operationalize the vision, identify clear ways to overcome environmental constraints, and energize and inspire the staff of the organization to achieve organizational objectives. They encourage development and change, as opposed to control and status quo. These characteristics, argue Osborne and Gaebler, lead to mission-driven as opposed to rule-bound government.[5] One of the constraints on public sector management in developing countries has been a shortage of high-quality leadership in government organizations. Senior managers tend, due to constraints in their sociopolitical environment, to be conservative, unwilling to take risks, and inward rather than outward looking. The authoritarian nature of a national political system and the hierarchical controls discourage even those who have the aptitude and desire to lead.

3. **Strategic Management:** The strategic management of organizations in relation to their environment is another critical issue in the public sector management capacity. It deals with the determination of the mission and purpose of the organization, main policies and plans to achieve the mission, and activities aimed at its products and services in the interest of stakeholders. The interdependence of mission, policies, and activities can enable the organization to position itself within its environment, build its identity, and use its strengths to carve out a niche for the organization.[6]

Governments recognize usefulness of strategic management. In the case of Tanzania, for example, as a part of the national civil service reform program, several strategic activities were undertaken—the establishment of the Civil Service Department in the Office of the President to lead the reforms in the civil service, the reduction in the size of civil service through retrenchment, the introduction of user charges and other cost-sharing measures, and the abolishment or amalgamation of a number of parastatals. The case studies in this chapter of Malaysia and Singapore illustrate the significance of strategic management in the process of public sector reform.

4. **Human Resource Management and Training:** Another critical issue is human resource management that includes organizational structure and culture, personnel selection and placement, training and development, job design, and performance appraisal. In many developing countries, human resource management continues to focus on administering rules and regulations instead of introducing a proactive approach to improve performance.[7] Some of the recent success stories of human resource development include Malaysia and Singapore. As the case studies in this chapter show, human resource management—one of the key pillars of the reform efforts in both countries—was designed and implemented to meet both the short-term and long-term needs in response to the changing role of the state.

The shortage of skilled and well-trained managers is a major constraint on effective public sector management in developing economies. To respond to this problem, developing countries and external partners have invested a huge amount of funds in management training and development. Public administration institutions were established in most of the countries to introduce new—largely Western—management techniques for government organizations and to train government officials at senior, middle, and lower levels. The results of the past management training and development programs have been mixed. There are many reasons for that. Many of the training programs, especially those of short duration, have focused on lectures and have not provided a forum to analyze practical issues in real-world situations. Even when the training programs are based on sound methodologies and practical problems, the participants are not able to use the experience in the sociopolitical environment in which they perform their day-to-day activities.

There are, however, some examples of successful management development institutes. The National Institute of Public Administration (INTAN) in Malaysia offers training programs at all levels as an integral part of the public sector reform in the country. The Eastern and Southern Africa Management Institute (ESAMI) seeks to improve the performance and effectiveness of management in the public and the private sector.

5. **Improving Service Delivery:** The need to improve the quality of and access to public services is another critical issue in public sector management. Total Quality Management (TQM), a Japanese-inspired management practice, implies continuous improvement of products and service quality, a shorter and more reliable response time throughout the process of production, a sales and service provision, and constant concern about customers and efficiency. These principles are applicable, with modification, to all public sector organizations in all cultures. In the case of Uruguay, for example, in his annual report to the parliament, the president pointed out that the "TQM in Uruguay—the National Debureaucratization Program" led to savings of over \$20 million in public services because the program introduced a new accounting and financial management law and new administrative procedures. The computerized registration of revenue-generating organization and individuals "reduced fiscal evasion and simplified record keeping."[8] Malaysia has emphasized TQM to improve service quality.

6. **Interorganizational Relations:** In addition to intraorganizational issues in public sector management, there are a number of issues concerning interorganizational and intergovernmental relations that significantly influence the performance of individual government organizations. One of the most important issues concerns central-local government responsibilities and relationships. In order to build effective partnership between different levels of government, it is essential to streamline and clarify areas of primary and secondary responsibilities of each level of government and administration. While the constitution in each country—whether federal or unitary—provides a list of principles on which these relationships are to be based, in actual practice the areas of responsibilities need to be understood and acted upon by government functionaries at different levels. One of the problems in most government organizations—lack of coordination— usually emanates from a lack of clarity in the division of responsibilities among different levels. In most cases, however, government officials at different levels need to work together to complement each other's activities.

The rapid growth of urbanization and of the number of cities of all sizes highlights the complexity of governmental and interorganizational relations. The review of experiences gained through the Urban Management Program, one of the largest UN programs of technical assistance in this sector, shows that while a great deal of progress has been made in interorganizational and intergovernmental cooperation in the process of urban management, several urban governance challenges continue to affect service quality and service delivery—the need to reconcile the national planning processes and systems with those at the level of urban local government, the need to match the distribution of roles and responsibilities between the central and urban local government based on the comparative advantage and capacity of each level, and the need to provide financial resources to urban governments by expanding their powers to levy additional local taxes as well as through central government grants and transfers.[9]

There are four "building blocks" to improve public sector capacity in developing countries: (1) strong central capacity for formulating and coordinating policy,[10] (2) reform of institutions for the delivery of services,[11] (3) motivated and capable staff selected based on the highest qualifications at the entry level, intensive training, merit in the system of promotion and incentives, and the commitment of political leadership, and (4) effective mechanisms for interface between the public sector agencies and organizations of the people.

In addition to the above aspects of public sector management capacity, globalization has highlighted the significance of three other issues—accountability and transparency of the financial and administrative procedures and processes, new skills among the civil servants to cope with the global implications of national and local policy and program choices, and effective regulatory frameworks and judicial systems. These topics are discussed in chapter 3 and chapter 8.

THE MAGNITUDE AND IMPACT OF GLOBALIZATION

Globalization is a dominant force in the 21st century. It is shaping a new era of interaction—and interdependence—among nations, economies, and people. Most of the command economies of the past have been transformed into market-oriented economies. Integration is taking place not only in the economy but also in technology and governance. New technologies are developing rapidly. Knowledge-based industries and skills are growing in importance. The world economy is being increasingly integrated through an accelerated pace of trade and investment. Though globalization is not a new phenomenon, the present era is generating profound and far reaching changes in new markets (foreign exchange and capital markets linked globally), new tools (such as Internet links and media networks), new actors (such as the World Trade Organization and networks of global NGOs), and new rules (including multilateral agreements on trade and intellectual property).[12]

Globalization is providing new opportunities to millions of people around the world. To varying degrees, economic growth and improvements in people's living conditions are taking place due to increased trade, new technologies, foreign investments, expanding media and Internet connections.[13] For example, more than $1.5 trillion are exchanged each day in the world's currency markets. About one-fifth of goods and services produced each year are traded. Foreign direct investment topped $400 billion in 1997, seven times the level in the 1970s. Thus, rapid economic integration is taking place by the liberalization of trade, investment and capital flows, technological change, and an information revolution. Foreign direct investment provides capital and contributes to the transfer of skills and technology. A global consensus on shared values is emerging on such issues as fundamental human rights, gender equality, and protection and promotion of the environment.

Yet, global wealth has not led to equitable benefits for millions of people around the world. Nor are services and activities vital for human well-being ensured through a competitive market, which inevitably rewards those with access to assets and skills. Financial pressures are forcing governments to cut back on the supply of basic social services. For example, more than a quarter of the 4.5 billion people in developing countries still do not have some of life's basic choices such as survival beyond age 40. Nearly 1.5 billion people lack access to clean water and over 2.3 billion people live on incomes of less than $1 a day.

The inequalities between countries and among groups within countries have increased. For example, the income gap between the fifth of the world's people living in the richest countries and the fifth in the poorest countries was 74 to 1 in 1997 as compared to 30 to 1 in 1960.[14] As a result of globalization, people are facing new threats to human security—such as the financial turmoil in East Asia during 1997 to 1999—insecurities in jobs and income emanating from economic and corporate restructuring, the spread of HIV/AIDS, illicit trade in drugs, weapons and money laundering, and environmental degradation. The poor people and poor countries, states Oxfam's Policy Paper, "are being left behind in increasingly marginalized enclaves of deprivation within an ever more prosperous global economy. The rules of globalization have neglected the needs of those least equipped to benefit from new opportunities."[15] For example, the income gap between Sub-Sahara Africa and the industrialized countries is continuing to increase. Capital market liberalization has negatively affected the poor in some developing countries. Foreign direct investment has been concentrated in a few countries—especially in East and Southeast Asia.

Many countries fear the erosion of state sovereignty as transnational bodies such as the World Trade Organization and the United Nations Commission on Human Rights play a more active role in mediating on issues of national concern and enforcement of international laws. Trade liberalization creates "winners" and "losers"—sometimes generating unemployment in selected industries and producing more inequality among unskilled and skilled labor forces. It could also be one of the factors for political instability in the country. Other negative consequences of globalization are environmental degradation, the breakdown of indigenous societies, cross-border corruption, global reach of terrorists and extremist organizations, and crime and narcotics.

A large number of countries lack adequate access to new information and communication technologies, which are instrumental in the process of globalization. South Asia, with 23 percent of the world's population, for example, has fewer than 1 percent of the world's Internet users. Average cost to purchase a computer vis-à-vis income is much higher in less developed countries than in the West.[16]

Table 2 shows changes resulting from globalization and the effects of these changes on governance systems and processes.

The discussion on the positive and negative consequences of globalization leads to one conclusion: because globalization is a reality that can not be reversed, the challenge to the world community is to delineate rules and institutions for stronger governance at the local, national, regional, and global levels in order to take advantage of opportunities provided by it but also provide resources to ensure that it "works for people—not just for profits."[17] This entails ensuring that globalization protects human rights, reduces disparities within and between nations, diminishes the marginalization and poverty of people, and provides for social security and the sustainability of the environment.[18] National policies and institutional frameworks play a critical role in the process of globalization and the way it affects the poor in developing countries. Where trade liberalization and the deregulation of a market takes place without adequate redistributive measures, the poor are left behind and those with assets and greater entrepreneurship benefit from globalization. In practice, opportunities from globalization are unevenly distributed. Many countries have been benefiting from globalization—Malaysia, Chile, India, Poland, and Turkey, for example. However, a large number of countries—most of them in Africa such as Niger and Madagascar—are benefiting little—and in some cases becoming even more marginal.[19]

ROLE OF THE STATE—THE PARADIGM SHIFT

Development outcomes often vary widely among countries following reforms to open up their markets. The central factor accounting for the difference in development effectiveness is the ability of the state to influence this in many ways—by providing a macroeconomic and microeconomic environment to create incentives for efficient economic activities; by establishing and enforcing institutional arrangements such as law and order and rules and property rights to domestic and international investment; and by providing basic social services such as education, health, and infrastructure to promote economic activities and to protect the environment.[20]

The role of the state in developing countries has been evolving for many decades.

Policymakers and planners assumed that the state could effectively mobilize resources and people and teach them how to eradicate social and economic injustice. After independence, governments in Asia, Africa, Latin America, and the Middle East initiated comprehensive programs in most sectors of the economy to respond to the "revolution of rising expectations" of the people who expected their new governments to improve their living conditions. Governments initiated programs to improve infrastructure, provided basic services such as education and health, and established semiautonomous economic enterprises in different sectors of the economy. The rapidly expanding role of the state was encouraged by the popularity of the central planning model such as the one in the former Soviet Union. Many policymakers and development practitioners in developing countries strongly believed in the merits of state-dominated economic development. Therefore, "by the 1960s, states had become involved in virtually every aspect of the economy, administering prices and increasingly regulating labor, foreign exchange, and financial markets."[21]

The oil price shock of the1970s affected the role of the state in two ways. It provided huge sums of money to the oil-exporting countries, which they invested in the rapid expansion of state programs. The oil-importing countries, however, continued their state-funded programs, often borrowing heavily from the petrodollars. In the 1980s, the debt crisis faced by many developing countries and the decline of oil prices put tremendous pressures on the state's capacity to govern. The collapse of the Soviet Union highlighted the failure of government intervention in the economy and "sounded the death knell for a developmental era."[22] This was followed by government policies to reduce the extent of state intervention in the economy and to promote market-friendly strategies. The shift from heavy state intervention in the economy to "the minimalist" state had many negative consequences. One was that in order to balance budgets, many governments cut such social programs as primary health care and education. Such cuts were politically unpopular and adversely affected the poor groups. In some countries the resulting crisis led to the collapse of the state. In most cases the civil society organizations assumed some of the functions previously performed by the state.

The case of India presents an interesting example of the evolution of the role of the state over the past 50 years.[23] From 1947 to 1964, the focus was on industrialization and a strong state with a planned economy to achieve self-sufficiency. The period 1966 to 1977 was characterized by an emphasis on agriculture through state activism in subsidizing new seeds and fertilizers, agricultural credit and rural electrification, as well as increased state control on every aspect of the economy including the nationalization of banks, more restrictions on trade, and price controls. From 1977 to 1991, some of the controls on imports and industrial licensing were relaxed

Table 2: Globalization and Public Sector Capacity

Changes Resulting from Globalization	Effects of the Changes
Greater and faster increase in exchange of goods, services, and capital	Better choices, quality, and prices for consumers; but requires new skills and attitudes of public officials to manage change emanating from globalization Only strong firms will survive, causing short-term unemployment and potential for civil unrest in poor countries
Economic and cultural boundaries between states are more porous and more ambiguous	Richer access to a wider variety of ideas, values and successful practices (such as democracy and human rights) Strength and appeal of liberal-democratic model is sometimes perceived to threaten local values and traditions
Freer mobility of individuals affecting balance of human capital	Greater opportunities for individuals with access to rich, advanced, and well-integrated states; but requires new human resource development strategies in the public sector Potential increases in brain drain and human capital losses in poor, less integrated economies
Logic of the market dominates decision-making globally and nationally	More efficient and less bureaucratic production and productivity; shift from control to the "enabling" role of the state Lower regard for the national public good especially in transboundary domains, such as the environment, etc.; some protectionist policies, such as agriculture in the northern markets and the low capacity of developing countries impede utilization of opportunities provided by globalization

Table 2: Continued

Changes Resulting from Globalization	Effects of the Changes
Information technology is increasing access to knowledge and shrinking time and space	Decision-making is more informed, timely, and effective; but access to information technology limited in most developing economies Use of IT for illicit activities increased (money laundering etc.); knowledge-gaps and digital divide among countries
New actors, rules and tools; the establishment of worldwide social networks	Increased opportunities for innovative solutions to age-old problems, especially those of a global nature; concern for democracy, human rights, poverty, and the environment; increased role of international NGOs and civic responsibilities of transnational corporations Increasing debate on the capacity of the public sector to manage the wide range of pressures; current arrangements favor well-established economies; a large number of people and many countries are marginalized

Sources: Compiled from Department for International Development, UK. *Eliminating World Poverty: Making Globalization Work for the Poor,* London, White Paper on International Development, 2000; UNDP, *Human Development Report 1999;* Oxfam, *Globalization,* London, Oxfam G. B. Policy Paper 5/00; United Nations Department of Economic and Social Affairs, *World Public Sector Reports 2001 and 2003.*

and anti-poverty programs were expanded. The reform period began in 1991 and continues to the present. Private and foreign investments were encouraged and the state began to emphasize its role as the facilitator of entrepreneurship. Among other reforms, the government reduced import tariffs, liberalized the financial sector, and abolished many of the industrial and import licensing sectors.

The experience of developing countries over the past 50 years shows that while state domination of the economies has failed, development cannot take place without the state. Therefore, "the consequences of an overzealous rejection of government have shifted attention from the sterile debate of the state versus market to a more fundamental crisis in state effectiveness."[24] The strengths of the state are that it can create an enabling environment for people-centered development; it has the mandate to coerce and exert force; it can maintain a stable legal and regulatory framework; it can safeguard the rights of vulnerable groups by maintaining standards of public health and safety for all citizens; and it can regulate the protection of the environment. Its weaknesses, however, are that powerful vested interests manage to shift the focus of the government actions in their favor, often at the expense of the poor and other marginalized groups; that it is difficult to enforce national standards in such government-initiated programs as environmental protection, primary health care, and education; and that government officials assume disproportionate discretion in the process of implementation that leads to a lack of accountability and corrupt practices.

Effectiveness of the government and the efficiency of markets are closely interrelated. Countries that attract higher levels of investment and trade are those that have relatively better government systems—where rules and policies are predictable, where law and order is maintained, where the governments invest in human capital in health and education, and where property rights are protected. The maintenance of law and order and the upholding of contracts are essential components of an environment conducive to business. An effective legal, institutional, and regulatory framework is essential to promote financial sector stability, to protect the environment, and to enhance human rights including labor standards. However, excessive regulations increase discretion of government officials and might stifle entrepreneurship and investment. Combating corruption and promoting accountability and transparency are essential to build investor confidence.

Many implications of the rapid pace of globalization on the changing role of the state are discernible.

Shift from Control to Regulation, with Emphasis on Accountability and Transparency

As mentioned earlier, control orientation has been one of the characteristics of public sector management in many developing countries, especially during the early post-colonial period. Government officials often saw their role as guardians of the state in the process of enforcing state regulations and maintenance of law and order. This control orientation was also triggered in many cases by the feudal structure of societies, wherein an overwhelming majority of the poor were lacking education and unaware of their rights. Globalization has been instrumental in changing that in many ways—through access to global media, through revolution in information technology, through the global movement for transparency and accountability, and through increased pressure from below for better access to government services. For example, Transparency International (TI), a Berlin-based international NGO, has national chapters in about 70 countries that provide a forum for the civil society, the private sector, and government functionaries to interact with each other to create public awareness about corruption in the country. The United Nations General Assembly has passed a resolution requesting Member States to design and implement strategies to combat corruption. The Organization for Economic Cooperation and Development (OECD) has approved an anticorruption convention that has been endorsed by the member countries making bribery of public officials in developing countries by multinational corporations a criminal offence. The international business sector wants regulations that are conducive to investment and not state controls that stifle private sector initiatives. Each of the above and related actions emanating from the rapid pace of globalization have shifted the focus of the public sector from control to accountability and transparency in government actions—a trend that is likely to continue and expand.

Shift from Inward Orientation to Protecting the Public Good

Globalization has led to both opportunities and crises—an economic miracle in East Asia that was followed by financial turmoil and social cost; the end of the Cold War followed by an increase in civil strife and conflict; prospects of healthy lives resulting from progress in medicine followed by new diseases such as HIV and AIDS; technological advances followed by ecosystems overloaded with waste and pollution.[25] Many issues, such as the environment, which were traditionally considered to be national issues, now require actions by more than one nation state. In the case of the environment and the protection of heritage, for example, major strides have been made in policy development at the national and global levels and in technical cooperation to respond to global environmental concerns including the Montreal Protocol and Global Environment Facility. The process of consensus building on global public goods requires the state to look beyond its borders. Increasingly government ministries and departments have international cooperation units and divisions to prepare national strategies as a part of global concerns. The shift from inward-looking attitudes of public officials to the recognition of interdependence of nation states in effectively dealing with public goods is one of the key outcomes of globalization. Over the past few years, the celebration of the 50th anniversary of the Declaration of Human Rights, the human rights initiative of the Secretary General of the United Nations, and the proactive role of national and international human rights institutions—both governmental and nongovernmental—have been instrumental in building pressures from the local as well as global levels to promote and protect the civil and political rights of all individuals, especially marginalized groups, the poor, and women.

The rapid pace of globalization requires governments to make decisions in a global environment of uncertainty, heterogeneity, and high levels of complexity. The governments, therefore, need to possess requisite capacity in terms of institutions, knowledge, skills, and information flows.[26]

Shift from Government to Governance: Roles of Civil Society and the Private Sector

Effective governance is the process of fostering interaction between actors from the civil society, the private sector, and the state. Traditionally, mistrust—and in many cases hostilities—between the public and the private sector have constrained complementary actions on both sides. Similarly, lack of trust and goodwill characterizes relationships between the state and the civil society actors. The practice in developing countries shows that each of these actors has its strengths—the state in providing an economic and legal framework, the private sector in creating jobs that provide income to improve living conditions, and the civil society in protecting the rights of all citizens and facilitating their participation. Where they work together—as in the case of Japan and Korea—the capability of the society to deal with its economic and social problems is enhanced. Of particular importance is the role of the civil society, which is increasingly called upon to play an important role in ensuring proper accountability of the state, in some cases to serve as an alternative channel for the provision of basic services, and to defend the interest of the poor in national and global fora. At the national level, the civil society has been recognized as a significant partner in governance. There is thus added pressure to enhance its capacity for policy level interaction with institutions of the state. Civil society will be increasingly called upon to play an important role in ensuring proper accountability of the state and the private sector, defend the interests of the poor in national and global fora and to facilitate the participation of people in decision-making. At the global level, civil society is playing an increasing role in strong advocacy for global concerns such as protection of the environment, protection of human rights, gender equity, trade negotiations, and debt relief.

As the main engine of economic growth, the private sector has an increased responsibility for the creation of employment that brings high value added, higher income and subsequently added state revenue that could be used for social spending. Opportunities for joint ventures firms from advanced countries promote new technology and knowledge in developing countries. One of the areas of close interaction between the state and the private sector is the need for the private sector to be more socially responsible as it improves productivity and for the state to create an enabling environment—including policy, legal and regulatory frameworks—that promotes competitiveness in the economy. The state institutions are assuming added responsibility in the formulation of and adherence to new global rules dealing with such matters as protecting the public goods and enhancing the equity of exchange between firms from different countries.

Shift from the Focus on Growth to the Reduction of Interregional and Social Inequalities

With globalization, the state has to play an even more important role—though differently than was done traditionally—to reduce social inequalities and interregional disparities. There are many reasons for that. Experience suggests that in most cases globalization has increased disparities among different groups because those with better skills, assets, and entrepreneurship are more likely to gain greater benefits. Furthermore, globalization facilitates the flow of information to all segments of the society, thereby generating greater pressures on the state to effectively respond to intergroup disparities. The same is true in the case of interregional disparities. Therefore, instituting measures to reduce disparities among groups and regions will continue to be an important role of the state. Yet this role needs to be performed not by controlling the economy but by "steering" and facilitating the functions of the state—enforcement of standards to maintain national standards dealing with such issues as the environment, human rights, and education; interaction with the national and international business sectors to promote corporate social responsibility; and compensation of the displaced and vulnerable groups.

Shift from State Control to Matching the Role of the State to Its Capability

Matching the role of the state to its capability is essential to ensure the effective and efficient use of public resources. It implies identification of what states do and how they do that. The World Bank in its 1997 *World Development Report* has identified three types of functions of the state—"minimal functions," "intermediate functions," and "activist functions."[27] The report argues that countries with low state capability should focus first on the provision of "pure public goods"—macroeconomic stability and the provision of basic services such as safe water, control of infectious diseases, law and order, and property rights. The second category of functions includes "management of externalities (pollution control, for example), regulation of monopolies, and the provision of social insurance (pensions, unemployment benefits)."[28] The "activist" functions include the state's role in the promotion of markets through industrial and financial policy.

With the rapid pace of globalization, the state's regulatory role has become more complex with respect to environmental improvement, the financial sector, information and communication technologies, and traditional areas such as monopolies.[29]

The administrative capacity of the state needs to be strengthened to cope with globalization. This may include the capacity to manage change and strengthen the role of the state as a "learning organization" and to enhance leadership skills and strategic planning capacities, as well as the need for both performance standards for management development and training of top-level managers to perform significant tasks on a supranational level. Competencies needed to cope with the challenges of globalization include a combination of knowledge, skills, behavior, and attitudes.

Shift from the Traditional to the New Skills for State Capacity

Public sector management is one of the pillars that supports democracy and good governance and enables the society to benefit from the process of globalization. To do this, however, the public sector must have the capability to perform its new tasks and the public servants should have a new "mind-set" to assume their responsibilities in the changing world. New norms, values, rules, and behavior patterns are needed to create incentives for state institutions and organizations to work for collective interests and to facilitate program implementation.

The first element of the new state capability is the rule of law including restraints on arbitrary behavior. An independent judiciary, the separation of powers and oversight of executive branch strengthen—instead of weaken—the type of state capability required for promoting good governance and benefiting from globalization. The second element consists of competitive pressures through such measures as recruiting public officials based on merit and allowing private sector organizations to compete with the public sector agencies through trade. Competition in the public sector, however, does not mean for the state to disengage from assisting the vulnerable groups or ensuring the enforcement of public standards in such areas as environment, public health and education. The third element is the participation and voice of all segments of the society—civil society organizations, business councils, women's organizations, for example—in decision-making processes. The decentralization of powers and resources and institutional arrangements for the participation of community-based groups can enhance state capability, as discussed in chapter 6.

CASE STUDIES IN PUBLIC SECTOR MANAGEMENT INNOVATIONS

There are many elements of public sector reform that affect the institutionalization and consolidation of democracy as well as the ability of a country to benefit from what globalization can bring. The trend towards containment and retrenchment of the size and scope of the public sector in the 1980s led to a new approach. Its key elements were reducing the tax burden while improving the quality of public services, decentralizing (including devolving) power and resources, making the processes of governance more inclusive, fostering greater use of information technologies, and protecting the rights of individuals and groups against a "paternalistic bureaucratic state."[30] The New Public Management and "Reinventing Government" emphasize results over process; downsizing, contracting out, and outsourcing; "steering rather than rowing"; empowering rather than serving; and earning rather than spending.[31] The "Reinventing Government" movement, in addition, focuses on e-government development, the decentralization of authority and resources, the accountability of government, and innovations, especially in service delivery. Many elements of these movements are emphasized to varying degrees—depending upon the context of the public sector organizations—to encourage the "entrepreneurial manager" instead of the conventional bureaucrat; to introduce business principles and values such as total quality management; to promote professional ethics in public service; and to introduce performance budgeting.

Case 1: Public Sector Reform in Uganda

In 1989, the government of Uganda established a commission to examine the structure and the role of the public sector and to suggest strategies for reforming it. The idea for reform emanated from the new political elite—a rebel movement—in order to transform economic and social life in Uganda. There were seven sets of the comprehensive reform package.

The rationalization of government structures and functions including decentralization was aimed at improving the performance and accountability of the government organizations performing core functions. Reforms consisted of refining roles, structures, and staffing of ministries, redefining functions between central and local governments, giving more powers and resources to local governments, and reducing the size of ministries and government departments. The purpose of decentralization policies was to promote community empowerment and to introduce democratization at the grass roots. To achieve this, financial, personnel, and planning responsibilities were transferred to the elected leaders of Local Government Councils. Decentralization policy has been successful in many areas. It has made local leaders aware of and sensitive to the aims of the policy and the role of local leaders. It has strengthened local capacity through training and information dissemination, planning and budgeting skills, and increased consultations with community-based groups. It has reduced the "dependency syndrome" because many districts have taken local initiatives to mobilize additional resources and provide services. Many districts have introduced innovative service delivery mechanisms such as contracting services to NGOs and establishing development committees in such areas as production and marketing, health and environment and transport.

The second component dealt with reduction in size of the public service. In addition to voluntary retirement, the reduction was to be achieved through a recruitment freeze and the removal of nonperforming workers including ghost workers and those who joined through irregular means. The size of the public service was reduced from over 300,000 in 1990 to about 150,000 by 1997.

The third component was to enhance salaries of civil servants in order to increase motivation and result-orientation in government organizations. This consisted of increasing salaries, improving salary administration to avoid delays and salaries paid below or above the grade, and increasing the amount of salary increase based on promotion. The increase in salaries between 1993 and 1997 was 930% for a primary teacher, 1,175% for a nurse, 1,004% for a policeman. One of the significant reforms was to put money value to such noncash benefits as transport and housing, which made the remuneration more transparent, fair, free of abuse, and flexible to the needs of the employees. The result of these changes was that the public sector wage bill as a percentage of the recurrent expenditure increased from 21% in 1993–1994 to 35% in 1996–1997.

The fourth component involved training, capacity building, and human resource development. The training of personnel at different levels included skills such as information technology, communication, office record management, performance appraisal, and result-oriented management. The training improved efficiency in financial management and accounting, the submission of final accounts of the central government transfers, and adherence to financial and accounting regulations such as annual estimates of revenue and expenditure.

The fifth component focuses on a system of management information and control. This component of the reform was aimed at providing the managers and decision-makers with relevant information dealing with service delivery, performance budgets, costs and revenues, personnel, and assets. This component of the reform included (1) payroll and personnel management systems to clarify the exact number of staff in government ministries and departments; (2) budgeting and financial management systems to equip government departments with financial management systems and skills; (3) pensions management; (4) records management to improve access to information; and (5) health information management to provide an integrated system of relevant information and to assist the Ministry of Health in planning, managing and evaluating health care service delivery.

The sixth component was constitutional reform. The 1995 Constitution of Uganda decentralized government functions and delegated powers to local governments, encouraged the participation of all citizens in governance, and provided an enabling environment for civil society organizations. It promoted fundamental human rights.

Finally, major reforms were introduced in the health and education sectors. In the health sector, the reforms included shifting from curative to preventive health care support by introducing community-based health care and primary health care. In addition, health units were rehabilitated, user charge schemes were introduced, and health services were decentralized.

The reforms in the education sector consisted of improving the access of women to educational facilities in order to reduce gender imbalance, and introducing universal primary education. The result was a significant increase in the number of females enrolled at the university level as well as in the proportion of female students entering professional courses in science.

The factors that led to the success of the above reforms were:

- the commitment of political leaders,

- the coordination of ministries and departments through the president's office,

- the involvement of local expertise and civil society organizations,

- the phasing of the reforms, and

- the support of international development partners.[32]

Case Study 2: Civil Service Reform in Malaysia

Malaysia has over 40 years of experience in designing and implementing public sector management improvement initiatives. During the 1960s and 1970s the objectives of the public sector reform were to transform the country's law and order administration, to improve development administration, to introduce a planning system with "top-down"and "bottom-up" inputs, and to promote strong interaction and discussion among the representatives of the federal, state, and local government on national strategies in order to effectively respond to development challenges. During the 1980s and 1990s, the government liberalized the economy, leading to an active role of the private sector in economic growth. Furthermore, the government initiated concrete steps to improve the quality of public sector management. A series of reforms were introduced to transform structures, management technologies, skills and knowledge, attitudes, and systems and procedures. These measures were in support of three stages in national development strategy—the 1971 New Economic Policy that was aimed at creating national unity by reducing interethnic and interregional economic disparities; the New Development Policy established in 1993 to consolidate and expand the gains from the first period; and Vision 2020 to make Malaysia a fully industrialized and developed country over the next three decades.

Vision 2020 identified four challenges to improve public sector management in the country—to develop a mission-oriented administrative system with an ability to provide high quality public services; to develop an institutional capacity to promote and sustain creativity and innovation; to enhance the ability of public officials to respond effectively to rapidly changing demands emanating from the increasing pace of globalization; and to develop the quality of human resources necessary for the country's transformation.

One of the key features of the Malaysian reforms for structural changes was continuity over the past several decades. In the early 1960s, the Development Administration Unit in the prime minister's department was established to introduce and monitor reforms in civil service. The Malaysian National Institute of Public Administration (INTAN) was established in 1972 to provide short- and long-term training along with overseas training of senior officials. The Malaysian Administrative and Manpower Planning Unit (MAMPU) was created in 1977 to study key issues of administrative development and to make recommendations to the government. Both INTAN and MAMPU continue to play a proactive role in promoting modernization and change in Malaysia's public service, as it continues to benefit from globalization including increasing foreign investments.

In order to improve productivity and the delivery of services, MAMPU created a special division within the organization to enhance the awareness of agencies concerning productivity measurement and improvement, to provide advisory services to agencies, to undertake studies on attitude and behavior, and to coordinate and monitor the productivity improvement initiatives of government organizations. The government began its privatization program in 1980 to sell public enterprises and to consolidate departments and statutory bodies. Nearly 150 public enterprises were privatized, amounting to about ten percent of the public service. In addition to privatization, the government also set out to redefine the role, size, and structure of the government at the federal, state, and local levels—resulting in a new remuneration policy to rationalize salaries and incentives of civil servants, establishing growth rates that identified sectors in which posts could be increased, and abolishing 9,253 posts by 1994.

A number of measures were introduced to improve the performance of individual civil servants, including new practices to recruit and retain staff, a new performance appraisal system, a remuneration system that provided performance incentives, increased opportunities for staff training and development, equal employment and promotion opportunities for women, and a new public service code of conduct. The New Remuneration Policy led to the reduction from 574 to 274 job classifications, grouped into 19 service categories. In-service training has become a requirement for career development. New employees have to go through an induction course. Public Service Innovation Awards and Excellent Service Awards were introduced to encourage and reward innovations and performance level.

In addition, the government has been awarding scholarships for advanced study abroad to develop technical skills and specialization to meet the requirements of a global economy. The government encouraged the participation of civil servants in workshops and seminars organized by the private sector to improve their understanding of the corporate world and its management culture. Some government officials were seconded to private firms identified by multinational corporations.

In 1993, the government of Malaysia issued a new code of conduct for public service to enhance the discipline and commitment of staff, and to improve their job performance including productivity and the quality of services. In addition to the code of conduct, procedures for disciplinary actions were identified.

In order to improve the quality of public services and the responsiveness of officials, several complementary reforms were also introduced. "Client/counter services" included one-stop counters on the ground floor of each office building, electronic queuing, one-stop bill payment centers, a single counter for collecting fees for all public services, an online, realtime government-wide computer system, and telephone lines to provide information about government services. "Client Charter" was introduced in 1993 to create customer orientation among public officials. Government agencies undertake review of their work processes and systems. Officials are expected to provide information about the quality of services to be provided by them. Total Quality Management emphasizes the need for satisfaction of all customers and stakeholders in all government operations. In 1991, the government issued the Guidelines on Quality Control Circles, which required the government agencies to establish circles for mobilizing expertise, experience and employee creativity in order to provide better services to the people. In 1992, Guidelines on Total Quality Management were issued that included a quality suggestion system, a quality process, a quality inspection, a quality day, a quality slogan, feedback on quality, and quality information.

Attitudinal and behavioral changes were sought through its "Look East Policy" that encouraged government officials to follow the approaches and role models of Japan and Republic of Korea and, subsequently, sent a number of senior officials to the two countries for training and internship. Other measures concerning attitudinal and behavioral changes were to instill Islamic values in public sector management, "leadership by example," the use of name tags and punch clock systems, and "Malaysia Incorporated Policy" to promote public and private sector cooperation for economic development.

There are many internal and external factors that led to the success of the Malaysian model of public sector management. Some of the critical factors were as follows:

- Continuity in political leadership for over 40 years led by a national coalition of three ethnic groups—Malays, Chinese, and Indians—that enabled the country to introduce incremental and experimental approaches within a holistic framework;

- Rapid expansion of the economy—fueled by high local resource base and local entrepreneurship—that enabled the country to invest heavily in human resource development and the training of civil service personnel;

- Increased foreign investment—especially from Japan—that led to a transfer of new skills and technologies to improve the productivity of the country;

- A proactive government that took major steps to reduce interregional and interethnic disparities but took the timely steps to reduce the scope of government intervention in the economy and built a stable partnership with the local private sector to generate new jobs;

- Heavy investment in education, health and infrastructural development;

- Emphasis in the 1960s and 1970s on rural and agricultural development that led to reduction of poverty and more effective rural-urban linkages.[33]

Case 3: Public Service Reform in Singapore

Singapore's civil service is one of the most efficient and least corrupt in the world. The salaries of the civil servants are pegged to the private sector. Twelve Government Parliamentarian Committees, each chaired by a Member of Parliament, serve as a feedback mechanism and a link between the ministry and the people concerning the government policy and services provided by the ministry. Each government ministry or department has a "quality service manager" with a toll-free line to ensure effective feedback from the people.

In the early 1970s, the government established a Management Services Department (MSD) to improve the efficiency and effectiveness of the public sector. The administrative reforms in Singapore can be divided into two phases. During the 1980s, the government introduced performance budgeting, management accounting and activity-based costing, and performance indicators that were being published in the budget book. During the 1990s, corporatization and the Public Service in the 21st Century program were introduced.

Meritocracy is the single most critical aspect of the civil service in Singapore. Lee Kuan Yew, the former Prime Minister, took pride in the fact that both the process of recruitment, and the promotion of the civil service were based on merit. The government provided scholarships for the brightest students to attend the best universities in the world with the condition that they had to serve the government for at least eight years after graduation.

The MSD served as think tank and trouble shooting arm of the government providing in-house consulting services and undertaking organizational reviews. The department was placed under the Ministry of Finance. The MSD introduced performance budgeting, management accounting systems, the privatization and establishment of statutory bodies, and computerization. It established Work Improvement Teams in government departments. In 1995, the MSD was transformed into a company, thereby requiring it to compete for jobs on an equal basis with private sector consulting firms. The MSD also reviewed the mission objectives, functions, and performance indicators of ministries and departments; determined the organizational structure and manpower requirements of each ministry and department; identified areas of privatization and contracting out; and reviewed systems and procedures for computerization.

One of the innovations introduced by the MSD was the introduction of performance budgeting. Because of this, funding for every department and ministry is determined by a performance budget. Examples include cost per every student trained in the case of education, cost per dollar collected in the case of the taxation department, and the cost per patient day in the hospital in the case of the health department. With the pegging of the salaries of the civil servants to the private sector, the salaries of civil servants increased substantially. In view of this and in order to encourage a high level of performance, marginal performers were encouraged to retire early.

Government ministries were encouraged to corporatize some of their departments. For example, the Inland Revenue Department of the Ministry of Finance has been converted into a statutory board and is funded on the basis of percentage of tax collected. The Ministry of Defense established a statutory board dealing with defense technology. The Ministry of Health has corporatized most of its hospitals with subsidies for each class of ward on a per patient basis. Public housing is provided by the Housing and Development Board, a statutory body. One of the key characteristics of public sector management in Singapore is that state-owned enterprises are run on a commercial basis, managed by professionals who are rewarded like the private sector employees.

The initiative entitled Public Service in the 21st Century was launched in 1995. Its aims are to create an orientation of excellence in service through high standards of quality, courtesy, and responsiveness and to establish an environment that promotes continuous change in order to achieve greater efficiency and effectiveness through the use of modern management tools and through continued attention to the morale and well-being of civil servants. The need for change on a continuous basis is recognized as essential to meet the demands emanating from the rapid pace of globalization.

The experience of Singapore shows that many critical factors accounted for its success. The first was the high level of political support on a continuous basis from the top political leadership. The second was the role of the Management Services Department as the "champion" of reform in the public sector. The MSD consisted of young professional employees most of whom had returned after getting their degrees abroad. The third was the emphasis on the need to ensure that the departments and ministries concerned fully understood and supported benefits they would get from the reform, which made it possible for them to support the new initiatives. Finally, perhaps the most critical factor was linking the rewards for each employee with his or her performance.[34]

CONCLUSION AND LESSONS OF EXPERIENCE

This chapter has examined the key issues in policy and program responses to strengthen public sector management capacity—which is necessary for promoting good governance and democracy and for taking advantage of opportunities provided by globalization. Civil service reforms, leadership and vision, human resource management and interorganizational relations continue to be key challenges in developing countries. The rapid pace of globalization has led to the need for a paradigm shift in the role of the state. Some of the lessons that can be learned from the case studies and other good practices follow.

First, there is no one model of public sector management reform that suits all situations. Program designers should pay attention to the political, legal and sociocultural context of the reform interventions. There is the need for an interdisciplinary approach to better understand socioeconomic and political factors that facilitate or impede the success of reforms. For the reforms to succeed, many systemic variables are important, including congruent culture, institutional framework conducive to organization level reform, continued political support at the highest level, and the involvement of stakeholders in program design and implementation.

Second, best practices are a useful tool to share experience and knowledge. They highlight some of the common reform issues discernible in most situations, relationships between systematic variables—the extent of political support at the highest level and the resource base of the country, for example—and the various elements of the civil service reform. Furthermore, knowledge of global experience and best practices facilitates a critical review by national and local development practitioners of their own context and feasible options.

Third, an incremental approach to building the capacity of the state might be essential in some cases to sustain reforms. The capacity of the state and that of the private sector are interrelated, if the objective is to ensure the promotion and protection of public goods such as the environment. The state capacity is vital, whatever the scope of the role of the private sector. The challenge today is to strike a balance between the state capacity and the scope of its functions.

Fourth, governments must be in control of the process of change even though the civil society and the private sector are actively involved. The government alone is ultimately responsible for protecting the public goods such as environment, enforcing human rights standards and norms, and defending the interests of the poor and the marginalized.

Finally, building the national ownership of reforms and the public trust is essential to consolidate public sector reforms in support of effective governance and to cope with globalization. Consensus-building among societal actors—politicians, representatives of civil society organizations, parliamentarians, entrepreneurs etc.—is key to the design and implementation of sustainable public sector reform programs.

ENDNOTES

1. Yehezkel Dror, *Capacity to Govern* (London: Frank Cass 2001), 7–32.

2. United Nations, *Globalization and the State* (New York: United Nations, 2001), 12.

3. UNDP, *Public Sector Management, Governance and Sustainable Human Development*, Discussion Paper 1, Management Development and Governance Division (New York: UNDP, 1995), 55.

4. Ibid., 55–57.

5. For key elements of this approach, see D. Osborne and T. Gaebler, *Reinventing Government: How the Entrepreneurial Spirit is Transforming the Public Sector* (New York: Penguin), 1993.

6. UNDP, *Public Sector Management, Governance and Sustainable Human Development*, 68.

7. H. Taylor, "Public Sector Personnel Management in Three African Countries: Current Problems and Possibilities," *Public Administration and Development*, 12, (1992), 193–207.

8. UNDP, *Public Sector Management, Governance and Sustainable Human Development*, 79.

9. Babar Mumtaz and Emiel Wegelin, *Guiding Cities* (Nairobi: UN Center for Human Settlements, Urban Management Program paper no. 26, 2001), 28–31.

10. World Bank, *The State in a Changing World* (Washington, DC: World Development Report, 1997), 80–85. While politicians identify broad vision and goals they want to achieve, it is only through effective institutional arrangements that these goals can be translated into policy priorities of the government. Uncoordinated political pressures from politicians and the inability—or unwillingness—of civil servants to translate a government's political vision into policy priorities are more likely to take place where institutional arrangements for formulating and coordinating policy are vague or not adequately followed. An effective public sector exists where there is strong central capacity for macroeconomic and strategic policy formulation as well as strong institutional links with stakeholders outside the government to ensure accountability. The central capacity for policy formulation and coordination is weak in many developing countries. One example is the difference between the budgeted and actual recurrent expenditures in countries such as Uganda, Tanzania, and Nigeria. Sometimes, the central capacity is further weakened because of the prolif-

eration of foreign funded projects, especially when bilateral donors and development banks reach agreements with the government without adequately examining the sustainability of these projects in terms of the government's ability to meet recurrent costs on long–term basis.

11. Ibid., 86–92. The challenge is to identify services that can be more effectively provided by the market as well as those for which the public sector should assume direct responsibility. Institutional mechanisms to improve delivery include contracting out service delivery to private firms or NGOs, the establishment of performance-based agencies in the public sector, and user participation and client surveys to increase citizens' voice and inputs. The "new public management" reforms focus on market mechanisms to provide services.

12. UNDP, *Human Development Report* (New York: Oxford University Press, 1999), 1. For the impact of globalization on human conditions, See Department for International Development, U.K. *Eliminating World Poverty: Making Globalization Work for the Poor,* London: White paper on International Development, 2000; UNDP, *Human Development Report 1999;* Oxfam, *Globalization,* London: Oxfam G.B. Policy Paper 5/00; United Nations Department of Economic and Social Affairs, *World Public Sector Report 2001,* New York: United Nations, 2001; Robert Isaak, *The Globalization Gap: How the Rich Get Richer and the Poor Get Left Further Behind* (New York: Prentice Hall, 2005).

13. Ibid.

14. UNDP, *Human Development Report 1997,* 3.

15. Oxfam, *Globalization,* Oxfam G.B. Policy Paper 5/00, 2.

16. UNDP, *Human Development Report 1997,* 6.

17. UNDP, *Human Development Report 1999,* 2.

18. Ibid., 3.

19. Ibid.

20. World Bank, *The State in a Changing World,* 30–31. The World Bank's 1997 World Development Report points out three findings based on surveys of 94 industrial and developing countries covering about 30 years and over 3,600 domestic firms—first, government policies and institutional capability are critical for both economic growth and the improvement of quality of life; second, institutional "capability" affects uncertainties felt by domestic firms as well as their perceptions of the state; and third, institutional capability influences the overall framework and setting for development performance.

21. World Bank, *The State in a Changing World*, 23.

22. Ibid., 23.

23. Ibid., 24.

24. Ibid., 25.

25. For a review of global public goods, see Inge Kaul, I. Grunberg and M. Stern, eds. *Global Public Goods: International Cooperation in the 21st Century* (New York: Oxford University Press, 1999).

26. Yehezkel Dror, *The Capacity to Govern* (Rome: The Club of Rome, Society for International Development, 2001), 7–32.

27. World Bank, *The state in a Changing World*, 26–28.

28. Ibid., 27

29. Ibid., 27

30. United Nations, *Globalization and the State*, 2001.

31. Ibid.

32. P. Langseth, Katorobo, Brett, and Munene, eds. Uganda Landmarks in *Rebuilding a Nation* (Kampala: Fountain, 1995); A. Nasibami, ed. *Decentralization and Civil Service in Uganda: The Quest for Good Governance* (Kampala: Fountain, 1998); S. W. Kisembo, "An Overview of Financial Performance of Districts in the 1995–96 Financial Year" (Paper presented in a Decentralization Implementation Review workshop, Kampala, Feb. 12 to 14, 1996); James Katorobo, "Civil Service Reforms in Uganda" (New York: UNDP, 2000).

33. A.T. Rafiqur Rahman, *Reforming the Civil Service for Government Performance* (Dhaka: the University Press, 2001); *Government of Malaysia, Vision 2020* (Kuala Lumpur: Government of Malaysia); Johari bin Mat, "Coordination, Institutional Capability and Development Performance in Malaysia" in G. Shabbir Cheema, ed. *Institutional Dimensions of Regional Development* (Hong Kong: Maruzen Press, 1981).

34. Janet Tay, "Singapore's Public Administration Experience" (New York: UNDP, 2000).

CHAPTER 8

JUDICIAL REFORM
IMPROVING ACCESS TO JUSTICE

Effective judicial systems and processes are necessary to strengthen democracy and good governance. Some of the problems that constrain the effectiveness of judicial systems and processes are the lack of independence of the judiciary, court delays, outdated laws and slow procedures, corruption in the judiciary, increased crime and violence, crisis in prison systems, and the lack of legal training facilities or outdated curriculum in law schools. Governments in developing economies, multilateral institutions, and bilateral donors, therefore, have over the past few years focused on providing targeted assistance to improve legal and judicial systems—introducing new methods and structures to improve judicial selection, increasing judicial budgets, promoting public safety, and streamlining case management by courts. Furthermore, they have established judicial training schools, supported bar associations as agents of change, improve people's access to public- and private-sector justice services, and attempted to foster alternative methods of dispute resolution.

This chapter examines the judicial reform necessary in developing countries to promote and strengthen democracy and good governance. It discusses the significance of the rule of law, the impact of globalization, and constraints on the independence of the judiciary. It also reviews key issues in the management of the justice system and innovative approaches to improve the access of the poor to justice.

RULE OF LAW AND DEMOCRATIC GOVERNANCE

The rule of law is the foundation of democratic governance. It includes the effective administration of justice, respect for political and civil liberties, the subordination of government power to legal authority, and consistent application of laws. It deals with the established rules that determine relationships among individuals in the society ("rule by law") and between the state and citizens ("ruling bound by law").[1] It includes control mechanisms to hold the state and power holders accountable in accordance with the constitution. Citizens and political officials obey laws because of their duty as well as because of incentives to do so. Political officials in democracies have strong incentives to obey laws because doing otherwise puts their future at great political risk.[2]

In addition to the above elements, there is an economic rationale for the rule of law. Effective judicial systems are required to enforce property rights, check abuses of government power, and enable exchanges between private parties.[3] To benefit from the global economy and increase of foreign investments, a country should have an effective and efficient legal and judicial system. The investors should be able to get justice in the country's courts. Investors also want to ensure that contracts and property laws are enforced, and that there is a system of checks and balances and horizontal accountability. A World Bank survey of 3,600 firms in 69 countries, for example, showed that over 70 percent of the respondents considered an unpredictable judiciary to be a major problem in business operations and that there was a correlation between the effectiveness of the judicial system and the level of investment.[4]

The judiciary is the guardian of the rule of law and legal accountability in accordance with the constitutional norms. In this capacity, it undertakes many functions—guarding the law and constitutional principles, providing a mechanism for the settlement of disputes, and administering the criminal justice system. The courts thus play a vital role in democratic consolidation.

The above political and economic reasons for judicial and legal reform are widely accepted by scholars, policymakers, and development practitioners. Amartya Sen makes even a stronger case by asserting that we should "value the emergence and consolidation of a successful legal and judicial system as a valuable part of the process of development itself—not just for the way it may aid economic or political or some other kind of development."[5] He argues that capitalism emerged after the evolution of law and order; that ownership-based economy became feasible after the legal acceptance of property rights; that enforcement of contracts through legal reforms led to the efficiency of exchange; and that the development of credit institutions came before smooth financing of businesses.[6]

GLOBALIZATION AND THE RULE OF LAW

Sound legal frameworks and an effective and independent judiciary are the conditions for a country's ability to benefit from globalization. An independent judiciary is an important factor in creating a stable environment for entrepreneurship, and to ensure that the system of checks and balances within the government work effectively. The judiciary is increasingly involved in transnational illegal activities involving cases of terrorism, transnational crime, corruption, trafficking in human beings, drugs, and money laundering. This requires greater capacity of the judicial system at the national level and enhanced cooperation at the global level. In view of this, the United Nations Convention Against Transnational Organizational Crime was adopted by the General Assembly of the United Nations at its Millennium Summit in November 2001. This new UN instrument identifies mechanisms through which countries can improve cooperation among them on such matters as extradition, mutual legal assistance, transfer of proceedings, and joint investigations.

Over the past few years, with the liberalization of economy in many developing countries and the countries in transition, commercial courts and constitutional courts have been .established for the speedy resolution of commercial conflicts and conflicts between different branches of government in accordance with the constitution. The case studies that follow provide the context and outcome of some of these efforts.

Case 1: Tanzania's Commercial Court

In Tanzania, the commercial court was established in 1999 as a specialized division of the High Court. The court rules in cases that involve the establishment and governance of business firms, the restructuring or payment of commercial debts, and liabilities from the firms' business activities.[7] The main reason for creating the commercial court was the shift of the economic policy of the government from central planning to market-oriented liberalization. This required a new legislative and regulatory framework. There were serious deficiencies in the judicial resolution of commercial disputes due to case backlog, inefficient case management practices, a low budget, corruption, and inadequate physical infrastructure. Furthermore, there was an inadequate understanding of applicable commercial laws and legal principles.[8] The commercial court was established to respond to these problems. The primary objective was to increase the confidence of investors and promote the development of the private sector by providing a reliable and speedy mechanism for the resolution of commercial disputes.

Though it is still early, several outcomes of the commercial court are discernible. The Court has resolved the commercial cases with greater speed than was the case with the High Court. For example, whereas it took an average of four to five years to resolve cases through the general division of the High Court, the

Commercial Court took an average of 89 days during its first year of operations. The reasons for this speed and efficiency are that the court is well funded and enjoys better facilities, and that the judges and the staff have built a culture of timeliness among advocates and the parties. However, the impact of the court on the environment for commercial dispute resolution or on the overall business climate of the country has not been significant, partly because the court can handle only a small percentage of the commercial disputes.[9] The question still remains, however, whether the court would be able to sustain this level of performance, given several limitations in the environment of Tanzania including lack of adequate recurrent funding and slow reform of the commercial laws.

Case 2: The New Eastern European Constitutional Courts

The new Eastern European Constitutional Courts provide a good example of ensuring the accountability of different branches of government that violate the principle of separation of powers, of the national government that might violate the principles of federalism and local autonomy, and of any branch of government violating individual or group rights.

The Polish Constitutional Tribunal was established in 1986 due to pressures from Solidarity and other groups. Its decisions were subject to be overridden by a two-thirds majority of the parliament, which was intended to reduce its power under the communist control. Yet, the tribunal continued to move beyond what the legislature had intended it to do. It decided on such cases as human rights, nullification of increases in apartment rents, and quotas for women in medical colleges, government statutes concerning tapping phones and screening letters and the efforts of the former President Lech Walesa to expand his powers beyond the constitutional limits. The new Constitution of 1997 reduced some restrictions on the tribunal—such as making its ruling final after two years. Since 1989, the court has played an important role while the country went through many problems in the consolidation of democracy—excesses of the executive with respect to the rights of citizens, and frequent conflicts between the president and the parliament.

The Hungarian Constitutional Court—established in 1989 based on discussions between the "Reform Communists" and the opposition—was empowered to accept complaints about the "abstract" unconstitutionality of laws and legal norms that, in effect, makes it look like a chamber of the legislature. Its decisions have focused on statutes enacted by the parliament, and the encroachment by the executive branch on free speech in those pertaining to radio and television media. Given some ambiguities in the separation of powers between the president and the prime minister, the court has been called upon to interpret the constitution.

For example, on the question of nomination of six vice-presidents of radio and television, the court decided that the president did not have the power to veto candidates submitted by the prime minister for high-level state posts. The court has been most active on the issues of political, social, and economic rights.

Despite these successful cases of constitutional courts, there are others in the region that did not do well: examples include Belarus, where the decisions of the Court were defied by the executive branch, Albania, where the court did not exercise independent judgment, and Romania, where the court "rubber-stamped" decisions of President Ion Iliescu.

In many cases, however, the impact of constitutional courts on promoting horizontal accountability and the rule of law in the region has been positive even though in some cases "the circumstances were unfavorable to these efforts, such as political attacks on the courts, retaliation, stringent national economic circumstances and lack of public awareness, to mention but a few problems."[10]

INDEPENDENCE OF THE JUDICIARY

The independence of the judiciary—including objectivity in its operations, its accessibility, its transparency and predictability, and its ability to protect human rights, private property rights, and legitimate interests of the state—is a necessary condition for courts to effectively perform their primary functions. There are four aspects of judicial independence: (1) political autonomy from other branches of government to make sure that the decisions of judges dealing with the constitutionality of legislation and legality of the actions of the power-holders are not influenced by political considerations, (2) the detachment and "insularity" of judges from the conflicting parties to ensure the neutrality of their decisions, (3) the detachment of judges from specific ideologies to ensure that they are impartial in making their decisions, and (4) the avoidance of public pressures on the judiciary through the media and other means to preserve the neutrality of judges.[11] The independence of judges in practice depends largely on "the institutional setting" of the judiciary—procedures and processes for their appointment, transfers, disciplinary proceedings, and career patterns.[12]

The independence of the judiciary is affected by weak political institutions. In Pakistan, political institutions have been weak, as reflected in four military coups in the 55-year history of the country, which in turn has affected the independence of the judiciary. During the government of former Pakistani Prime Minister Nawaz Sharif, a serious rift took place between the executive and the judicial branches. One of the contentious issues was the procedure for the number of judges who could be appointed. The Chief Justice contended that the executive branch was trying to influence the judiciary by unilaterally adding to the number of judges. In addition, differences existed between the two branches about the process of appointing new judges. This led to the constitutional crisis in the country. Eventually, the military took over and issued the Provisional Constitutional Order, amending the constitution.[13] The Supreme Court observed that the armed forces had no power to amend the salient features of the constitution relating to the independence of the judiciary and the federal and parliamentary form of government as specified in the constitution. The court also observed that the prolonged involvement of the army in civilian affairs could lead to politicization of the army, which was not in the long-term interest of the country. The court, however, conferred legitimacy on the regime on the "doctrine of state necessity," without "the abdication from the exercise of the power of judicial review in the transient suspension of the previous legal order."[14]

Sometimes there is tension between democratic rules and the independence of the judiciary. On the one hand, partisan and public pressures on judges must be avoided and they must have the institutional mechanisms to hold accountable those in power. On the other hand, judges should also be subject to democratic accountability through political controls because their decisions have profound implications for lawmaking and social norms and standards. In view of this, most systems attempt to achieve "optimum rather than a maximum degree of institutional independence."[15] Judicial independence is achieved through at least three institutional mechanisms—appointment procedures that determine the extent of political influence on those who get elected or appointed to judicial office; a tenure system that determines the degree of independence from those appointing the judges; and decent salaries and financial autonomy of the courts in order to avoid pressures from political groups and litigating parties. The role of the judiciary is also affected by other factors including judicial review and legal control powers and "the political environment in which a legal system is embedded."[16]

In many developing economies, the judiciary is dominated by the executive branch of the government. In some countries such as Argentina and Peru, surveys show "distrust" of the judicial system.[17] Judicial systems in Latin America, argues Pilar Domingo, "reproduce an image of corruption, and inefficiency and are not viewed as impartial administrators of justice or autonomous agents of constitutional and legal control."[18] The 2004 survey of 18 countries in the region sponsored by the United Nations shows that one of the critical reasons for the erosion of confidence in elected governments is an ineffective legal system including abusive police practices, politicization of the judiciary, and corruption in the judiciary.[19]

In some developing countries, the judiciary has been the cornerstone of democracy. In the case of India, for example, the judiciary has resisted encroachments on its independence—defending citizens' fundamental rights, safeguarding the environment and other public goods, and ensuring the accountability of the executive branch.[20] Other examples of judicial independence include the annulment by Mali's Constitutional Court of the first round of 1997 elections in response to a petition from the opposition parties, and by Gabon's Constitutional Court of a presidential decree dealing with the appointment of the country's Economic and Social Council.[21] In South Africa, because of an independent judiciary and the Constitutional Court, the separation of powers between the three branches of government is ensured. Furthermore, the Independent Judicial Service Commission has made the courts "more representative."[22]

IMPACT OF POLITICAL ENVIRONMENT

Independence and performance of the judiciary are directly affected by the political environment in the country. In a military dominated or other form of authoritarian government, the independence of the judiciary is the first victim. Lack of national consensus on the constitution triggers conflicts between the executive and judicial branches. The weakness of political institutions—including parliaments and political parties—weakens trust between the executive and judicial branches. Above all, the absence of a political culture of tolerance and accountability and of a tradition of democratic practices leads popularly elected leaders to act in an authoritarian manner. In view of these and related aspects of the national political process, the constitution and other legal documents that define the relationship between the branches of government might not be followed in practice. Indeed, the constitutional guarantees of independence of the judiciary are necessary but not sufficient.

In Latin America, for example, the past authoritarian regimes were not conducive to the development of strong judicial institutions. Furthermore, the countries of the region have a strong presidential system of government at the national level which historically played a predominant role in the executive-judicial relationships. However, with a consolidation and deepening of democracy, the role of the judiciary was strengthened and its independence increased. With the introduction of a democratic system, the judicial branch started to play a more active role, sometimes confronting the executive branch—as in Brazil, Bolivia, and Mexico.

In Africa, the groups and lobbies for the independence of the judiciary are weak. Business groups, for example, have traditionally been divided based on ethnicity and competing political leaders. Members of the bar have not been able to influence the relations between the executive and the judiciary. However, as Jennifer Widner's review of building judicial independence in common law Africa shows, chief justices can pursue several strategies to increase the independence of the judiciary—offering impartiality, improving effectiveness, building constituencies, refashioning jurisprudence, and creating alliances with international organizations.[23]

The experience in Africa demonstrates that countries with similar provisions about the recruitment, promotion, and dismissal of judges show different levels of judicial independence. Some of the factors that explain this are the extent to which democratic culture has taken root and the influence of groups such as bar associations, the media, and business groups in lobbying for the independence of the judiciary in practice.

In Tanzania, the judiciary was seen as a threat by some in the one-party government of the 1980s. When strong anticorruption measures were enacted that removed some offenses from the jurisdiction of courts, the chief justice played an important role in presenting the point of view of the judiciary, arguing that even though the Tanzanian constitution had given supreme powers to the party, it was necessary for the judiciary to have the final say in order to eradicate corruption in government. In the case of Uganda, the National Resistance Movement sought to restore judicial independence in order to create a new political base and to promote commercial and investment activities, after the previous regime of Idi Amin had stifled the role of the judiciary and killed a chief justice.[24]

The impact of the political environment on the independence of the judiciary and on legal and judicial reforms is clear from the recent experience of some countries from the former Soviet Union. In Estonia, for example, with the abolishment of the Soviet-era Supreme Court in 1993, Chapter 13 of the Constitution provided for the independence of the judiciary through the Courts Act, Status of Judges Act, and the Procedural Code. Inexperienced judges, especially at the lower levels, constrained the accessibility and effectiveness of the judiciary. In response to this, significant training programs were initiated to improve the quality of justice. This led to a positive assessment by the European Commission of the legal and judicial reforms in Estonia. In its 2000 report on Estonia's progress towards the European Union (EU) accession, the Commission reported that Estonia had "made considerable progress in consolidating a truly independent judiciary, both by establishing formal arrangements and creating a spirit of respect for the principle of judicial independence."[25] One of the critical driving forces in the success of the legal and judicial reform efforts in the country was the political priority of the government to vigorously seek accession to the EU by fulfilling the necessary requirement for the accession.

In Uzbekistan, on the other hand, the executive branch at the central government level continues to dominate the political life under President Islam Karimov. Chosen in the 1991 election, which was not considered fair and free by many observers, he had his tenure extended to 2000 by 1995 plebiscite. He was again elected with "token" opposition, with 92.5 percent of the votes. This election was not considered free and fair by most observers either. Even though the country has a Western-style judiciary, its practice does not reflect the written policy and formal structure. For example, Article 221 of the Code of Criminal Procedure empowers the police to detain a suspect with police alone determining the justification of grounds for detention. Even though Uzbekistan has formal institutions for free and fair elections, a free press and the constitutional provisions for the independence of the judiciary, their enforcement has been lacking because of the absence of political will to ensure that these institutions perform their assigned functions effectively.

INSTITUTIONAL AND ORGANIZATIONAL PRACTICES

Institutional and organizational factors that affect independence and the impartiality of the judiciary include mechanisms and procedures for appointment, promotion, and tenure of judges; a process of budgetary allocation and controls; and procedures for judicial administration.

Effective and efficient management of the judicial system requires increasing the judiciary's budget, improving the physical infrastructure, and reforming judicial selection and judicial career laws. Other measures to improve the efficiency and effectiveness of the judiciary are training judges and other court personnel, strengthening bar associations, instituting curriculum reform in the universities, increasing the availability of legal materials for judges, and strengthening case management and other administrative tasks.

Financial autonomy is an important determinant of the independence of the judiciary. In the case of Latin America, adequate data about budgets are not available, which in itself shows lack of adequate transparency concerning the internal operations of the judiciary. In many cases judiciaries are underfinanced. This has many consequences in the region—low salaries and poor working conditions leading to corruption and bribery, the tendency on the part of more qualified jurists to move to the private sector, weak infrastructural deficiencies that lead to judicial inefficiencies, and delays in court proceedings.[26]

In the Arab region, as in most developing countries, there are historical reasons for underdeveloped institutional mechanisms of accountability—the determination of the ruling elite to build a strong state to deal with internal and external security, strong government intervention in the economy, and the avoidance of a strict separation of powers. More recently, however, some progress has been made. An increasing number of policymakers and development practitioners, under pressure from increasingly vocal citizenry and in response to the requirements of globalization, have begun to recognize the need to ensure the independence of the judiciary and effective mechanisms of accountability.

The approach adopted in the Arab region is to ensure that the judiciary as a corporate body is independent from the other branches of government.[27] It has been difficult, however, to realize this independence in practice. For example, in many countries the constitutional texts are too vague to provide protection to the judiciary. Among the countries where the constitutional provisions guarantee the independence of the judiciary but with few detailed provisions are Algeria, Egypt, Jordan, Kuwait, Syria, Tunisia, and the United Arab Emirates. Judicial review of the constitutionality of legislation is provided in the UAE, Yemen, Egypt, and Morocco. Specific judicial councils exist in Algeria, Egypt, Kuwait, Morocco, Sudan, Tunisia, and Yemen.[28] Due to the internal and external security environment, huge security apparatuses, however, have been constructed which the executive branch does not want to bring under judicial scrutiny to ensure their perceived effectiveness. The composition and competencies of judicial councils are the subject of debate among reform-minded groups. In practice, some states "maintain administrative matters affecting the judiciary under the control of the ministry of justice; others allow their judicial councils far more direct oversight over the internal affairs of the judiciary."[29] In most of the countries in the region, the judiciaries are organized in a hierarchical structure, with the diminishing number of courts at each level and the supreme court at the apex. In addition, a number of courts with specialized jurisdiction exist outside this hierarchy—including those dealing with juvenile, constitutional, military, administrative, security, and religious courts.

The 1999 Beirut Declaration for Justice was adopted at the First Arab Conference for Justice. It provided for a regional Program of Action consisting of four components—safeguards of the judiciary based on the United Nations Basic Principles on the Independence of the Judiciary in the Arab constitutions and laws, independent budgets for the judiciary, and immunity for judges associated with their jobs; the election and appointments of judges through an open and transparent process; the training of judges through specialized centers in order to prepare them for their responsibilities; safeguards for the rights of defense and a fair trial; and support of gender equality under the law in the appointment of judges and practice of the judiciary.[30]

Procedures for the recruitment and evaluation of judges and the relationship of the judiciary with the Ministry of Justice are important dimensions of judicial management. There are significant variations among countries, even in the same region, concerning these dimensions. In most cases the executive branch of the government including the ministries of justice plays a significant role in the appointment and evaluation of judges and in administration and budgetary matters. However, to varying degrees, judicial councils are directly involved in the appointment and evaluation of judges. Administration and budgets are the primary responsibility of ministries of justice.

Judiciaries in many developing countries have outdated personnel practices, procedural requirements, and equipment. Furthermore, they perceive their professional roles and responsibilities differently from those of career government officials. "The civil judge may be a career bureaucrat," Linn Hammergren points out, "but she shares with her common law counterpart an independent, craftsman's approach to her work which conflicts with such basic management techniques as standardization of procedures, organizational guidelines for prioritizing attention to tasks, or quantified output targets."[31] Judges usually are reluctant to delegate authority to professional managers, to have their performance monitored, and to deal openly with disciplinary issues.[32]

One of the important areas of judicial management, especially in Latin America, is alternative dispute resolution—usually through mediation and arbitration—to keep many cases out of the courts, ease the backlog, and reduce cost for the persons involved. Revitalizing or reshaping the role of public prosecutors and public defenders is an important complementary element of most judicial reform programs. This is particularly important in post-conflict situations such as those in Bosnia, Rwanda, and Somalia.

Civil society organizations (CSOs) play an important role in enhancing the efficiency and responsiveness of the judiciary. CSOs (1) work for public interest law reform such as political and civil rights, government transparency, and the environment; (2) seek to help groups such as farmers and tenants through legal advocacy at local government officials, judges, and other authorities; (3) try to promote and advance judicial reform, police reform, and other institutional reform, and (4) are involved in media training teaching journalists about legal and judicial reform and legal aid clinics assisting the disadvantaged to gain access to justice.

In the Arab region, over the years many changes in the management and administration of courts have led to improvements—including the establishment of a professional judicial corps, the identification of procedures to improve access of citizens, improvement in the professionalism and integrity of judiciaries, the increase in judges' salaries, improvement in the training of judges, and the allocation of more independence to judicial councils. Serious problems, however, remain—inadequate administrative support for the courts, the continuation in some cases of exceptional courts that negatively affects a unified judicial system, overworked and underpaid clerks and other personnel, and tensions between the judiciary and the Ministry of Justice over the budget and administrative support for the courts.

ACCESS TO JUSTICE

One of the key principles of democracy is providing a fair mechanism by which groups and individuals can solve their disputes regardless of their political and economic influence. In many cases, the primary reason for a lack of adequate access to justice is poverty. What is needed is to give a voice to the poor through legal means in order to promote and protect their interest like other citizens. The judicial systems in developing countries, however, do not adequately protect the judicial rights of the poor who consider the judiciary and the police unresponsive. It is not uncommon to see corrupt police officers making false arrests and harassing street vendors. These biases are reinforced where the judicial systems fail to punish the police abuses. For example, in Brazil, one study found that only 30 out of 1,730 cases of politically motivated killings of peasants, trade union workers, religious workers, and human rights lawyers were brought to trial.[33]

In many low-income communities in developing countries, nonlawyers—often paralegals—are playing an important role in educating and assisting women, farmers, the urban poor, indigenous peoples, and other disadvantaged groups concerning legal issues affecting them directly. In many cases, paralegals try to resolve conflicts without going to courts through alternative dispute resolution and community action. In other cases, they assist the poor in gathering evidence, constructing affidavits, and using legal arguments to support their clients. Furthermore, they enhance people's access to justice by strengthening their capacity to use legal process, applying pressures to ensure the implementation of existing laws, and raising the awareness of the disadvantaged groups about their rights.

In practice, the poor's access to justice is affected by many factors. The payment of lawers' fees determines the quality of legal advice. Public defense focuses more on criminal cases than on other cases. The facilities for legal aid for the poor are usually inadequate. Equally important are the obstacles experienced by the poor in accessing justice—internal organizational structures and the location of courts, the lack of awareness on the part of the poor to their rights, the cost and time needed to go through the judicial process, and the fear of the poor of those in power.[34]

The following case studies of programs supported by the Ford Foundation show the potential of the civil society in improving the poor's access to justice.

Case 1: Alternative Law Groups and Participatory Justice in the Philippines

Alternative Law Groups (ALGs) in the Philippines seek to promote popular participation in lawmaking, policy formulation, and governmental activities to enhance the social and economic progress of disadvantaged groups. The ALGs consist of small groups of lawyers, law students, and development practitioners interested in protecting the interests of the poor. In many cases they work in close collaboration with NGOs and grassroots associations. Among the issues that ALGs address are agrarian reforms, violence against women, shelter and services for the urban poor, illegal logging, and the rights of indigenous people. They promote and advocate for the interests of the poor in the process of lawmaking as well as monitor the implementation of laws. Furthermore, they train paralegals, provide legal assistance and guidance, and negotiate with the corporate leaders on behalf of the poor concerning environmental and labor issues. In the Philippines, those with resources and family connections can get access to justice, while others must seek out local power brokers, pay bribes, or turn to ALGs and related organizations.

The performance of ALGs in policy advice, regulatory reform, legal implementation, and accountability has been impressive. They were actively involved in the main legislative initiatives in the 1990s to protect the needs and priorities of disadvantaged groups by providing information to legislators and strengthening the legal expertise of NGOs and community-based groups.[35]

Case 2: Legal Education and the Problems of the Poor in Bangladesh

In Bangladesh, one of the initiatives with regard to legal activism was to work directly with NGOs and community-based groups. The Ford Foundation in Bangladesh adopted this "constituency creation" approach by supporting groups and individual activists to respond to legal constraints faced by the disadvantaged groups. These groups included the Bangladesh Women Lawyers' Association (BNWLA), Madaripur Legal Aid Association (MLAA), and the Bangladesh Environmental Lawyers' Association (BELA). It provided grants to these groups and promoted interaction among them. It organized meetings of law students and professors with the legal service organization. The groups supported by the Ford Foundation used media to increase public awareness about legal issues affecting them directly such as police brutality, and the trafficking of females for prostitution.

The above and related groups significantly contributed to employing mediation in legal services, and to engaging the mainstream legal community. The MLAA, for example, used *shalish* (mediation), one of the indigenous practices of using outside expertise to resolve disputes. Other groups too have used this practice for the resolution of disputes. While a useful practice to resolve conflicts, it has not always been a fair mechanism for gender equity because of the male-dominated nature of the society. The practice can work against a client who is not well connected. In some cases, the village middlemen *(touts)* who sell their influence can work against the interests of the poorer segments of the society.[36]

Case 3: The Role of the Centre for Applied Legal Studies and the Legal Resource Centre in South Africa

The 1973 Ford Foundation Conference on "Legal Aid in South Africa" held at the University of Natal brought together leading human rights activists and provided a forum for them to discuss responses to the worsening human rights situation. Eventually, this led to the establishment of two organizations—the Centre for Applied Legal Studies (CALS) in 1978 and the Legal Resource Centre (LRC) in 1979—by two of the activists. The two organizations were supported by the Ford Foundation, Carnegie Corporation, and other international institutions. The LRCs challenged the local implementation rules of acts of parliament such as those dealing with barring family members of black employees living in white towns. The CALS played the "trailblazing role" concerning public interest litigation, which created an environment in which the press could criticize security forces and more people began to resist abuse. The LRC and CALS did not challenge the Act of Parliament concerning the incorporation of indigenous Africans into "ethnic homelands"—because that would certainly have failed—but focused on narrower issues of implementation by the government taking advantage of the courts' partial independence. Public interest litigation strengthened the role of antiapartheid activists and encouraged the involvement of prominent lawyers. Furthermore, it increased pressures on prosecutors who were trying to enforce unjust laws, expand the judicial understanding of NGOs regarding human rights, and promote partnership and dialogue among lawyers' groups, NGOs, community-based groups, unions, and the media to protect the rights of the disadvantaged groups. CALS also supported the black labor movements, which were an important political force in the country, contributed to South Africa's interim and final Constitution, enhanced negotiation skills of the labor movement, and developed data and strategies to challenge the apartheid regime nationally and internationally.[37]

REFORM PROCESSES AND INSTITUTIONAL ARRANGEMENTS

The reform of the judiciary requires many new processes and institutional arrangements. The core of a judicial reform program consists of measures to improve the effectiveness of the judicial branch of government. These measures aim to (1) strengthen the judicial branch by introducing changes in the selection, evaluation, and discipline of judges to avoid improper influences; (2) speed the processing of cases by providing training equipment and resources to judges and court personnel; (3) increase access to dispute resolution mechanisms by creating mediation and conciliation services and other mechanisms to reduce court costs; and (4) professionalize the bench and the bar through in-service training for judges, lawyers, and other legal professionals.[38] Efforts of national governments and international development partners have led to changes in the legal framework, organization, and budgetary resources in many developing countries and increased the involvement of a variety of national, regional, and external actors in the dialogue about the role to be played by the judiciary in the process of democratization and, more specifically, the role of the related entities including police, ministry of justice, legal aid societies, and bar associations.

   Legal and judicial reforms in Latin America have dealt with two interrelated categories—those that concern justice administration including structures, procedures, and the administration of justice including mechanisms for the appointment, assessment, and internal accountability of judges; and those that attempt to modify existing relationships between the judiciary and other branches of government. One of the key features of reforms in the region is the creation of judicial councils including those in Costa Rica (1989), Colombia (1991), Paraguay and Ecuador (1992), and Bolivia, Argentina, and Mexico (1994). To varying degrees, these councils are responsible for the appointment of judges, the establishment of procedures for judicial appointments, promotion, and discipline, and the administering of the judicial budget. Another feature of the judicial reform in the region includes laws such as the General Code of Procedure in Uruguay

(1989) that was aimed at shortening and simplifying court procedures and processes to improve efficiency; and the use of professional managers to reduce the administrative tasks of lower court judges (such as in Bolivia, Costa Rica, Honduras, and Panama).

Countries in the region have followed different strategies and approaches concerning the horizontal relationship between the judiciary and the executive. In Bolivia and Mexico, the focus was on reducing the powers of the executive by changing the appointment procedures. In Brazil, Bolivia, and Colombia, the emphasis was on increasing the powers of the high tribunals or the creation of constitutional courts. The experience in the region suggests that while institutional reform is necessary, past legacies of judicial subordination, authoritarian rule and weaknesses of democratic institutions influence the degree of judicial independence. One can discern several positive trends concerning independence of the judiciary in the region—the increasingly political role being played by the supreme courts including judicial decisions concerning corruption cases involving the highest levels of political leaders.

The period from 1990 to 1997 saw a significant reorganization of the justice sector in Mozambique. The Mozambican Constitution of 1990 conceived of the judiciary as a fully independent branch of government. The fundamental change was a part of the larger pattern of growing political pluralism. The constitutional independence of the judiciary dramatically reinforced the principle of the separation of powers, one of the pillars of the rule of law. These changes were taking place in the larger context of ending the Mozambican civil war and building multiparty democracy. During the 1990s, Mozambican institutions and a few international aid agencies began to make substantive investments in strengthening the capacity of the judiciary and the police including training, rehabilitation of the court system, and sponsorship of legal reform work.

In India, as in many other developing economies, domestic violence against women is a major social problem. To respond to this problem, amendments have been made to the Indian Penal Code (IPC)—the main law describing crime and punishment in the country—and the Criminal Procedure Code (CPC)—that describes the procedures for the police and courts and the Indian Evidence Act (IEA). These amendments include Section 306 of the IPC dealing with suicide by women. If a woman commits suicide within seven years of marriage and evidence of cruelty can be shown, the presumption of abetment is provided by Section 113A. Where the death of a woman is caused by burns and/or bodily injury and there was evidence of harassment for dowry, such death "will be called a dowry death and husband/relative shall be deemed to have caused death."[39] Another amendment of the code provides for a mandatory postmortem examination where the case involves the suicide of a woman within seven years of marriage or where a relative makes a request or where there are doubts about the cause of death.[40] In addition to the above amendments to the law, the response of the government agencies to violence against women has also been through community-policing initiatives, counseling, all women police stations, and family courts.

The problem in the implementation of the above laws and other initiatives remains—misuse of the law to take revenge against the in-laws, the reluctance of the police to file complaints under this section, and the difficulty of the complainant to get access to her matrimonial home after she files a case. The conviction rates under this section are very low.[41] Women face many stumbling blocks in their quest to secure justice through the judicial system. Most of the domestic violence cases come within the purview of the criminal system that is based on the premise that the accused is innocent until proved guilty. In the case of domestic violence in the country where the parties are bound by ties of marriage, extended family relations, and social pressures, it becomes extremely difficult to gather adequate evidence. In addition, there is the serious problem of case backlog in the Indian judicial system. Sometimes the cases take so long that the memory of the witnesses might be affected and they might be unwilling to provide the evidence. Other constraints on women to secure adequate justice from the judicial system are high workload on the investigation officers and prosecutors, inadmissible evidence, time-barred complaints due to the lethargy of the police, and compromise agreements due to pressures from family and relatives that usually result in the charges of violence being dropped.

Many examples presented in this chapter show the progress that has been made in improving the administration and management of the judicial system, reviewing laws, improving access of the poor to justice, providing new roles for the civil society organizations, and enhancing the independence and autonomy of the judiciary. Furthermore, in many countries budgets allocated to the judiciary have been increased, there are more opportunities for the professional development of the staff, and procedures for monitoring and evaluation have been improved. Bilateral donors, multilateral development organizations, financial institutions, and civil society organizations have over the past few years been playing an important role in supporting government efforts to reform judicial and legal systems and processes. Legal and judicial reforms in many regions such as Latin America have become a central part of the reform agenda of the governments at the national level. There is greater public interest in the issues of access to justice. The increasing scrutiny by the media has been instrumental in pressuring the policymakers and development practitioners to invest even more resources to improve the effectiveness of the courts and to reform the outdated laws.

LESSONS OF EXPERIENCE

Many lessons have been learned from experiences of developing countries in designing and implementing judicial reform programs. The case studies and analysis in this chapter and other recent studies including those supported by the US Agency for International Development point to the following critical factors that determine the success or failure of judicial reform efforts.[42]

1. **Support at multiple levels is essential.** Active civil society participation—including bottom-up initiatives through NGOs, community-based organization, public interest law groups, and human rights organizations—is crucial from the beginning. Reforms should be driven and owned by actors at the national level. The international organizations can act only as international advisors and facilitators of resource mobilization to achieve national objectives. Global policy work is crucial as long as it is in tune with national realities and facilitates cross-fertilization of experiences and ideas.

   Political leaders and judicial institutions lack the political will to reform on a sustained basis. It is usually difficult to mobilize people to put pressure from below on the issues related to legal and judicial reform. Even when a senior politician is truly committed to legal and judicial reforms, his/her efforts are thwarted by vested interests—to continue corrupt practices, keep control of personal fiefdoms, and influence judicial decisions in his/her favor. The experience suggests that small group of lawyers and NGO leaders have been playing an important role in mobilizing support for legal and judicial reforms. However, many of their efforts are focused on providing legal assistance to the poor and disadvantaged groups.

2. **There has been a serious gap between the magnitude of the problem in this sector and the amount of investment made by national governments and the international community.** Many countries lacked adequate infrastructure, salaries for judges and other personnel, and operating budgets. Under such circumstances, internationally funded projects become islands of innovation in the

otherwise broken system—and once the external funding is withdrawn, these are not sustainable.

3. **Reforms in the judicial system are more difficult than in the agencies and departments of the executive branch** because of the tendency of judges of the superior courts to be independent, unwilling to decentralize to the subunits, and reluctant to support reform initiatives for fear of ceding powers to the executive branch. Even when assistance is provided to the leadership at the top and when this leadership is committed to change, implementation is stifled at lower levels because of the traditional ways of doing business, especially in transitional countries.

4. **Reforming institutional structure is the key to ensuring the independence of the judiciary.** The selection process should be transparent including a broad-based judicial council and merit-based selection process with recognition of the diversity of the society. Other elements of the institutional structure for judicial independence are the security of tenure with effective procedures for performance evaluation and promotion, length of tenure (life tenure and fixed-term), and the structure of the judiciary—including adequate budget and the role of private lawyers and bar associations. Adequate training and skills of the judges and their commitment to the independence of the judiciary are important components of judicial reform strategies. To enhance the capacity, skills, and commitment of judges requires training programs (including continuing judicial education and university legal education), access to legal materials, codes of ethics, improvements in the public's perception of the status of judges, and proactive judges' associations.

5. **Enhancing societal respect for the role of an impartial judiciary is an important ingredient of successful reforms.** This can be facilitated where the courts have the authority to declare laws and executive actions unconstitutional, where the judiciary decides cases efficiently and fairly where the judiciary has strong internal leadership, and where the judiciary has the managerial capacity to undertake its responsibilities.

6. **The design of judicial reforms should specify procedures and processes to ensure a balance between judicial independence and judicial accountability.** While the judges are expected to render their decisions independently and impartially, their decisions should not "stray too far" from the public sentiments.

CONCLUSION

Rule of law and effective judicial systems are required to protect civil and political liberties, check the abuse of authority, and to take advantage of opportunities provided by globalization such as the promotion of foreign investments. Judicial independence is the core of effective judicial systems. The practice in developing economies shows that the independence of the judiciary is directly affected by the political environment in the country— whether the country has a pluralistic government, "guided democracy," one-party system, or military-dominated government. It is also affected by procedures for the appointment, promotion, and tenure of judges; the process of budgetary allocation and controls; and procedures for judicial administration. To varying degrees, progress is being made in promoting the independence of the judiciary in Africa, Asia, the Arab region, Eastern Europe, and Latin America. Though poverty continues to be the main constraint, civil society organizations and community-based groups are playing a significant role in improving the access of the poor to justice.

ENDNOTES

1. Robert Barros, "Dictatorship and the Rule of Law: Rules and Military Power in Pinochet's Chile" in *Democracy and the Rule of Law,* Jose Maria Maraval and Adam Przeworski, eds. (Cambridge: Cambridge University Press, 2003), 188–222.

2. Barry R. Weingast, "A Postscript to Political Foundation of Democracy and the Rule of Law" in *Democracy and the Rule of Law*, 109–110.

3. Richard E. Messick, "Judicial Reform: The Why, What and How" (paper presented, Conference on Strategies for Modernizing the Judicial Sector in the Arab World, Marrakech, Morocco, March 15–17, 2002), 2.

4. Ibid., 4.

5. Amartya Sen, "What is the Role of Legal and Judicial Reform in Development" (keynote address, Global Conference on Comprehensive Legal and Judicial Development, Washington, DC, June 5–7, 2000), 14.

6. Ibid., 16–17.

7. David Louis Finnegan, "Observations on Tanzania's Commercial Court: A Case Study" (paper presented, World Bank Conference on Empowerment,

Security and Opportunity Through Law and Justice, St. Petersburg, Russia, July 8–12, 2001), 4.

8. Ibid., 6.

9. Ibid., 8.

10. Herman Schwartz, "Surprising Success: The New Eastern European Constitutional Courts" in *The Self-Restraining State: Power and Accountability in New Democracies*, Andreas Schedler, Larry Diamond and Marc Plattner, eds. (Boulder, CO: Lynne Rienner Publishers, 1999), 210.

11. Pilar Domingo, "Judicial Independence and Judicial Reform in *The Self-Restraining State*, 153–154.

12. Carlo Guarnieri, "Courts as Instrument of Horizontal Accountability: The Case of Latin Europe" in *Democracy and the Rule of Law*, 225.

13. Irshad Hasan Khan, "Judicial System of Pakistan: Measures for Maintaining Independence and Enforcing Accountability" (paper presented, International Conference of Legal and Judicial Reform, Washington, DC: 2000), 3.

14. Ibid.

15. Ibid., 154.

16. Ibid., 154.

17 Maria Dakolias, *The Judicial Sector in Latin America and the Caribbean: Elements of Reform* (Technical paper 319, Washington, DC: World Bank, 1996), 4.

18. Domingo, "Judicial Independence and Judicial Reform," 156.

19. UNDP, *Democracy in Latin America* (New York: UNDP, 2004), 1–20.

20. UNDP, *Deepening Democracy in a Fragmented World* (New York: Oxford University Press, 2002), 72.

21. Ibid., 72.

22. Ibid., 72.

23. Jennifer Widner, "Building Judicial Independence in Common Law Africa" in *The Self-Restraining State*, 177–194.

24. Ibid., 183–84.

25. *2000 Regular Report From the Commission of Estonia's Progress Towards Accession*, November 8, 2000, http://europa.eu.int/comm./enlargement/Estonia/.

26. Domingo, "Judicial Independence and Judicial Reform," and Dakolias, *The Judicial Sector in Latin America and the Caribbean*.

27. Nathan J. Brown, *Mechanisms for Accountability in Arab Governance: The Present and Future of Judiciaries and Parliaments in the Arab World* (Beruit: Programme on Governance in the Arab Region, UNDP, mim. December 2001), 2.

28. Ibid.

29. Ibid., 9.

30. UNDP, *Arab Human Development Report* (New York: UNDP, 2002), 116.

31. Linn Hammergren, *Fifteen Years of Judicial Reform in Latin America: Where We Are and Why We Haven't Made More Progress* (Washington, DC: USAID Global Centre for Democracy and Governance, 2002), 3.

32. Ibid., 4.

33. UNDP, *Deepening Democracy in a Fragmented World*, 66.

34. Ibid., 202.

35. Stephen Golub, "Participatory Justice in the Philippines" in *Many Roads to Justice*, Mary McClymont, ed. (New York: Ford Foundation, 2000), 197–232.

36. Stephen Golub, "From Village to the University: Legal Activism in Bangladesh" in *Many Roads to Justice*.

37. Stephen Golub, "Battling Apartheid: Building a New South Africa" in *Many Roads to Justice*.

38. Richard E. Messick, "Judicial Reform: the Why, the What and the How" (paper presented, Conference on Strategies for Modernizing the Judicial Sector in the Arab World, Marrakech, Morocco, March 15–17, 2002), 5.

39. V.S. Elizabeth, "Law Reform to Combat Domestic Violence in India" (paper presented, World Bank Conference on Empowerment, Security and Opportunity Through Law and Justice, St. Petersburg, Russia, July 8–12, 2001), 4.

40. Ibid.

41. Ibid.

42. Thomas Carothers, *Aiding Democracy Abroad* (Washington, DC: Carnegie Endowment for International Peace, 1999), 172. For guidelines to promote judicial independence based on project experience, see US Agency for International Development, *Guidance for Promoting Judicial Independence and Impartiality* (Washington, DC: USAID, January 2003).

CHAPTER 9

GOVERNANCE IN CRISIS SITUATIONS

The most effective systems of governance are fundamentally well-developed conflict management mechanisms that help to balance conflicting interests and needs in a way that benefits the human development of the majority without sacrificing that of the minority. When conflict becomes violent, systemic, or long lasting, however, it threatens both democracy and human development. It has become obvious that failed governance is both a cause and a consequence of conflict. Therefore, strengthening the institutions and processes of governance is an important tool for conflict prevention, recovery, and reconciliation.

This chapter reviews the causes of conflict and its effect on human development and democracy. It then explores the potential of democratic governance as a tool for conflict prevention, management, and resolution, looking at specific components including rebuilding fractured communities, approaches and methods of political reconciliation, security sector reform, reintegration programs, and the role of the civil society during the conflict and post-conflict situations. Finally, the chapter examines some specific cases in rebuilding fractured communities that bring together issues of governance and conflict in a practical manner.

CAUSES OF CONFLICT

There is a difference between the root causes of conflict and its triggers. Root causes tend to be structural and include things such as scarcity of resources and protracted macroeconomic crisis; artificial boundaries and political geography that do not reflect traditional social patterns; and/or the institutionalized exclusion of particular groups from political or economic decision-making or from access to opportunities.[1] Conflict triggers, on the other hand, tend to be more isolated events. Often, they involve the manipulation of ideological, religious or ethnic differences, or perceptions to exacerbate the perception of differences between groups and incite confrontation between constituencies.[2]

Today, more and more conflicts are internal. The origins of many violent conflicts can be attributed to domestic factors.[3] Internal conflicts can range from low-intensity guerilla insurgencies, to full-scale civil war, to state-sponsored campaigns of genocide. Although the term "internal" is used to describe these conflicts, it is rare for a conflict within a state not to cause repercussions in neighboring states. In 1994, for example, following the massacres of hundreds of thousands in Rwanda, over 250,000 Rwandans fled into Tanzania in one day.[4]

It is usually difficult, if not impossible, to trace conflicts to a single source as they tend to owe their genesis to diverse causes. In recent years, however, certain trends have emerged that suggest, as noted above, strong linkages between scarcity, inequality, and institutional weaknesses in societies and their abilities to ensure peace and security. Indeed, recent research on complex humanitarian emergencies (CHEs) concluded that "horizontal inequalities" between groups are the major cause of most recent civil conflicts.[5] These horizontal inequalities do not necessarily determine which countries will become CHEs; they simply represent commonalities that appear among CHEs and in that way can be useful predictors on which to base preventative policies and efforts. Important areas in which horizontal inequalities are found include politics, economics, employment and income, and social access and situation. Not all countries with horizontal inequalities in these areas will become CHEs. Much depends upon the policies of individual leaders. In some countries, such as Rwanda and the former Yugoslavia, bad leadership pushed already vulnerable countries the rest of the way towards conflict.

A number of variables can be used in analyzing the risk factors in CHEs.[6] These include:

Income and Food Output: The first correlation is between stagnation and decline in average income (or GNP per capita) and increased vulnerability to CHEs. A 10 percent growth rate in a given country has been found to translate to an 8.5 percent decline in the probability of that country experiencing a CHE. Likewise, the global economic crises of the late 1980s translated into a sharp rise in the number of CHEs. As the food output per person in a given country falls, the vulnerability to CHEs rises.

Inequality: Horizontal inequalities between ethnic and social groups constitute a major variable in CHEs. The greater the number of inequalities between these groups, the higher the risk of CHE.

Inflation and Military Spending: As inflation increases, so too does a country's vulnerability to CHEs. A rise in military spending, when combined with inflation, serves to further exacerbate a country's vulnerability to CHEs.

Past Conflicts: A country's history of past conflict is also a variable—that is, whether there exists a history of conflict and how that conflict was resolved. Countries with a history of past conflict are more prone to CHEs. Yet, within this group, those countries that developed a tradition of peaceful dispute resolution fared better than did those with a history of settling conflict through the use of force.

Breakdown of Interethnic and Interregional Dialogue: Ethnic heterogeneity and interregional economic disparities per se are not the root cause. It is only when the dialogue between the groups and regions of the country breaks down that the risk of CHEs becomes more critical.

Current research disproves the role of ethnicity per se as a root cause of conflict. Ethnic variables do not emerge in any significant way as causes of CHEs, but they are used as extremely destructive triggers that can then perpetuate a cycle of violence and hinder efforts at reconciliation. In this sense, the manipulation of ethnic differences, combined with a pattern of ethnic inequality and unequal access to resources, can become a root cause of future conflict. Indeed, if the research shows anything it is that the complexities of conflict—intrastate and interstate alike—defy a simplistic explanation such as "ethnic hatred." If this were a legitimate root cause of conflict on its own, why did Bosnia implode where Belgium did not? And why have the Abkhazians tried to secede violently from Georgia where the Québecois have not tried to do the same from Canada? Why did East Timor secede from Indonesia while multiethnic Malaysia has been politically stable for the past three decades? Why have various groups in Tanzania lived in relative harmony while some multiethnic societies in Africa are falling apart?

Consequences of Conflicts on Development Performance

The negative effects of crisis on development are universally recognized. A short but destructive conflict can undo decades of human development gains. Preventing and mitigating the worst effects of crisis and ensuring recovery increase the likelihood that countries will move toward human development. During the past 10 years or so, the nature of conflicts has changed fundamentally. They are now increasingly internal, total, and protracted.[7] More conflicts feature significant regional impact and incur higher civilian casualties than ever before. Hence, the social, economic, and environmental consequences of these conflicts are considerable and long lasting, and have disastrous effects on the human development of affected countries.

For example, Sub-Saharan Africa, one of the regions most affected by conflict and natural disasters during the past two decades, experienced a cumulative decline in real GDP. Total losses in the Central American countries worst hit by Hurricane

Mitch in 1998 were estimated at US$6 billion, representing 13 percent of the region's 1997 GDP.[8] Countries such as Haiti and Sierra Leone, already among the poorest in the world, have seen their Human Development Indexes drop precipitously.[9] And Mozambique, which had experienced steady recovery and economic growth since the end of civil strife eight years ago, saw the 2000 floods displace 300,000 people and affect as many as 1.9 million.[10] Over two decades of conflict in Afghanistan—triggered by both serious internal divisions and external interventions—have devastated the economic, social, and political infrastructure and institutions of the country, leading to the lowest levels of human development in the world.

It is the poor who bear a disproportionate share of the conflict's burden in terms of human and environmental costs. The poor are more likely to be deprived of their means of livelihoods, to suffer from the inability of the government to maintain law and order, and to be subject to human rights abuses. They are also likely to be displaced from their houses, depriving them of even the rudimentary services accessible to them. Most importantly, conflict fractures communities, depriving people of their immediate support groups.

IMPACT OF CONFLICT ON DEMOCRATIC GOVERNANCE

Systemic and long-term conflict short-circuits democratic governance, undermining the institutions and processes upon which it is based. In a conflict situation—particularly an intrastate conflict—traditional or prewar governance and social safety structures are destroyed or disabled. This often leads to the innovation of new governance structures and processes located closer to the grass roots that can deliver services and protection in the absence of state authority. Further, the impact of conflict on governance does not end with the conflict itself. Once peace is established, citizens have high expectations that the quality of governance and of their lives will improve appreciably. At the same time, fragile postwar governments are often beset by authoritarian or military legacies, and tempted by authoritarian solutions given the scale and urgency of the challenges facing them and the imperative need for direction, unity of approach, and authority. Post-1994 Rwanda presents an example of this phenomenon.

The specific effects of violent conflict on various institutions and processes of democratic governance are discussed in more detail below.

Human Rights: As discussed in chapter 5, basic human rights are often the first things to be sacrificed in a conflict situation. In many countries, if a conflict is internal, a government can assume extraordinary powers that curtail normal constitutional provisions against arrest without evidence, detention without charge, prohibition on movement, etc. If a conflict is international, the rules of war are sometimes not adhered to, resulting in heavy civilian injuries and casualties. In East Timor, for example, 60,000 people (10 percent of the population) were killed within the first two months of Indonesia's 1975 invasion.[11] In Iraq, large numbers of civilians have been killed over the past year. While little is often done to ensure that human rights are protected during a conflict situation, the defense of these rights in the post-conflict environment is crucial to stability and long-term reconciliation. In a number of countries emerging from deep-rooted conflict—such as Cambodia, Afghanistan, El Salvador, and Haiti—the United Nations and other organizations have deployed human rights monitors with good effect. These monitors can encourage local populations to regain confidence in their governing institutions and thereby return from refugee camps. Such human rights monitoring missions usually form part of a larger umbrella UN peacekeeping mission in a given country.

Access to Justice and Security: The restoration of justice by itself does not heal relations, although it is likely to contribute to healing by attributing responsibility and punishing perpetrators of violence. True reconciliation requires the capacity to repent and the capacity to forgive, at individual and collective levels. Exposing and admitting the facts is a necessary precondition for this, which is why truth and historical verification commissions can play such an important role. Equally important, for the victims, is the belief that similar horrors will not occur again, and this in turn implies that new governance and judicial structures are seen as credible and legitimate. In post-conflict environments, there is a need to reform not just laws, but institutions as well (and, in some cases, to create new laws and institutions). As discussed in chapter 8, basic human rights and specific minority rights need to be enshrined in the constitution and access of the poor to justice needs to be improved.

Some recent experiences show the complexity of establishing a judiciary and the rule of law in crisis and post-crisis situations. In Kosovo, for example, the international community did not receive sufficient local support because of the inability to establish a "responsive and efficient judicial system as part of the transitional administration."[12] The cases of Rwanda and Sierra Leone show the difficulties in the reconstruction of legal and judicial systems due to the political crises. Based on his analysis of the two countries, Chris Mburu identifies three challenges. The first is that the demand for immediate justice "overwhelms" the capacity of the government established in post-conflict situations making it difficult to start comprehensive legal and judicial reforms. The second challenge to comprehensive reform efforts is a serious shortage of lawyers and other legal professionals. In Rwanda, over 80 percent of the judges, prosecutors, magistrates and other trained legal personnel had either been killed or fled the country after the 1994 war—leading to situations where many legal tasks were undertaken by persons with inadequate legal background and training even though the international community initiated programs to train a new group of legal personnel. The third challenge is to build new legal and judicial institutions and infrastructure in response to the collapse and destruction of the old ones. In both countries, programs were initiated to build the capacity of the legislature, strengthen the police force, reform the prison system, strengthen the capacity of the justice ministry, and improve the infrastructure and capacity of the court system.[13]

Electoral and Legislative Systems and Processes: During conflict, electoral and legislative processes and systems are often either defunct or operating at the bare minimum. While the legislature often plays a role in involving a state in conflict or in crafting a compromise to emerge from it, conflicts tend to consolidate power in the executive at the expense of the legislature. War can leave behind unresolved power struggles, particularly if a cease-fire was imposed on an unfinished civil war. Elections do not necessarily put an end to these struggles. In the absence of a mature democratic system and of organized civil society, elections rarely lead to sustainable power-sharing arrangements, but rather to one party simply dominating another. "Winner takes all" electoral systems tend to aggravate this problem.

The outcomes of elections in post-conflict situations do create a new set of problems. In the case of Cambodia, for example, between 1991 and 1994, the establishment of a freely and fairly elected government was the primary objective of the United Nations. The post-election arrangements—including co-premiership and sharing of senior posts in each ministry among the two parties and the coalition government—resulted in further politicization of the civil service, an increase in the government budget, and constraint on the effectiveness of the public sector because of the need to keep the "fragile political balance."[14] In Rwanda, when the Transitional National Assembly was appointed it represented nine political parties. The assembly lacked the capacity to legislate and perform its oversight function vis-à-vis the executive branch of the government. The members of the assembly and the staff were inexperienced and, according to Chris Mburu, "they were dealing with a government that was essentially trying to recreate itself."[15]

Decentralization and Local Governance: Service and resource delivery and management is usually crippled in conflict situations, particularly in internal conflicts. Often what resources are delivered and utilized bypass formalized decentralization and local governance structures. Informal economies and systems spring up. In times of crisis, there is a general tendency for governments to avoid decentralization, especially in those crises caused by internal struggle for power between groups of people concentrated in different geographic centers. The reason for this is that governments do not wish to weaken even further the common social identity or increase regional or "nationalist" sentiment within their borders. At the same time, it should be noted that regional inequalities in governance within a given country have contributed to intrastate conflict. In this way, decentralization poses a potential solution to this root cause of conflict. A number of countries, such as Uganda, have taken this approach of using decentralized governance to reduce such regional disparities and contribute to the elimination of the cause for conflict. In post-conflict situations, key municipal services and instruments such as basic health, education, sewerage, water and solid waste removal need to be reestablished. Being centers of market interactions, it is also pivotal that cities function in order to generate resources for sustainability and recovery, both for individuals and state institutions.

Public Administration: Conflict directly impacts the state's capacity to govern. In some cases the state implodes altogether (e.g., Somalia in the late 1980s and early 1990s); in others it is only able to function minimally or exert influence over part of the state's territory (e.g., the late days of Mobuto's Zaire). In Rwanda and East Timor, the public administration system was broken down. Conflict disrupts the normal cycle of public administration functioning, including the recruitment and training of the civil service, the creation or restructuring of various government agencies and departments, systems for payment of salaries to government employees, and other civil service reform initiatives. In most countries emerging from crisis situations, such as Afghanistan, the reconstruction of post-conflict public administration systems has been given first priority by the international development community. Moreover, conflict tends to make states aid dependent, which also interferes with the normal productivity and flow of resources from the center to the regions and back. The executive branch in crisis situations wields too much power in the day-to-day processes of decision-making and policymaking and, as such, has often been at the center of criticism on the part of minority groups.[16] Because exclusion from involvement in public sector institutions of certain minority groups (or of the majority) often constitutes one of the structural causes of conflict, it is important to address it in post-conflict rebuilding. Any number of methods can be used to do this, including a review of quotas and other systems of preferential treatment based on ethnicity; decentralization; or the inclusion of civil society organizations and the private sector in public administration reform.[17]

Accountability and Transparency: Under wartime and other special measures the accountability and transparency of governance are compromised. The normal means of checking government power—the legislature, judiciary, media, civil society watchdog groups, etc.—are often either suspended or persecuted in conflict situations. As discussed in chapter 3, in addition to upholding the separation of powers and strengthening the roles of inspectors-general, auditors-general, and the judiciary and essential legislation, assistance also needs to be provided to strengthen civil society organizations that can serve as watchdogs and can help to democratize the process of ensuring accountability.[18]

Media: Countries have long sought to encourage the "masses" to fight by carefully crafted propaganda campaigns. Such campaigns control access to the fighting; exclude neutral correspondents; and muster support in the name of patriotism. In Rwanda, "hate radio" helped to incite the killing of almost one million Tutsis and moderate Hutus in 1994. After such manipulation, the media is often hard pressed to rehabilitate a reputation for independence and fairness. That said, the media has an extraordinary potential to promote reconciliation in a post-conflict setting. Particularly through the use of radio, media has been used successfully to provide balanced and objective reporting; to give humanitarian information; to promote peace building initiatives; and to develop over the long term free, independent, and responsible media in countries prone to conflict.[19] In Burundi, for example, UNESCO, UNDP and UNHCR have worked with the media to promote reconciliation and peace education. An American NGO named Search for Common Ground went one step further and helped the Burundians establish the country's first independent radio station in 1995.

CONFLICT PREVENTION, MANAGEMENT AND RESOLUTION IN THE CONTEXT OF DEMOCRATIC GOVERNANCE

Democratic governance is an excellent tool for conflict prevention, management, and resolution because of its powers to promote maximum popular participation and effective power sharing.[20] Perhaps most significant to its conflict linkages, democratic governance provides the mechanisms and processes for citizens and groups to articulate their interests, mediate their differences, and exercise their legal rights and obligations.

Democratic governance also provides a number of outlets for resolving disputes, including the police, the judiciary, or the legislature. However, in a society where these institutions are crippled or nonfunctional, disputes will be resolved by violent means.

This is why it is crucial to enhance the capacities of at-risk countries to analyze vulnerability trends, development risks, and societal tensions, and to take early preventive actions consonant with the principles of good governance. This would help to secure the structural stability of these countries. In some countries, for example, the United Nations regularly issues "Early Warning Reports" based on a set of inter-related indicators, designed to monitor the dynamics of the overall economic, social, political, religious, and ethnic environment. In some countries the information is based on monthly opinion polls, data from governmental institutions, and information in the press. The basic assumption that overall stability in a given country predominantly depends on social and economic issues has determined the set of phenomena and indicators monitored on a monthly basis, like employment and job security, political stability, ethnic and religious tensions, and personal security.[21]

While democratic governance has proven the best system for preventing, managing, and resolving conflict within and between states, there are naturally some situations in which more coercive means are necessary to accomplish these goals. These more robust methods include nonviolent, though not victimless, means such as sanctions and economic embargoes. These methods serve three purposes: they send a signal of international concern to an offending state that may be menacing a neighbor or its own citizens; they try to modify this behavior; and they hold the promise of stronger action if the state fails to comply.[22] It goes without saying of course that sanctions and embargoes remain within the purview of individual states to enforce; international organizations such as the United Nations can only authorize their use. These methods have more often been used as a means of conflict prevention to change the behavior of a state that is violating the rights of its own citizens (e.g., South Africa, Haiti, and Iraq), rather than as a method of managing or resolving conflict on an international scale (e.g., the former Yugoslavia).

Where peace and order is broken down and communities fractured, tensions between restoring peace and establishing democratic control are much more pronounced than in an environment of peace within the society. The cases of Cambodia and Bosnia and Herzegovina show that holding national and local elections in the context of violence and mistrust among communities can delay the peace process. On the other hand, the cases of El Salvador, Mozambique, and East Timor demonstrate that because of a conducive environment within the society, progress can be made in reforming or creating a professional military and police, demobilizing and reintegrating combatants, and creating an environment of reconciliation among various segments of the society.[23]

REBUILDING FRACTURED COMMUNITIES

Rebuilding societies after wars is highly complex because of the "legacy of the conflict (physical destruction, lack of resources and manpower, institutional fragility, political volatility, social trauma), by the urgency of the problems and by the simultaneous challenges of humanitarian relief and of military security."[24] There are three primary governance imperatives in crisis and post-crisis countries that directly and immediately affect the fractured communities. These are (1) recreating or consolidating the institutional foundations of the state (e.g., constitution, parliament, public administration, etc.) and promoting democratization; (2) promoting broad-based and equitable social cohesion and enabling an enhanced role for the civil society and the private sector; and (3) guaranteeing human security and the right to development including political, social, and economic rights.

Countries emerging from conflict have unique governance and development needs. Post-conflict rebuilding therefore must include not just bricks and mortar assistance for the physical environment, but also less tangible assistance for the social fabric so communities can reconcile and equitably share limited economic and social resources. Approaches need to be found to mend relations among communities, and to restore dignity, trust, and faith between former adversaries.

In the case of Kosovo, for example, it is recognized by all parties—including those inside and outside of Kosovo—that restoring trust between Kosovar Albanians and minority groups including Kosovar Serbs is the most fundamental issue to be resolved to ensure peace, development, and stability in the area. In view of this, the United Nations Mission Interim Administration in Kosovo (UNMIK) recognized the need to improve the relationship between ethnic Albanians and Serbs in Kosovo and to protect ethnic minorities.[25] This was made the central goal of the "Institution-building Pillar"—a key program of the UNMIK. Three strategies to achieve this goal were adopted. First, in order to encourage the members of the smaller communities to remain in Kosovo, capacity development and institution-building programs were to be designed to correct individual and systemic discrimination. Second, reconciliation and tolerance was to be promoted through confidence-building measures. Third, the strategies promoted the right to return of all internally displaced persons and refugees. Among specific actions taken by the UNMIK to improve ethnic relations were the enhancement of freedom of movement through the issuance of Kosovo license plates to ethnic Serbs, a guarantee that civil service would be multiethnic and multilingual, the establishment of an Office for the Returnees, and instituting a faster process to resolve property issues. Furthermore, the number of ethnic Serbs in the justice system was increased, 10 percent of the parliamentary seats in Kosovo's assembly were reserved for ethnic Serbs, and the Small Investment Minorities Fund was established.

The improvement of ethnic relations in Kosovo, however, continues to be difficult due to historical and deep resentment of various communities towards each other. Leaders of all Kosovo communities and external actors continue to face new challenges in rebuilding fractured communities. The March 2004 interethnic riots, which led to the death of several civilians, showed difficulties in reconciling the aspirations and demands of a majority—which is lukewarm in its support for minority rights—and the minority—which is extremely reluctant to recognize the aspirations of the majority and looks to Serbia for its own identity.

An important element to any successful strategy, if implemented with the help of outside actors, is to base interventions and programs on local consultative and decision-making structures.[26] With this is mind, the War-torn Societies Project (WSP), a collaborative project of the United Nations Research Institute for Social Development (UNRISD) and the Program for Strategic and International Security Studies (PSIS) of the Geneva Graduate Institute of International Studies, was launched in June 1994. Its first aim was to help clarify policy options in societies that are emerging from major social and political conflict.[27] WSP was launched in Eritrea in June 1995, in Mozambique in July 1995, in Guatemala in August 1996, and in Somalia—after a prolonged preparatory period—in January 1997.

Several lessons—concerning the understanding of the challenge, the actors, and the response—have been learned from the case studies of the War-torn Societies Project.[28] To begin with, it is essential to understand and recognize the complexity and difficulty of rebuilding war-torn societies. Mending relations among the parties and restoring trust and faith are also essential to rebuild war-torn societies. In Somalia, for example, mistrust among groups was seen to be the primary obstacle to the restoration of administration. Deficits in political development—including lack of clarity in the division of powers, and weak political institutions—made it difficult to mend fragile relationships between people and institutions. In Angola, elections did not bring about peace. Instead, the reinforcement of group cleavages led to the outbreak of war again.

As the case of Eritrea shows, post-war political systems often lead to authoritarian modes of decision-making, even when there is a broad recognition of the need for popular support for the rebuilding strategies. In other cases, such as Guatemala, the return of the demobilized soldiers to their villages politicizes their communities, sometimes leading to more local conflict.

The post-conflict governments are usually overwhelmed by the magnitude of the problems of reconstruction. Urgent tasks related to the reconstruction are given first priority. The promotion of dialogue and active engagement of the civil society are not given adequate attention—which is necessary to strengthen trust—and this leads to a breakdown of formal agreements. Reconciliation among people and communities is extremely difficult in situations where memories of the conflict are still painful, such as is the case in Rwanda and the former Yugoslavia. Because of the political instability in post-war societies, solutions or policy responses to problems are seen more in terms of power and relationships than technical soundness. Building relationships among people and between people and institutions is central to dealing with humanitarian issues such as displacement, security presence, and health and sanitation problems.

The project findings show the importance and the role of internal actors—local citizens, the private sector, women, and community-based organizations—as the main forces to establish trust and rebuild societies.

POLITICAL RECONCILIATION: APPROACHES AND METHODS

It is generally recognized that, depending upon the unique prevailing variables in any given country, political reconciliation requires a certain number of prerequisites, without which success could not be achieved. These can include:

Recognition: Mutual acceptance of the political legitimacy of each of the other key political actors and acceptance of the possibility that other political actors have legitimate claims that may have to be, at least in part, accommodated.

Amnesty: Any peace negotiation involves a tacit willingness to grant at least a degree of amnesty to opponents for wrongdoing during the armed conflict. This may include, but is not necessarily limited to, human rights abuses during the height of the conflict. Fear of legal or more violent retribution for human rights abuses on the part of one or more of the parties has frequently provoked either a breakdown of talks or withdrawal of one or more of the parties.

Vulnerability: There is always some form of vulnerability on the part of all of the negotiating parties in the absence of a negotiated settlement. Actors must perceive their own vulnerability, but must also be willing to appreciate that of others.

Willingness: Willingness on the part of all of the different militarized parties to pursue a negotiated settlement for a durable, demilitarized solution. Most frequently, particularly in the case of protracted conflict, this has meant the occurrence of a significant event to upset the military and/or political equilibrium.

Internal and External Mediators: Conflict is the demonstration of the breakdown of communication and trust among the parties. The role of internal and external mediators is essential to create at least a minimum level of trust among the parties in order to create an environment where they begin to talk with each other.[29]

Just because people enter into negotiations with each other does not necessarily mean that they are ready to forgive or forget. States emerging from conflict—either internal or external—are faced with the dilemma of somehow punishing those who committed abuses without sabotaging a fragile peace. Between impunity and international prosecution lie numerous alternatives for achieving partial accountability within a framework of reconciliation. Along the continuum, there are perpetrator-centered mechanisms and victim-centered mechanisms.[30] The former determines the guilt and accountability of those who violated the laws. The latter can include anything from reparations to symbolic gestures by way of compensating victims for the perpetrators' transgressions.

Between the two models are truth commissions. These national or UN-led voluntary self-examinations sometimes have the power to accuse and bring individuals to trial, but often they only have the power to bring to light past abuses and to validate the victims' suffering. South Africa, Ethiopia, and Argentina are just a few of the countries that have used different models of truth commissions. Other countries have initiated low-level inquiries, and still others have been subject to international criminal tribunals (e.g., Bosnia and Rwanda). Whatever strategy for reconciliation is adopted, it must be carefully calibrated to the situation at hand—either too stringent or too lenient a policy of accountability can derail a lasting peace. Also, consideration must be given to resources and whether their best use is in adjudicating war crimes and human rights abuses or in rebuilding tattered judicial systems.[31]

When tackling political reconciliation in post-conflict situations, one essential decision that must be made is whether all groups are treated equally, or whether some (e.g., ex-combatants or returnees) are given preference over those who stayed behind and may have less pressing needs. If there is a distinction in how different groups are treated, it should be recognized that there will also be consequences of this course of action. For example, in Mozambique 95,000 ex-combatants—many of whom had no marketable skills or experience in market economies—were demobilized following years of civil war, and more than two million refugees and displaced persons were resettled. The demobilized ex-combatants had access to resources to which local communities did not, and they sometimes sought to resettle in different areas than their origins. Both factors affected the level of acceptance among local communities.

Many factors may influence the parties to the conflict to move the genuine dialogue—the change in the military balance, the creation of sudden imbalance due to external military intervention, the breakdown of military alliance among the parties, and the defection of military personnel. Demobilization and disarmament of combatants is a prerequisite for political reconciliation, as the cases of Angola, Mozambique, and Cambodia show. Yet, this is difficult to achieve because the negotiating parties want to start with a position of strength and are usually reluctant to give up arms due to the fear of the breakdown of political dialogue. In the end, it is the extent of the lack of trust among the parties emanating from years of internal conflict that determines the extent to which the parties are willing to demilitarize. Furthermore, at least an initial peace agreement should be negotiated before the former combatants can be realistically expected to demobilize.

Long internal conflicts transform societies because of the displacement of local populations, the breakdown of the family structure, the destruction of infrastructure, and the weakening of social networks. Political reconciliation and sustainable peace can be achieved through all or a combination of measures which have been used in many countries—the establishment of a Human Rights Ombudsman (as in Bosnia and Herzegovina, East Timor, and Guatemala), the oversight of police conduct and prison conditions (El Salvador), the administration of community trials (East Timor), and the creation of Truth Commissions (Argentina, Chad, Haiti, and South Africa).

Designing and adopting a new constitution is an important step in rebuilding a society. This is usually done in two stages—an interim constitution or the transitional charter and a more permanent constitution. In many African post-conflict countries (Ethiopia, Uganda, and Mozambique), new constitutions were designed to strengthen democratic governance.

SECURITY SECTOR REFORM

UNDP's 1994 *Human Development Report* addressed the concept of human security. It approached the concept broadly, as more than just physical safety and inclusive of two main aspects: safety from chronic threats such as hunger, disease, and repression; and protection from sudden and hurtful disruptions in the patterns of daily life— whether in homes, jobs, or communities.[32] Thus, both humans and nature can be at fault when human security is eroded. Today, job, income, health, environmental, and crime securities are each an emerging concern for human security all over the world. As the world becomes more globalized, what were once primarily internal concerns are now borderless phenomena. Famines, ethnic conflicts, social disintegration, terrorism, pollution, and drug trafficking are no longer isolated events, confined within national borders. Their human security consequences are felt worldwide.

When tackling the issue of security within a country emerging from conflict, it is usually the security sector institutions that need reform first and foremost. Insecurity constitutes a major obstacle to the progress of any peace process. However, strengthening security forces is complicated by the fact that in a number of countries abuses of human rights, political allegiances, and repression by security forces were triggers to the conflict in the first place (e.g., Haiti, South Africa, Guatemala, Chile, Argentina, Afghanistan, etc.). Furthermore, in countries emerging from a long history of internal conflict or civil war, internal security has, as a rule, been transferred to the purview of the armed forces. In many instances, it is the armed forces who have been directly responsible for some of the most heinous human rights abuses.

In post-conflict societies where responsibility for security is ceded from the army to the police, the police force is rarely in a position to fulfill its duties and will consequently require a degree of capacity development. In other countries, security sector capacity is entirely destroyed or otherwise absent.

After the tragic events of the 1994 genocide in Rwanda, for example, security was one of the main concerns of the Rwandese government. The former armed forces had been implicated in the genocide and had consequently fled the country or were imprisoned. As a result, the government that took power after the genocide had to establish a new security mechanism from scratch.

During internal conflicts, the distinctions between the military and the police break down because of the need to restore order using all branches of the security apparatus. This requires appropriate policies and strategies for armed forces, police, intelligence agencies, and other parts of the security forces. Many countries, including South Africa and Sierra Leone, have taken steps to reexamine the role, mission, and composition of their militaries, and have absorbed the former combatants into their armed forces. The goal in Afghanistan is to establish a multiethnic army. The experience in El Salvador, Mozambique, and Rwanda shows that the transition from internal war to peace requires police forces that are accountable, depoliticized, and composed of different groups.

REINTEGRATION PROGRAMS

The reintegration of refugee populations and ex-combatants is an important component to any post-conflict rebuilding and institutionalization of the democratic processes. The demobilization and integration of combatants have taken place in many countries that have gone though internal war—including El Salvador, Ethiopia, Guatemala, Haiti, Mozambique, Nicaragua, Sierra Leone, and Uganda. Of course, refugees and others cannot be forced to repatriate. In Cambodia, for example, with the close scrutiny of the press, the United Nations High Commissioner for Refugees (UNHCR) was required to give refugees free choice of their ultimate destinations. No mechanisms could be put in place to actively prevent secondary migration within the country.

The reintegration of refugees, internally displaced people, or demobilized soldiers and militias illustrates the importance of locally prompted action. Experience shows that people who return to their homes of their own free will rather than at the prompting of governments or international agencies are far more likely to be successfully reintegrated. Similarly, local communities, particularly in rural areas, have a remarkable capacity for receiving and reintegrating returning groups, as long as their "absorptive capacity" is strengthened with minimal assistance.[33]

The integration of some ex-combatants into new national armed forces is often an option for gainfully employing soldiers.[34] This was done in Mali, for example, where Tuareg rebel soldiers were guaranteed a certain quota within the national army as part of the negotiations to end their insurgency in the northern provinces of the country.

Area-based programs have emerged as one of the most effective options for the economic and social recovery of the war-affected populations. One of the early and successful examples of this is the Area Development and Peace-Building in Central America (PRODERE) Program. The purpose of the program was to improve the human development conditions at the local level for displaced persons, refugees, and returnees in Belize, Costa Rica, El Salvador, Guatemala, Honduras, and Nicaragua. The program consisted of six national projects and three regional subprograms. Among the activities the program supported were the resolution of legal issues including land ownership and resident permits, the creation of the civil society organizations including development committees, and employment and income-generation activities including microenterprises and agricultural development. The program also supported the creation of local development agencies, the building and rehabilitation of schools, the training of teachers, adult education, and community health care services. Though the program started with humanitarian assistance in 1990, its scope had expanded to a multisectoral human development program by 1994.

The Area Development Program in Cambodia, among others, was aimed at strengthening local government institutions, constructing health clinics, schools, roads, and irrigation schemes, and developing capacity for agricultural production. It also supported land redistribution, reforestation, and agriculture-related industries and established a local planning process to prepare village plans. Since the end of the Cold War, area-based programs—adapted to suit the local environment—have also been established in Bosnia, Croatia, Eritrea, Guatemala, Mozambique, Somalia, and Tajikistan. Most of the area-based programs have exclusively focused on rural areas.

ROLE OF NONGOVERNMENTAL ORGANIZATIONS AND COMMUNITY-BASED ORGANIZATIONS

Nongovernmental organizations (NGOs) and community-based organizations (CBOs) intervene in important areas in post-conflict countries. NGOs, and, in particular, women's NGOs, play an important role in organizing women—who are more often than not the head of households in conflict or post-conflict settings—and building their capacities to manage post-conflict rebuilding. They are also important outlets for peace and reconciliation education programs. Education is a major factor in socializing individuals, particularly in their formative years. Many conflict-prevention NGOs, both national and international, target women because it is women who inculcate values early on in the lives of their children. Women in crisis countries need to be viewed not as victims but as actors for building peace culture. Also important are NGOs that focus on community education projects for the prevention of domestic violence within the context of building a society's capacities for incorporating respect for human rights culture.

The case of Serbia and Montenegro provides an example of the role the NGOs can perform in crisis and post-crisis situations. As per a survey conducted by the United Nations in 2001, there were more than 20,000 active NGOs operating in Serbia and Montenegro.[35] They were organized around civic development, the provision of services, and environmental protection. They have been at the forefront of the democratic revolution and continue to make significant contributions to the consolidation and sustainability of democracy. Their specific strengths have been operational flexibility, the maximization of available technical and financial resources, and a high degree of solidarity—which has in the past enabled them to promote accountability and transparency of the government and to undertake basic tasks related to the provision of services and civic responsibilities. Their weaknesses have been a poorly defined mission, low accountability to stakeholders, inadequate monitoring and evaluation, and weak internal management.

ROLE OF EXTERNAL PARTNERS

International partners can play an important role in helping countries avoid, manage, or resolve conflicts. Some, such as those within the UN system, focus assistance on almost every aspect of the conflict cycle, depending upon the organization's mandate. One of the most critical aspects of the role of the United Nations is that it provides legitimacy for global actions in support of the crisis situation in a country. Others, such as the Bretton Woods institutions, are constrained by their mandates from engaging in peacemaking, peacekeeping, disarmament, or humanitarian relief. Still others, such as international NGOs, lend specific relief or assistance before, during, or after conflicts. What more and more international partners are realizing, however, is that conflicts rarely have well-defined beginnings, middles, or ends. Rather, they are protracted and recycled. Indeed, emergency, relief and development coexist in times of conflict and interact in many ways. Therefore, the lines between relief, and development in reality do not exist. Development assistance must take place in harmony with relief assistance and vice versa, if international partners hope to have a lasting positive impact on conflict.

In 1992, Secretary-General Boutros Boutros-Ghali published an *Agenda for Peace*, calling for a greater UN role in peace and security issues, particularly intrastate peace and security issues. The report advocated the use of preventive diplomacy and peacemaking; peacekeeping; peace building; disarmament; sanctions; and peace enforcement to control and resolve conflicts between and within states.[36] The *Agenda* also asserted that there is "an obvious connection between democratic practices— such as the rule of law and transparency in decision-making—and the achievement of true peace and security in any new and stable political order."[37] Therefore, the report concludes, the United Nations is obligated to support the transformation of "deficient national structures and capabilities" and to strengthen new democratic institutions as a means to prevent, manage, and resolve conflicts over the long term.[38]

The *Agenda for Peace* sparked a great deal of debate over the UN's role in intrastate conflicts, given the tension between upholding international human rights standards and respecting the sovereignty of member states. Of course, there are myriad other options open to the United Nations in terms of conflict prevention, management, and resolution. Most fundamentally, the support of good governance is a key mechanism through which the United Nations can help member states avoid conflict in the long term. In the shorter term, the use of peacekeeping, economic sanctions, arms embargoes, judicial enforcement measures, and even military force have all been used by the United Nations—with varying degrees of effectiveness—to resolve, manage, or prevent intrastate and interstate conflicts.

Violent conflict is something that will likely never be vanquished entirely. Its occurrence can be contained, however, by furnishing states with the tools to share power and resolve disputes before they reach the level of violence. By addressing the root—structural causes of conflict with the systems and institutions of good governance—states can do just this and reduce their risk for complex humanitarian emergencies, intrastate conflict, or interstate war. In this way they can end the impractical and unrealistic settlement of differences through the use of force.

Sustainable and just peace in conflict-prone countries requires a mix of appropriate responses—including a strong and transparent state, professional and civilian-led security forces, respect for the rule of law, an open civil society, and a culture of tolerance and respect for individual rights. These responses reflect "the essence of democratic peace building."[39] The situation in conflict-prone countries presents security dilemmas to policymakers. For example, democracies are expected to provide institutional mechanisms for different groups to express their viewpoints and concerns. Yet, democracies have not been able to eliminate violent conflicts such as recent conflict in Gujarat, India, and the conflicts in Northern Ireland and Sri Lanka.[40] Many groups in the established Western democracies—the United States for example—have shown serious concerns about the violation of human rights for security reasons. As a recent UNDP report argues, "the respect for human rights lies at the heart of what it is to be a democracy and at the heart of democratic civil control of the security sector."[41]

Societies in conflict situations need the support of the international community to enable them to start rebuilding their economies and institutions. In this process, however, such intervention can also do harm. For example, in Somalia and Afghanistan, relief and rehabilitation resources were diverted by the warlords for their armed militias. In Rwanda, massive support was provided to the refugees in the camps of Goma, which were under the mafia-type control of persons who had committed genocide in Rwanda.

CONCLUSION AND LESSONS LEARNED

Violent conflicts negatively affect human development. Democratic governance provides a useful set of tools for conflict prevention, management, and resolution—including rebuilding fractured communities, political reconciliation, security sector reform, reintegration programs, and the enhanced role of the civil society during the conflict and post-conflict situations. For long-term peace and stability, rebuilding fractured communities is essential.

The world community has learned many lessons concerning the rebuilding of institutions of governance and repairing the ruins of the failed states.[42] Some of these are as follows:

- There are limits to what the United Nations or any one country can do. What is needed is a homegrown solution facilitated by external partners. The need is to make sure that international development partners continue to be engaged in the second and third phases of the reconstruction (Somalia, Afghanistan).

- Quick introduction of an outside force is essential to create necessary conditions for the United Nations and other external partners to provide humanitarian assistance, maintain human security, and support the process of nation-building (East Timor, Sierra Leone).

• External partners may provide a forum for discussion among the parties but should always take a backseat, enabling the local parties to talk to each other on their own (South Africa).

• It is essential to involve all parties to the conflict. Negotiations involving one segment or excluding major groups do not lead to positive results. Even though short-term agreements can be reached, these are not sustainable (Afghanistan, Palestine, Iraq).

• National leaders with skills and wisdom make a real difference in the final outcome (South Africa).

• Fracture of communities as a result of long internal conflict, inequalities, and poor governance makes it extremely difficult to build durable peace. There is, therefore, a strong case for "democratic peace building," i.e., to resolve conflicts before they lead to internal war (Yugoslavia, Rwanda, Congo).

• There is a strong need for a balance between security imperatives and open and transparent governance processes including support for vulnerable groups and the strengthening of grassroots institutions for conflict resolution (Afghanistan, Mozambique, Kosovo, Sierra Leone).

ENDNOTES

1. UNDP, *Governance Foundations for Post Crisis Situations* (New York: UNDP, 2000), 19–20.

2. Ibid.

3. Among others, see Michael Brown, ed. *The International Dimensions of Internal Conflict* (Cambridge: Harvard University Press, 1996); and UNDP, *Governance and Conflict* (New York: Management Development and Governance Division, 2000).

4. Ibid.

5. The impact of intergroup inequalities on humanitarian emergencies is examined in Jeni Klugman, "Social and Economic Policies to Prevent Complex Humanitarian Emergencies: Lessons from Experience" Policy Brief #2, United Nations University/World Institute for Development Economics Research, 1999; and UNDP, *Governance Foundations*.

6. Ibid.

7. Freedom House, *Freedom in the World 2000* (New York: Freedom House, 2000).

8. On the linkage between peace and development, see Michèle Griffin, "Development, Peace and Security" working paper, Emergency Response Division (ERD), UNDP, 1999, and "Working for Solutions to Crises: the Development Response" (Emergency Response Division, UNDP, 1999).

9. Ibid.

10. Omar Bakhet, "Crisis and Development" in UNDP, *Choices* (December 2000).

11. Michael Cranna, ed. *The True Cost of Conflict* (New York: The New York Press, 1994).

12. Scott Carlson, Wendy Betts and Greg Gisvold, "The Post-Conflict Transitional Administration of Kosovo and the Lessons-Learned in Efforts to Establish a Judiciary and Rule of Law" (paper presented, World Bank Conference on Empowerment, Security and Opportunity Through Law and Justice," St. Petersburg, July 8–12, 2001), 14.

13. Chris Mburu, "Challenges Facing Legal and Judicial Reform in Post-Conflict Environment: Case Study from Rwanda and Sierra Leone" (paper presented, World Bank Conference on Empowerment, Security and Opportunity Through Law and Justice," St. Petersburg, July 8–12, 2001).

14. UNDP, *Governance Foundations for Post-Crisis Situations*, 38.

15. Mburu, "Challenges Facing Legal and Judicial Reform," 14.

16. UNDP, *Governance Foundations.*

17. Ibid.

18. Ibid.

19. "Working with the Media in Conflicts and other Emergencies" (Department for International Development, Issues Paper, London, August 2000).

20. UNDP, *Governance and Conflict.*

21. Griffin, "Development, Peace and Security."

22. John Stremlau, *Sharpening International Sanctions: Toward a Stronger Role for the United Nations* (New York: Carnegie Commission on Preventing Deadly Conflict, 1996).

23. UNDP, *Deepening Democracy in a Fragmented World* (New York: Oxford University Press, 2002), 95.

24. UN Research Institute for Social Development, "Rebuilding After War: A Summary of the War-torn Societies Project" (Geneva: UNRISD, 1998), 12.

25. Among others, see International Crisis Group, "Kosovo's Ethnic Dilemma: The Need for a Civic Contract" (Balkans Report number 143, May 2003), 2–20; Chris Hedges, "Kosovo's Next Masters," *Foreign Affairs* (May–June 1999).

26. War-Torn Societies Project Report (Geneva: UNRISD, 1998).

27. War-torn Societies Project (WSP) Case Studies on Eritrea, Guatemala, Mozambique, and Somalia. United Nations Research Institute for Social Development (UNRISD), Geneva 1998; and UNRISD, Rebuilding After War: A Summary of Report of the War-torn Societies Project, 1998.

28. Ibid.

29. UNDP, *Governance Foundations.*

30. UNDP, *Governance and Conflict Prevention: Proceedings of Expert Group Meeting* (ERD/UNDP, March 7–8, 2000).

31. Ibid.

32. UNDP, *Human Development Report,* 1994.

33. Fractured Communities Programme, "Summary Report 2001" (New York: UNDP, 2001).

34. US Agency for International Development, "After the War is Over What Comes Next: Promoting Democracy, Human Rights and Reintegration in Post-conflict Societies" (Washington, DC: USAID Conference Report, 1997).

35. UNDP, Common Country Assessment for Serbia and Montenegro (November 2003).

36. United Nations, *Agenda for Peace* (New York: United Nations, 1992).

37. Ibid.

38. Ibid.

39. UNDP, *Deepening Democracy,* 99.

40. Ibid.

41. Ibid., 100.

42. "How to Put a Nation Back Together Again," *New York Times,* November 25, 2001.

CHAPTER 10

SUSTAINING DEMOCRACY

CONTEXTUAL FACTORS

The previous chapters have shown that contextual factors affect the performance of democratic institutions—including electoral management bodies, parliaments, human rights institutions, anti-corruption commissions, and the judiciary. The chapters have also shown that similar institutional designs and reforms produce different outcomes from each of the democratic institutions—combating corruption from anti-corruption commissions, and overseeing the executive by parliaments, for example—depending upon such contextual factors as culture, ethnic heterogeneity, freedom of the press, the extent of poverty, and patterns of civil-military relations.

The next sections examine the role of culture, religion, ethnicity, and values in deepening and consolidating democracy with a focus on the analysis of the impact of Islam on democracy in countries with a Muslim majority. This is followed by a discussion of the impact of civil-military relations, media and freedom of the press, and poverty on democratic governance practice. The last section analyzes the role of external partners—including bilateral and multilateral organizations—in promoting democracy and good governance.

CULTURE AND VALUES

The relationship between culture and values and democratic governance is complex because culture covers many other relevant factors such as historical heritage and education. One point of view is elaborated by Lipset, who argues that historically there have been cultural prerequisites for democracy—Protestant European nations democratized earlier and more successfully than both European and overseas Catholic states and Islamic states, which have been more "demophobic."[1] Lewis, in his analysis of historical perspectives of Islam and liberal democracy and Huntington in his examination of traditional Confucianism

213

reach similar conclusions.[2] Huntington, for example, argues that unlike the separation of church and state in the West, the other great religious "civilizations" of the world lack a set of cultural characteristics that can sustain and promote Western-style democracy.[3]

The other school of thought is that, first, links between the emergence of democracy and culture are weak;[4] second, the colonial experience did not seem to be of critical significance;[5] and, third, weak democratic institutions in Islamic countries depend chiefly on other traits in countries where Islam predominates. The advocates of this school of thought argue that a series of democratic revolutions in the 1980s and 1990s—in Eastern and Central Europe, with vastly different religious and cultural backgrounds, and Latin America, with strong Catholic traditions, and Africa, with strong indigenous cultural traditions—are examples that invalidate the idea that a significant relationship exists between democracy and culture.

The practice of democracy in the world today shows that the role of culture and religion might not be as strong as some would suggest. For example, old authoritarian Catholic states such as most of Latin America have relatively free and competitive elections; South Korea is a vital democracy; Indonesia—the largest Muslim country in the world—has a competitive political process. It has been argued that the recent trends towards democratization may be due to the diffusion of information, the demonstration effects of economically advanced democracies and pressures from international institutions and the global community for the promotion of values of democracy and good governance.[6] Furthermore, one of the factors has been the change that has taken place within the church over the past three decades. Huntington has examined the influence of the change within the Catholic Church among countries including the Philippines, Brazil, Chile, El Salvador, and Korea. "All in all," he concludes, "if it were not for the changes within the Catholic Church and the resulting actions of the Church against authoritarianism, fewer third wave transitions to democracy would have occurred and many that did occur would have occurred later."[7]

Culture matters, though, in the process of democratization. Because of differences in their cultures, countries find their own mechanisms to achieve the basic principles and values of democracy and good governance—transparency, accountability, tolerance, individual freedom, devolution, and the rule of law. Culture and religions are part and parcel of the society where they are practiced— they are transformed as the society is transformed. Moreover, as Amartya Sen argues, every culture has a "heterogeneity of values," and there are liberal traditions and rich varieties of thought within Confucianism, Buddhism, and Islam that run counter to the dominant view of these cultures as illiberal and authoritarian.[8] About three-quarters of the countries that experienced a transition to democracy between 1974 and 1989 were Catholic countries.[9] The Catholic Church became a major force for democracy and social change, especially in the 1960s, opposing authoritarian regimes. The institutional and "principle" shifts in the Catholic Church over the past century have enshrined individualism, personal liberty, and popular participation—which in turn have influenced a departure from the historical role of the church and a new commitment to democracy.[10]

The evolution of democracy owes its origin to universal human yearning for freedom and life with dignity. That is the reason for democratization in diverse countries from Poland to Yemen, from Mauritius to Guatemala, and from Albania to Nigeria. Democratic governance in each of these countries has not taken the same route. Local cultures and traditions have had an influence on the way democratic values and systems are built and supported.

The debate on "Asian values" shows the complexity of the relationship between democracy and culture. Two points of view are usually expressed concerning this issue. One is that Asian values are characterized by the notion of community and collective rights, family orientation, respect of authority, and decision-making through consensus. Therefore, the people avoid extreme forms of individualism in their behavior. This, it is argued, negatively affects the process of democratization. The second is that principles of democracy and good governance are based on universal values that people in all cultures cherish and that the focus on "Asian values" is used by some authoritarian regimes to deny freedom of expression and other human rights to the people in order to perpetuate their power.

The debate about "Asian values" and its impact on democracy shows that societal values and the practice of democratic governance have an interdependent relationship in the process of the evolution of democracy—each influencing the other, sometimes in complementary ways and other times constraining the process. It is obvious that for a meaningful transformation to take place in Asia, it has to be rooted in the current value systems of the people—which is modified in the process of the transformation. Historically, Asian leaders have included those who introduced authoritarian and oppressive governance systems as well as those who introduced inclusive systems. Political structures introduced during the colonial period coexist with the traditional structures. Instead of promoting complementarities between the two, politicians sometimes exploit the symbols from religion or culture, especially where the modern political structures have not been able to address the economic, social, and political problems of Asian societies.

ISLAM AND DEMOCRACY

The terrorist attacks of September 11, 2001, in the United States have led to increased discussion worldwide about the impact of Islam on democracy in the developing countries with a Muslim majority. It is true that in the Arab world there is a serious "democratic deficit" with many countries ruled by kings (emirs) or strong men (sultans) who run for the office practically unopposed. A survey by Freedom House—Freedom in the World 2001–2002—shows that only 11 of the 47 countries (23 percent) with an Islamic majority have democratically elected governments, and that since the early 1970s the Islamic countries—especially its Arab core—have not seen significant improvements in political openness and transparency.[11] The survey also points out, however, that the majority of the world's Muslims live in electoral democracies because of the large size of such Muslim countries as Indonesia, Bangladesh, Nigeria, and Turkey. India, the largest democracy in the World, has a large Muslim population. One point of view expressed is that it might be difficult to reconcile the Islamic code affecting many aspects of life and enforced in a legal system with the key requirement of democracy, i.e., willingness to share power. In the case of the Arab region, it is also argued that the ruling families would be unwilling to give up their predominant powers and that it would be difficult to build consensus and a political culture of tolerance among the many tribes who historically have led fiercely independent and autonomous lives. While the rulers are willing to establish institutions and mechanisms to "consult" with different groups in the society—as in the case of Saudi Arabia and Kuwait—they would not agree to one person one vote. Furthermore, efforts at democratization are thwarted by some very tough conditions—extreme fundamentalism, international double standards to protect the economic and strategic interests of the developed countries, and extreme poverty in most of the Muslim world.

The other point of view is that with globalization and increased access to information, many of the countries in the Arab region would be forced to open up their political systems, pointing to the recent changes in Bahrain—amnesty for exiles, freedom for political prisoners, municipal elections held in 2002, parliamentarian elections in 2003, and the elimination of emergency laws. In Kuwait, the parliament was first established in 1961. It has the power to make laws and challenge the executive branch of the government. Since its first establishment, the parliament has been abolished three times to "silence liberal dissent," only to be reinstated under Western pressure.[12]

An examination of four of the world's largest Muslim countries—Indonesia, Pakistan, Bangladesh, and Turkey—shows that Islam is not a constraint on the deepening of democracy in these countries. Indonesia has over the past half century been a relatively tolerant Islamic society—notwithstanding recent intermittent riots among Christians and Muslims that are driven by a clash of economic interests and general political instability in the country. The ousted president of the country, Abdudrrahman Wahid, who was the head of the largest religious organization in the Muslim world before assuming the presidency, was particularly committed to the promotion of human rights and religious tolerance. The breakdown of democratic institutions is largely due to the influence of the military and its response to the communist threat in the 1960s.

In Pakistan, Islamic parties have never won more than a nominal number of seats—with only 2 seats in the National Assembly in 1997 elections and usually less than 15 percent of votes in most recent elections—even though they ended up with a majority in two of the smaller provinces of the country in the most recent provincial elections. Though Islamic parties are well organized at the grassroots level, they are not able to convince the voters about their political manifesto. The gains of these parties in the recent election have partly been due to their ability to mobilize segments of the population opposed to the Western policies in the Muslim world including the American military interventions in Afghanistan and Iraq.

In Bangladesh, too, the breakdown of democratic institutions in the past was due largely to the role of the military, the legacy of the war of independence, extreme forms of poverty, and the inability of politicians to provide leadership in developing democratic political culture. Islamic parties have not been able to mount a significant threat to the two predominant political parties, National Awami League and the Bangladesh Nationalist Party.

The 1992 Constitution of Turkey states that the Turkish Republic is secular. When the Welfare Party, led by Necmettin Erbakan, took office in 1996, the country had its first prime minister representing an Islamic party. In view of the secular nature of the constitution and pressure from the military, the prime minister resigned and his party was outlawed by the Constitutional Court. In the most recent national elections, a moderate Islamic party fully committed to the rule of law and democratic process came to power, reflecting a significant advance in democratic political culture in the country.

In many Muslim countries including Pakistan, Turkey, and Indonesia, "the greatest challenge to democracy is posed not by Islam but by the military and intelligence organizations unaccountable to democratic authority."[13] This, however, does not mean that Islamic parties are not influential in the political culture of Muslim societies. In Pakistan, the Government of Nawaz Sharif initiated the introduction of the Islamic law to respond to pressures from Islamists. In Egypt, the Muslim Brotherhood contested elections in 1984 and 1987 under the banner of other parties. In Algeria, the Islamic party—which was later banned—won a majority of seats in the parliamentary elections in 1991. These elections took place after decades of military-dominated, single-party socialism. In the absence of established opposition parties, Islamists had the popularity and organization to fill the vacuum. The secular ruling elite feared the constitutional reform that could have led to an Islamic state. The civil war started in the country after the military outlawed the Islamic Salvation Front and arrested many of its members. In 2004, however, the country elected a president to a second term in an election which was widely recognized as free and fair.

In practice, there are different stages of democratization in the countries with a Muslim majority. They include full-fledged democracies (Turkey, Indonesia, Bangladesh, Senegal), emerging democracies (Lebanon, Albania), limited democracies (Egypt, Pakistan, Yemen), authoritarian governments (Libya, Syria), and monarchies (Bahrain, Brunei, Kuwait, Qatar, Saudi Arabia).

Six lessons can be drawn about the relationship between Islam and democratic politics.[14] First, "political Islam" in many Muslim countries is a reflection of the protest against injustice, lack of economic opportunities, threats to collective identity, and repression. In the absence of open political process in the country, some groups are inclined to extremist fundamentalism and use Islam to achieve their political objectives.

Second, "the accommodative politics of inclusion" can facilitate reducing extreme expressions and radical actions by the Islamic militants. For example, if the Islamic party in Algeria—which won the majority—had been allowed to take over power, the civil war and violence that followed the elections could perhaps have been avoided. India's large Muslim minority—with the second largest Muslim population in the world—has not attempted to disrupt the institutions of democracy; indeed, the existence of such institutions provide them with the mechanisms to express their grievances and aspirations.

Third, voters in Muslim societies, like those in other countries, reward and reelect those parties—Islamic or secular—that deliver results in terms of improving the living conditions of the poor. The unpopularity of President Wahid in Indonesia, the head of the largest Islamic organization in the country, and the popularity of the Islamic Rafat party in Turkey, due to its effectiveness in managing large municipalities including Istanbul and Izmir, are examples. At the same time, in most other Islamic countries, the Muslim parties have failed to make significant electoral gains because of their inability to deliver basic services to the vast majority of the poor.

Fourth, because of the increasing integration of the international system, radical Islamic groups see many cases of Western double standards—the perceived reaction of the West to the massacre of Muslims in marketplaces in Bosnia and refugees camps in Lebanon, pro-Israel policies of most Western countries, and the West's support in the past for such authoritarian regimes as Iran's shah, Saudi Arabia's absolute monarchy, and Pakistan under Zia-ul-Haq. With the legacy of the West's colonialism, extremist groups turn their anger against both the authoritarian regimes and the Western countries.

Fifth, opposition to the government policy is often Islamic. Where secular opposition to the government is weak, Islamic parties increase their political and social influence. The rise of the Islamic Rafat Party in Turkey could be attributed to the community-level work undertaken by the party members in municipalities, towns, and rural communities in the country.

Finally, many Islamic societies are in the process of redefining the relationship between God and man and the role of religion in public affairs as the West experienced in the sixteenth and seventeenth centuries. This task can be facilitated if external actors support the democratic forces and recognize national sovereignty. More importantly, the national leadership needs to appreciate the inevitability of democracy due to pressures from the people for greater accountability and transparency and the necessity of good governance to benefit from the opportunities provided by globalization.

Since the beginning of the war in Iraq that led to the overthrow of the Saddam regime by external intervention, discussion has focused on concrete steps to promote democracy in the Arab and the Muslim world. On one extreme, it is argued that democracy is a value in itself and the world has an obligation to ensure that democracy and human rights are protected in all regions—thereby justifying external interventions. On the other hand, a view is expressed that the sovereignty of the country should be protected and that outside actors have no right to intervene in the internal political processes of a nation-state. Recent studies on democratization in the Arab world sponsored by the United Nations University show that some of the most critical points for consideration in the process of promoting democracy are as follows.[15]

1. Immediate and full-fledged Western-style liberal democracy is not possible in the Arab region. It might not even be desirable. Gradual steps toward more citizen participation in the political and economic development of the country would facilitate an orderly process of transition from authoritarian to representative regimes.

2. Democratic institutions of a country should be in harmony with religious norms and teachings respected in the society. This does not mean that the basic principles of democracy—transparency, participation, accountability, etc.—should not be followed. What this implies is that each country should follow its own path and speed in political transformations. Indeed, secularization and religiosity can exist in harmony when political leaders recognize both and create a balance between the two.

3. Democratization is a process. Each Arab country's journey to achieve the fundamental principles of democracy should be unique to its historical, cultural, economic, and political environment. The process and speed of democratization might be different in Saudi Arabia than in Egypt, for example.

4. The introduction of democratic norms and standards—even within the environment of each country—would provide channels through which grievances of various segments of society can be communicated to those who have power to make decisions at the national level. This would limit the reach of the extremist groups who thrive under the conditions of fear and oppression by the government. This is one of the best long-term strategies for responding to the threat of terrorism.

5. If democratic initiatives are to take hold in the Arab world, some key challenges should be met through collaborative efforts of the world community—economic development that provides jobs and opportunities to the marginalized groups; the restructuring of extremist educational programs that create hatred and cynicism; the negative role of external powers to achieve their short-term economic objectives; Israeli-Palestinian conflict; people-to-people exchanges between the North and the South to promote values of tolerance, harmony, and global interdependence. In order to be sustainable, the values and ideals of democracy should be embraced by broad sectors of the population. One indicator of this is an effectively functioning civil society.

ETHNICITY

Ethnic fragmentation and conflicts strongly influence the process of democratization. This is particularly the case where ethnic identities coincide with geographic identities. In many countries of Africa, Asia, and Central and Eastern Europe, ethnic conflicts impede the institutionalization of the democratic processes. On the one hand, democracy promotes national unity by providing institutional mechanisms by which different ethnic groups can express their views and influence the process of making political decisions in the country. On the other, ethnic tensions and mistrust impede the evolution of democratic culture and the deepening of democracy. The national political leadership and the level of economic development are critical factors in creating ethnic harmony. Malaysia is an example of how continuity in political leadership and rapid growth of an economy over the past three decades have led to a situation where all ethnic groups have a strong "stake" in the system. Rapid economic growth has enabled the federal government to design and implement redistributive programs—land resettlements and increase in ownership of assets by the indigenous people, for instance—to assist the economically less developed Malays and less developed regions. At the same time, the private sector–led growth has provided many opportunities from which Chinese and Indian Malaysians may benefit. This in turn has enabled the multiethnic National Coalition of three ethnic parties to continue to be the ruling party over the past three decades.

In many countries in Africa, the postcolonial states have frequent ethnic conflicts and domination of one group at the expense of others. In the case of Kenya, for example, differentiated treatment by the British increased tensions between Luo and the Kikuyu—the largest groups—and smaller ones such as Kalenjin. Kenyatta, the first President and a Kikuyu, isolated Luo in collaboration with smaller ethnic groups. The extensive use of political patronage and a "winner take all" orientation created further tensions and suspicions among the Luo. Tanzania, on the other hand, presents a good example of forging national unity and consensus. Julius Nyerere encouraged the use of one language, Kiswahili, deemphasizing dialects and ethnicity and laying the foundation of a legitimate state. The evolution of multiparty politics further increased political legitimacy.

The case of Southeast Asian countries too shows that ethnic considerations envelop the state institutions and the society, strongly influencing the internal dynamics of political authority and power. When delicate ethnic divisions exist as they do in Malaysia, for example, ethnic considerations are formalized as the basis of allocation for positions in the government and for ownership of economic assets, underscoring the political preeminence of Malays and affirmative policies such as the New Economic Policy that give priority to Malays in government jobs and in business. The desire on the part of the federal government to construct an effective state by centralizing powers and resources has in many cases been challenged by regional forces seeking greater autonomy or even secession—such as the demand for autonomy by southern Thai Malay Muslims, and the demand for an independent Muslim state in the southern part of the Philippines. Where the military was the major instrument for centralization, there has been violent backlash and revolt from the periphery. In Indonesia, for example, the Free Aceh Movement and the Free Papua Organization in the provinces of Aceh and Irian Jaya, respectively, spearheaded secessionist revolts against the central government. As in other regions of the world, the multiethnic nature of states in Southeast Asia has posed serious impediments to the process of democratization due to centrifugal forces that make the societal consensus more difficult.

It is beyond doubt that ethnic homogeneity is conducive to the sustainability of democracy. Ethnic diversities and conflicts have often impeded the process of democratization in Asia, Africa, and Eastern and Central Europe. While majority rule gives voice to the poor, elections with a free market sometimes lead to a predominant role of entrepreneurial minorities such as ethnic Chinese in Southeast Asia. In the Philippines, for example, ethnic Chinese are 1 percent of the population but control about 60 percent of the private economy including major airlines, hotels, banks, and major conglomerates. Ethnic tensions (and sometimes hatred) between the vast majority of the poor and the "market-dominant minority" constrain the emergence of a tolerant political culture—which is essential for political institutions to work effectively.[16]

CIVIL-MILITARY RELATIONS AND TRANSITION TO DEMOCRACY

One of the characteristics of a genuine democracy is the civilian command of the military through the executive branch of the government. The military should be subjected to the command of the elected civilian leaders, with the head of the government designated "the commander in chief." Where military gets involved in influencing or making political decisions, the role of political institutions in representing voters' preferences is negatively affected. However, while broad defense and national security goals should be determined by elected officials and top civil servants, the execution of the defense policies is the responsibility of professionally trained military—a cadre of citizens trained in the use of arms for the national defense. An ideal division of responsibilities in civil-military relations ensures that policymaking on national security by political leaders and the implementation of that policy by a professional military are separated.

One of the complicating factors in civil-military relations, however, concerns the separation of functions related to external defense and security from internal security including the maintenance of law and order in the country. Internal security should be the responsibility of a national police force, with different reporting lines than those of the military. Some of the conditions which should be met to institutionalize civilian supremacy are the exercise of the civilian authority continuously over a number of years, the specification of the civilian authority in the constitution or laws, the behavior of the military over a number of years that reflects the acceptance of the above, and one or more examples where the civilian leadership made a decision opposed by the military.[17]

The idealized model of professional military institutions in Europe focused on merit and capability-based recruitment and promotion, the career orientation of soldiers, and military training to enhance technical capability. In most of the developing countries, attempts were made, with varying degrees of success, to follow this model. In reality, with the exception of a few countries such as India and Malaysia, this model could not be sustained after independence. The result was a series of military takeovers—Egypt in 1952, Sudan in 1958, Pakistan in 1958 and Togo in 1963. By the 1980s, many of the states in Latin America and Africa had either military or military-led civilian governments. These included some of the pivotal states—Indonesia, Bangladesh, Turkey, and Syria.

Experience suggests that the military took power in many countries for a variety of reasons—inept and corrupt civilian leadership, political instability emanating from interethnic tensions, the breakdown of civilian governments due to their inability to meet the rising expectations from citizens after independence, and the political ambitions of senior officials. The newly independent countries faced many difficulties in establishing ideal civil-military relations: (1) creating military organizations with internal rules to match those of the nonpolitical ideal, (2) building and strengthening relationships between the professional military and the civilian political command, and (3) identifying separate roles and responsibilities of the police and the military.[18] In some cases, dysfunctional civil-military relations and weak internal structures of the military led to the collapse of the state such as in Somalia (after 1991), Sierra Leone (after 1992), and Afghanistan (after 1989).

Patterns of Civil-Military Relations

In developing countries where professionalism and institutional integrity of the military remain intact, civil-military relations can take many forms. Michael Chege, in his survey of civil-military relations under the "Third Wave," identifies three broad patterns—the military as a professional and neutral actor, the military as a supporter of democratic forces, and the military as an obstacle to democratic change.[19] The first is where the military acts as a professional neutral actor—for example the Russian military after 1993, the army in South Korea after 1988, Argentina since 1983, Uruguay since 1984, and Brazil since 1984. Since the demise of the former Soviet Union, the military in Poland, Hungary, and the Czech Republic have not intervened in the interparty conflicts. In Africa too there are some good examples of military neutrality—Senegal, in 2000, when political power was taken over from the dominant Socialist Party by the opposition; Ghana, when multiparty politics was introduced and political power shifted from the ruling party in 2000; and Benin, when opposition parties took power in 1990 and 1995. The South African army remained neutral when the historic change took place from apartheid to majority rule in 1994.

The second pattern of civil-military relations is where the military intervenes in support of democratic forces. There is a paradox in the intervention of the military to support democratic forces. On the one hand, armed forces have interceded to protect the constitution and the democratic forces in the country. On the other, this type of intervention can lead to indirect influence—and in some cases institutionalization—of the role of the military in the political process of the country. In the Philippines, the army supported the democratic movement against the Marcos' authoritarian regime. In 2001, the army again supported a popular uprising against President Joseph Estrada due to corruption charges against him. The Russian army supported Boris Yeltsin in his political struggle against the hardliners. In Ecuador the military indirectly supported a popular uprising in 2000 against the government of President Jamil Mahuad.

In Africa too the military has supported democratic forces in many countries—for example, the military's disarming in 1993 of the Paramilitary Young Pioneers in Malawi, who were linked to the Congress Party of the Hastings Kamuzu Banda; and the organization of the Nigerian elections in 1999 by General Abubakar which led to the country's most recent restoration of democratic institutions. Based on the fundamental principles of democratic governance, the defense and interpretation of the constitution and violation by the executive of the popular mandate are the responsibility of the judiciary. The danger, of course, is that in most cases, the military ends up indirectly influencing the political processes in the country or directly taking over the governance of the country in partnership with civilian leaders. In both cases, the impact of the military on the political institutions is increased—which makes it difficult to deepen and institutionalize democratic culture. Therefore, while there are situations where the military can play a constructive role in democratization by direct intervention, this is usually a mixed blessing.

The third pattern in developing countries is the role of the military as an obstacle to democratic change. There are too many cases in Asia and Africa where the armed forces have suppressed the democratic movements and overthrown popularly elected governments—which the international community is usually not able to reverse. In Myanmar, the military refused to transfer powers to the Burmese National League that won the multiparty elections of 1990 and put the leader of the party, Aung San Suu Kyi, under house arrest. Despite condemnation by the global community, the situation has not been reversed, though in 2001 the military initiated negotiations with the opposition party. In Africa there have been too many cases of reversing the transition to democracy by the armed forces—the 1993 overthrow by the predominantly Tutsi army of the elected government of Melchior Ndandaye whose electoral base was Hutu; the 1997 military takeover by the Sierra Leonian military from an elected government leading to chaos and bloodshed; the 1999 military takeover of the elected government in the Côte d'Ivoire; and the abrogation of the 1993 elections in Nigeria by General Sani Abacha who imprisoned Mashood A. Abiola, the winner of elections. Sometimes the opposition encourages the military to stage a takeover when the political dialogue between the ruling party and opposition parties breaks down.

The civil-military relations in Africa are a symptom of the lack of stable political institutions that can effectively control the military. Civil wars, ethnic violence, the movement of refugees, extreme forms of disparities between the rich and the poor, and severe economic problems have considerably reduced the ability of the civilian regimes to govern effectively, which creates conditions under which military intervention usually takes place.

Three critical factors influence civil-military relations and the process of democratization—"the type of authoritarian regime, the power of the military establishment, and the nature of the transition process."[20] In most of the regimes characterized by one-party dictatorships, the military was under the tight control of the party. In communist regimes, for example, most officers belonged to the party. After the transition in Eastern Europe, one of the challenges was to replace a military subordinated to one party with one subordinated to a multiparty democratic regime. Military coups also took place where an existing military regime had been overthrown, where the military had been defeated, or where there was factionalism within the military, and—to a lesser extent—where a democratic regime was in power. In Nigeria and Sudan, the military regimes were reestablished in the late 1980s. The coup attempts in Argentina in 1987 and Guatemala in 1988 were partly aimed at changing the top level of the military leadership. The democratic regimes that followed military regimes—in Chile, Brazil, Nicaragua and Turkey, for example—faced a series of problems in their relationships with the armed forces. These included (1) the insistence of the military on assuming constitutional responsibilities for law and order and national security, (2) previous actions of the military regimes that were irreversible, (3) the creation of governmental organizations dominated by the military, (4) the assumption of senior positions in the new democratic governments by the military, (5) and attempts to ensure military autonomy in personnel and finance issues.[21]

South America presents a good example of the impact of the nature of transition on civil-military relations. The evolution of civil-military relations can be divided into three phases—transition under military influence, diverse post-transition outcomes, and civil-military relations after the transition. From the late 1970s through most of the 1980s, "transitions often took under constitutional frameworks planned by military authoritarian rulers or under ad hoc rules prepared to oversee change."[22] In Peru, the armed forces supervised the 1978 elections of a constituent assembly and retained executive control for the next two years. In Argentina too the military stayed in power for over a year after its failed occupation of the Malvinas Islands in 1982 and used that period to pass a law ensuring that the successive governments were unable to try military personnel for the abduction and killing of civilians. In Chile, the Congress included those appointed by the outgoing president and the military. During the second phase, significant influence of the military over the transitions "has given way to greater diversity," even though the situation varies from one country to another.[23] One of the challenges of the regimes during this phase was to change the institutional patterns aimed at reducing or eliminating military influences that were contrary to the norms of civil-military relations in democratic governance. During the third phase, to varying degrees, the civilian authority has been consolidated.[24]

A disproportionate number of African countries have suffered from the reversal of the democratic process as well as chaos following the imposition of the military takeover. Based on his review of African experience, Chege has identified three reasons for the military takeover—state collapse, the inability of civilian institutions to govern, and military self-interest.[25]

Thirteen out of forty-six countries in Africa have experienced interventions by the armed forces. The examples of state collapse after the disintegration of armed forces are Somalia, Liberia and Sierra Leone. These cases showed not only the impact of military intervention but also the breakdown of professionalism in the military. The inability of the civilian leadership to govern due to various forms of factionalism is usually the cause of the military interventions in politics as shown by the cases of the Côte d'Ivoire in 1999, Niger in 1995, Gambia in 1994, and Guinea-Bissau in 1999. The dilemma in such situations is that while the long-term impact of the military interventions in the democratization process is not known, a majority of the people supported such interventions in order to ensure stability. The third reason in Africa for the military takeover is "self-interest" where the military elite wants access to state means of patronage and to assure its own economic interests. They make an alliance of convenience among vested groups in the society who also want to use their influence with the military to misuse—in some cases loot—the national treasury. The 1993 military takeover in Nigeria is an example, when General Ibrahim Babaginda did not want the restoration of democratic institutions in the country leading to the takeover by General Sani Abacha.

Reform of Civil-Military Relations

The reforms in civil-military relations to improve democratic governance can take many forms—building a legitimate army and police force where the state has failed, promoting human rights norms where civilian leadership has failed in its responsibilities, reducing military spending where the military becomes an obstacle to democratization, and promoting cooperation with countries where there are good examples of professional armies and responsible political leadership such as those in South Africa, India, Botswana, and Senegal.[26] Some of the measures which the democratic governments undertake to reduce the influence of the military are reducing its military budget, curtailing its autonomous economic activities, removing military officials from civilian posts, forcing the retirement of military officers, and prosecuting military officials for human rights violations.

There is a growing realization about the need for an effective working relationship between the civilian authorities and the military. The politicians realize that politicizing the military does not in the end serve their own interests. The military can see the benefits of civilian control. It also recognizes that there are no easy solutions to the economic and social problems and is, therefore, reluctant to intervene in politics except in extreme situations. In the final analysis, the civilian and military leaders have to work together. In that sense, top military officials do influence some political decisions, especially those affecting internal and external security.

The challenge for the new democratic regimes is to design comprehensive programs for the modernization and professionalization of the military in order to reorient the military to democratic values and norms. Some of the most critical measures to modernize and professionalize the military are changing military training and educational systems, clearly identifying the military mission, and reorienting the military to the changing needs of a democratic polity. Other measures include changing the leadership and organization of the military, determining optimal military size and equipment, and improving the status of the military including salary, housing, and other benefits.[27] The reconciliation approach in civil-military relations implies obligations on both sides—for the military to accept civilian control as one of the basic norms of democratic governance, and for the civilian authorities to enhance the military's professional autonomy through a well-defined military mission, an adequate defense budget vis-à-vis security considerations, and a willingness to refrain from unnecessary intervention in military affairs.

THE PRESS, MASS MEDIA AND DEMOCRATIC GOVERNANCE

Freedom of the press is essential to build and deepen democratic governance. It enables the identification of popular preferences, the expression of citizens' reactions to government programs and policies, and the enhancement of the political and civil rights of people. Reform of the media is the most critical factor in making democratic institutions work effectively and improving the quality of the democratic process. Free and independent media with mass access and unbiased information provide a useful basis for informed participation and representation. Free media give voice to different segments of the society for the discussion of different viewpoints, serve as a mobilizing agent to facilitate civic engagement of all actors, and check abuses of power; each of these benefits promotes the transparency and accountability of those holding public offices.[28] More specifically, "watchdog media" make democratic institutions work better by stimulating debate on public policies, monitoring elections, reporting on human rights abuses, bringing political corruption and scandals to the attention of citizens, and empowering women.[29] For example, the media played an important role in reducing corruption in Peru. A video broadcast by a local television station showing the national security chief bribing an opposition member of the legislature led to his dismissal and contributed to the eventual resignation of the president. The work of the Philippine Centre for Investigative Journalism (examined in chapter 3) provides another example of how the media can bring issues of corruption to the attention of citizens.

The wide circulation of newspapers in the late nineteenth century, the introduction of radio as a form of communication in the early twentieth century, television as the most effective mass medium in the middle of twentieth century, and more recent information and communication technology breakthroughs including the Internet have transformed the ways in which information about political events is discussed and communicated. Each type of communication contributed to a broadening of the base of politics which historically was limited to a small number of elites. Radio and newspapers with massive circulation were particularly instrumental in nation-building, promoting people's participation in elections and other political activities, and facilitating direct outreach by national political leaders to the man on the street.[30]

Television as a medium has influenced democratic governance in many ways. It has facilitated communication between politicians and the people. However, it has increased the reliance of the candidates on financial contributions from political supporters to pay for the television time in the more advanced democracies. This, in turn, led to too much influence of vested interests, favoritism of the incumbent as compared to newcomers and a reduction in the power of political parties. Furthermore, television as a medium focuses on personalities and styles of politicians instead of arguments in support of a policy and reduces direct interface between the politician and the voters.[31] Negative TV advertising sometimes results in the alienation of open-minded and independent voters. This can lead to the indifference of citizens to the whole political process. The use of satellite television such as CNN has increased tremendously over the past few years in developing countries, usually with mixed impact. In the "third wave" democracies, satellite television has contributed to fragmentation between transnational English-speaking elite and the often illiterate or semiliterate masses. At the same time, regional networks such as Al Jazeera in the Arab region are increasingly presenting alternative viewpoints and breaking down the dominance of the Western-controlled media.

A sound relationship between the government and the press facilitates democracy and good governance. The nature of this relationship depends on the type of democracy. In classical democracy, political participation was restricted to a privileged few. In other democracies—especially those under serious internal or external threat—the state justified its restrictions on the press for reasons of security and national unity. Even countries where democratic norms are observed, such as Malaysia and South Korea, the internal security act of the past regime remains on the books to serve as deterrent. Some call this type of democracy "illiberal democracy."[32] Most countries in such situations attempt to strike a balance between the need for security and to protect the civil and political rights of individuals. After the September 11, 2001, terrorist attacks in the United States, a shifting balance between "homeland security" and the political and social rights of individuals has become a major and highly controversial issue in most of the established democracies in North America and Europe.

The press and the mass media are the most important instruments to ensure the transparency of government actions. Citizens' understanding of government policies and programs is enhanced through reporting by the press about executive decisions, parliamentary debates and discussions in various political parties. Governments need the press and mass media to enhance their legitimacy among citizens, to gauge the concerns and demands of the people, and to explain the content of government policies to the people in response to the opposition's version. One of the problems is the determination of popular preferences. Each of the existing instruments—exit polls, Internet hits, opinion polls—has its weaknesses in knowing the popular preferences.

Governments in many developing countries impose restrictions on the freedom of the press. Many newspapers are partly owned by the government. Independent newspapers find it difficult to remain financially viable without government advertisements and sponsorship. In many ways, the relationship between the press and the executive reflects the same pattern as the civil-military relations, i.e., the integrity, efficiency, and democratic orientation of the civilian leaders set the trend. Where elected political leaders provide sufficient space for the press to play its role in the democratic process, the press is more likely to respond in a positive way. However, when the political leaders want to use the press as an instrument for state control or are not willing to tolerate dissent in political debate, antagonism is created between the two.

The Freedom House's survey on press freedom shows 72 countries rated free—more than in the past decade—62 rated not free, and 53 rated partly free. In Africa, six countries were rated free, 17 partly free and 30 not free. The lowest level of press freedom was in the Middle East with one rated free, two partly free and 11 not free. Latin America and the Caribbean had 18 countries rated free and one not free. The regional trends show that (1) in Africa, 15 countries improved within their categories and 9 declined; (2) four Asian countries improved within their own categories but seven declined; (3) seven countries in Latin America showed "slight improvements"; and (4) out of 27 countries in Eastern Europe and the Newly Independent States, the media was free in 9 states, partly free in 11 states and not free in 7 states.[33]

Freedom of the press is important both for the citizens and the government. From the citizens' perspective, the press and the mass media provide important information and news, enable them to influence political events, provide a forum for discussion to form collective preferences, and serve as a mechanism through which the people can play the role of watchdog to monitor government actions. For the government, the press serves many functions—a vehicle for agenda setting, influencing the collective views of the people, monitoring and mapping out citizen preferences and feedback.[34]

The introduction of the Internet broadens the information base, enables communication with a large number of people, and builds communities of practice. It also facilitates the implementation of programs designed to enhance the accountability and transparency of government services. The "integrity system" in Seoul Metropolitan Government is one example.

Over the past two decades, censorship and ownership controls in developing countries have been loosened. Advances have taken place in freedom of speech and information, resulting from the abolishment of restrictive press laws, the spread of global and regional multimedia companies, information technology, and the Internet. Between 1970 and 1996, the number of daily newspapers in developing countries increased from 29 to 60 copies per 1,000 people.[35] Despite this progress, serious problems in the independence of media, including state-owned media monopolies, remain in many developing countries. State-owned media monopolies continue in the Arab region. In Chile, the Democratic Republic of Congo, and Zimbabwe various measures are used to curtail the independence of the media—"contempt of authority" as a crime against state security in Chile, reporting that "demoralizes" the public in Congo, and legislation to curtail press freedom in Zimbabwe.[36]

There is an increasing recognition that state controls are not essential to promote higher standards of professionalism and responsibility in the media. Some of the other mechanisms that can be used for this purpose are the establishment of independent media commissions as in Ghana, the withdrawal of support by the people, and self-regulation through press councils, internal guidelines ombudsmen, codes of conduct, and training.[37] In Thailand, the government passed the Official Information Act in 1997, which guarantees people's right to have access to information held by the government, including the official information in the Government Gazette and agency plans and manuals.[38] The experience in developing countries suggests that effective media are those that are independent, provide high quality and accurate information to varied groups in the society, and have an extensive reach to a large percentage of the population.[39]

POVERTY AND SUSTAINABILITY OF DEMOCRACY

As explained in chapter 1, the relationship between democratic governance and poverty is complex. Przeworski, Alvarez, Cheibub and Limongi examined relationships between economic development and "political democracy" and between democracy and "material welfare" by reviewing the experiences of 135 countries between 1950 and 1990.[40] Some of the findings of the study are that (1) the regime type has no impact on the growth of total national income; (2) growth is affected by political instability only in dictatorship; (3) democracies have greater increase in per capita income because of faster increase of population under dictatorships and (4) even though there is no direct relationship between democracy and economic development, in practice democracies are more likely to survive in wealthy societies.

Amartya Sen argues that there are "extensive interconnections between political freedoms and the understanding and fulfillment of economic needs."[41] He suggests that political freedoms can provide incentives and information to solve acute economic need, that the degree of economic needs adds to the urgency of political freedoms, and that political and legal rights play a constructive role in identifying and understanding needs. The instrumental role of freedom and democracy is that those who have power are forced to listen to the views and aspirations of the people and respond to their needs.

The main reason for the complexity of the relationship between poverty reduction and democratic governance is that both of these are very broad concepts, each composed of many dimensions. While one component of democratic governance might be positively related to one or more components of poverty eradication (e.g., decentralization might improve access to services), others might be negatively related (e.g., authoritarian regimes might improve the implementation of significant land reforms). In the final analysis, the links between democratic governance and poverty reduction are strong but not automatic.

Furthermore, as a recent UN report argues, "certainly democratization does not guarantee social justice any more than it guarantees economic growth, social peace, administrative efficiency, political harmony, free market or the end of ideology," but the institutions and practices of democracy "have the capacity to challenge the concentration of political power and prevent the emergence of tyranny."[42] However, citizens who have been exposed to periods of authoritarian rule do expect the emergence of democracy to produce economic results and improve their living conditions. When this does not happen, street protests force duly elected leaders to resign, as was the case in Argentina, Peru, and Venezuela. Inequality and poverty are increasing in the new democracies of Eastern Europe, Central Asia, and Sub-Saharan Africa. The lack of progress in economic development has led to political instability in some countries in those regions, putting serious constraints on the functioning of democratic institutions.

While the debate about the relationship between poverty and democratic governance continues among scholars, this study argues that the practice of democracy is significantly affected by the magnitude of poverty in a country—i.e., it is extremely difficult to promote and sustain democratic governance in a stagnant economy with high incidences of poverty among groups, regions, and individuals in the country. This is reflected in the ways democratic institutions function and in the processes through which decisions about public allocation of resources are made. In other words, it is easy to see the impact of poverty on the practice of democracy—the way the legislature, electoral process, human rights framework, decentralization, and judiciary actually function.

Take the case of parliaments in developing countries—responsible for lawmaking, representation of different segments of the society, and the oversight of the executive branch (chapter 4). In many poor developing countries—Bangladesh, Nigeria, Nepal, Yemen, and Pakistan, for example—members of the legislature are usually composed of the landed or business elite with a very small percentage of members from other segments of society. These property owners tend to vigorously protect their vested interests. In the case of Pakistan, the members of the National Assembly opposed—with success for a long time—imposition of the agricultural tax because of the pressures from the overrepresented big landowners in the legislature.

The practice of electoral process is another example (see chapter 2). In most cases, the candidates are expected to spend their own funds. The TV and radio—and in some cases the print media—are controlled by the government. The predominant—if not the only—route to winning elections in most of the less developed countries is the personal wealth of the candidate and his/her willing-ness to spend it. It is not uncommon to find examples of vote buying through intermediaries or bribing influential persons. In rural constituencies, it is extreme-ly difficult for persons with limited means to effectively challenge big landown-ing families during national and local elections. Those who do are seriously threatened. Because of their wealth, the candidates from wealthy families are also able to influence the local functionaries of the government—including polling officers and the police—and the local media outlets. Once elected, some of the members use their membership in the legislature for personal gains. Many tend to be more interested in designing and monitoring local development projects—a task that ordinarily should be undertaken by provincial leaders and local gov-ernment councilors—than in focusing on national legislation, discussing policy options for national problems, and ensuring the oversight and accountability of the executive branch. One of the reasons for this is that it provides them with more opportunities for corruption including the misuse of public resources.

The practice of legal and judicial reforms (chapter 8) in developing countries shows that one of the most critical issues is the access of the poor to justice. Though progress is being made in many countries due to actions at the national level and interventions of the civil society organizations, the cost of the justice system is too high for the poor who are increasingly dependent upon informal and traditional modes of conflict resolution. The cost of recourse to the judicial sys-tem is too high for the poor, both in terms of their inability to pay lawyers and to spend time in the long delays of the court system. High levels of corruption in the judiciary also affect the poor segments of society more than the well to do. Small wonder, public confidence in the integrity and effectiveness of the judicial systems in many developing economies is extremely low, as chapter 8 shows.

The practice of human rights (chapter 5) in developing countries also shows that the poor and disadvantaged groups including women are most negatively affected. Many countries have national laws which are more or less in conformity with the international human rights standard. Yet, their implementation is impeded due to vested interests of the dominant groups, usually at the expense of the poor. The news media in many countries of Asia, Latin America, and Africa, for example, are full of incidences of police brutality and violence against women and minorities. Paralegal groups are, to some degree, supporting the poor in making them more aware of their rights and protecting their interests. Yet, the formal judicial institu-tions and the court system are not adequately accessible to the poor.

The practice of decentralization and local governance (chapter 6) clearly shows the marginalization of the poor and disadvantaged groups in the local decision-making process. In urban areas, slum dwellers and squatters lack adequate access to shelter, security of tenure, and basic urban services. Despite this, most urban local governments allocate a major portion of their resources to middle- and high-income neighborhoods due to the inability of the poor and disadvantaged groups to influence local decisions about the allocation of local resources. Local councilors disproportionately represent the urban business and industrial elite.

In view of the above practice, there is growing disappointment among the populations in developing countries about the economic and social results achieved by countries that embraced democracy. A recent UN survey in Latin America, for example, shows disenchantment with elected governments in the region.[43] According to this survey of about 19,000 citizens and 231 political, economic, and social leaders including 41 current and former presidents and vice-presidents, a majority of respondents (55 percent) would support the replacement of a democratic government with an authoritarian one provided it produces economic benefits. This points to two aspects of democracy—first, the democratic culture and values are not sufficiently internalized, and, second, economic development is considered more important by citizens than maintaining democracy. Since 2000, four elected presidents have been forced to resign because of a sharp decline in popular support. Among the states with higher potential for political instability are Guatemala, which struggles with paramilitary groups and the smuggling of people and drugs, Haiti where an interim administration took over recently after popular revolt, Venezuela with a deeply polarized population, and Bolivia where the present administration took over after popular revolt in 2003. Some countries, including Peru, Ecuador, and Bolivia, suffer from continuous protests from indigenous people. The above findings are startling because over the past 25 years all of the 18 countries surveyed have held regular and fair elections and enjoy a free press and basic civil liberties. A decline in the confidence of the people in the region's elected governments is attributed largely to slow economic growth, inadequate services, and social inequalities.

In some countries in other regions too, years after the establishment of democracy, the human conditions of ordinary people have not significantly improved, and income inequality and poverty have increased—including in Eastern Europe and Sub-Saharan Africa. This is putting enormous constraint on the sustainability of democracy and good governance in developing economies. The case of the Russian Federation (a developed country) is interesting. After the collapse of the former Soviet Union, conventional wisdom said that a free market and political pluralism will go hand in hand because a free market will create the necessary pressures for political transparency, freedom of the press, and accountability. In practice, ordinary citizens looked for strong central leadership in the post-Soviet era, which accounts for the strong support enjoyed by President Putin. As in the case of Latin America, economic development and political stability have been given higher priorities by the people.

ROLE OF EXTERNAL PARTNERS

Though consolidation of democracy is the result primarily of democratic institutions of a country and its internal factors, experience suggests that external partners—bilateral donors, multilateral development organizations, and the international civil society—play important facilitating and advocacy roles. They provide global frameworks and incentives, support capacity development and global advocacy for core values of democracy and good governance, and provide fora for the sharing of good practices and transfer of knowledge. External partners are key players in the global, and in some countries, national debate on the promotion of democracy and good governance.

Global Forces

Over the past two decades, the role of external partners in promoting democracy and good governance has been expanding.[44] Several forces have led to this.

1. With the end of the Cold War, developing countries are more willing to seek the support and advice of external partners—multilateral organizations, including the UN and financial institutions such as the World Bank, and bilateral donors—to improve the functioning and capacity of electoral systems, parliaments, human rights institutions, local government systems, the judiciary, and public sector management. Countries are more willing to engage external partners in policy- and program-level dialogue on such politically sensitive issues as the introduction of a multiparty system and the realignment of national laws with the global legal framework for human rights. The resulting interaction between international and domestic actors "generates new democratic norms and expectations from below."[45]

2. The UN Secretary General's Agenda for Peace, published pursuant to the statement adopted by the Summit Meeting of the Security Council on January 31, 1992, emphasized respect for human rights and fundamental freedoms; rights of minorities and vulnerable groups including women; the empowerment of the unorganized, the poor and the marginalized; and strong national and local institutions.

3. The *Agenda for Development*, adopted by the General Assembly in June 1997, resulted from extensive deliberations by the Member States and the Secretariats of the UN. It recognized the role of nonstate actors including the civil society in the "participatory approach to development."[46] It argued that "participatory decision-making, together with the rule of law, democracy, and transparent and accountable governance and administration in all sectors of society is an important requirement for the effectiveness of development policies."[47]

4. Over the past two decades, the UN has organized conferences and summits on key issues of global concern, including the environment, human rights, human settlements, social development, the status of women, children, and financing for development. Specifically, the United Nations Millennium Summit has been a landmark event leading to the United Nations Millennium Declaration, and the road map towards the implementation of the United Nations Millennium Declaration prepared by the Secretary General, which includes the Millennium Development Goals (MDGs). One of the most critical issues emerging from each of the above has been upholding the central role of governance systems and institutions in promoting economic development, increasing the access of services to the vast majority of the poor, enforcing human rights legislation, enhancing the participation of women in the development process, and protecting the quality of the environment.

5. As discussed in chapters 3, 7, and 8, in order to benefit from the opportunities provided by globalization, developing countries are seeking ways to strengthen new frameworks and tools for political and financial accountability including domestic and cross-border corruption; to develop human resource with emphasis on capacity and new skills of the public sector in such areas as trade negotiations, regional treaties, and policy analysis to assess the impact of globalization on vulnerable groups and public goods; and to promote legal and judicial frameworks for trade and investment, including property rights and the access to justice for the poor. In each of these areas, the external partners can assist developing countries.

6. Civil society organizations (CSOs) are assuming the role of advocate, watchdog and interlocutor between the government and the people and between the legislature and the people. CSOs are globalized in their membership and agenda. They are playing a vital role in issue-oriented advocacy concerning such issues as debt relief, open trade, investments in the Least Developed Countries (LDCs),

market protections by the industrialized countries, and the impact of liberalization of the economy on the poor and vulnerable groups. Through their global membership, they provide direct support to developing countries and also monitor and evaluate the donor-assisted democracy programs. Human Rights Watch and Amnesty International monitor the enforcement of civil and political rights around the world. Freedom House performs advocacy functions, among others, by publishing the survey Freedoms in the World. Oxfam has played a significant global advocacy role in issues related to the impact of globalization including debt relief for the LDCs. chapter 2 highlights the role of international civil society in monitoring elections.

7. Over the past few years the number of requests from the developing countries for democracy assistance has significantly increased. The United States Agency for International Development (USAID), The UN Development Programme (UNDP) and the World Bank, for example, experienced a sharp rise in requests from developing countries for assistance to strengthen the capacity of democratic institutions including parliaments, electoral management bodies, the judiciary, and local government systems. No fewer than 104 delegations referred to the importance of governance in their opening statements to the 53rd session of the UN General Assembly, an indicator of the willingness of most developing countries to discuss internal governance and public administration reform in global settings. Intergovernmental collaborative arrangements have been forged at regional and subregional levels to share good practices and experiences in the electoral process, legal and judicial reform, the roles and capacities of parliaments, and decentralization and local governance.

8. Good governance has been increasingly used as a conditionality to development assistance and foreign aid. The reasons usually given for this are that "development effectiveness" requires efficient, transparent, and participatory governance systems and processes; that democracy and good governance are universal values even though their practice might vary from one country to another; and that donors must show results to their own constituents, which requires benchmarks, close monitoring, and accountability of development assistance. While foreign aid is the most significant tool used by bilateral donors in their democracy promotion programs, other tools used in the name of democracy include diplomacy to achieve political and economic agenda, economic sanctions, and paramilitary and military intervention.

Donor Approaches

There is a wide body of literature on the effectiveness of democracy assistance programs of bilateral donors and multilateral organizations.[48] Frequently, donors have different approaches to democracy assistance—financial institutions such as IMF and the World Bank focusing on economic reform and public sector development, the UN Development Programme on democratic governance, specialized agencies such as the World Health Organization on the governance of health issues, and some of the bilateral donors on human rights and democracy. This section describes the approaches of the Nordic countries, Japan, the United States, the World Bank, and the UN. It should be pointed out that other bilateral donors with significant democracy and good governance programs include the United Kingdom, France, Canada, and Germany.

Nordic Countries: In the Nordic countries, cultural values and internal pressures emanating from the ideals of the welfare state are the main determinants of the promotion of democracy in developing countries. Many aspects of the Nordic assistance promote the sustainability of democracy and good governance in developing countries.[49] Usually, democracy assistance is not guided by economic and military interests. A major portion of democracy assistance is provided through multilateral organizations such as the UN Development Programme. Over the years, assistance to the promotion of human rights institutions and the participation of women in democratic processes have been emphasized. Since the 1990s, funding for multiparty politics—with some exceptions such as Uganda—and legal education has been significantly increased. The use of conditionality has not been a predominant feature of democracy assistance. However, in some cases the countries have refused to consider new projects or have channeled assistance through civil society organizations. Denmark, for example, phased out its assistance to Sudan in 1990 and to Indonesia in 1991 due to human rights violations in those countries.

All of the Nordic countries have prepared their policy papers on good governance. Nordic countries played a central role in the creation of the International Institute for Democracy and Electoral Assistance (IIDEA), which focuses on consolidation of democracy at the country level by providing a forum to the academic institutions, governments and nongovernmental organizations. The Institute undertakes democracy assessments at the country level and promotes training and research on selected themes. The Nordic countries also support research on democracy and governance in the universities and other research institutions in developing countries. Norway has been playing an active role in supporting conflict resolution initiatives such as the one in Sri Lanka. UNDP and the Government of Norway jointly established the Oslo Center on Governance to support exchange and sharing of experiences and good practices in governance, including access to justice. Other areas of Nordic support have been multiparty elections, and local NGOs.

Japan: The promotion of democracy has not been the focus of Japanese international assistance due largely to the cultural factors such as an unwillingness to export its own political values, an emphasis on harmony and avoidance of conflict, and the communal orientation of the society that partly limits the role of individual rights.[50] Another reason for the lack of emphasis on democracy promotion in the assistance from Japan is the belief that political stability and economic development are necessary to promote and sustain democracy. For many years the "iron triangle" of the Liberal Democratic Party, the business community, and the elite civil service focused on political and economic stability, dependable trading partners, and a friendly business environment. This necessitated working with some of the authoritarian regimes in developing countries. Other reasons for the lack of emphasis on democracy promotion were political constraints imposed on Japan concerning an assertive foreign policy. Some of the recipients of Japanese assistance who have violated the human rights of their citizens include some of the previous governments of Indonesia, South Korea, Peru, and the Philippines. The adoption of the 1992 Overseas Development Assistance (ODA) charter explicitly stated the use of economic assistance to promote democratization. Yet the implementation of this charter has been constrained by sensitivity to the criticism of internal interference by governments of developing countries and hesitation of policymakers about the long-term impact of democratization interventions. Japan has been following a relatively quiet approach to democratization, emphasizing different paths to democracy depending upon the peculiar circumstances of each country.

In 1996, however, Japan increased its commitment to democracy promotion and added the "partnership for democratic development" to its foreign assistance policy, including support for legal and electoral systems and institutions and human rights protection. Assistance was extended to Cambodia, Indonesia, the Central African Republic, Ecuador, Guinea, Lesotho, and Nigeria. In Myanmar, Japan imposed economic sanctions after the opposition civilian leaders were put on house arrest and suspended economic assistance to the country. In Eastern Europe and the ex-Soviet states, Japan provided significant international assistance, focusing on economic needs instead of politics.

United States of America: The US support for the promotion of democracy has gone through several phases.[51] After the end of the Second World War, the containment of the communist threat was the priority goal of the American Government. Therefore, in many cases, strategic interests—and not democracy promotion—were the main determinant of the national policy. The government forged close alliances with such dictatorial regimes as the Shah of Iran, President Suharto of Indonesia, and President Marcos of the Philippines. Under President Carter's administration, greater emphasis was placed on human rights, though the United States continued to forge alliances with many undemocratic regimes. President Reagan placed democracy promotion as the central goal of US foreign policy, which led to the establishment of the National Endowment for Democracy. Electoral and judicial assistance was provided to some of the countries in Latin America. With the end of the Cold War and the transition of Eastern Europe and the former Soviet Union from socialist to democratic systems, the Bush administration made democratization an important element of the "new world order." President Clinton's policy of "building democracy" was divided into four areas—the establishment of electoral processes; rule of law including drafting of constitutions and independent courts; openness and transparency of government and combating corruption; and support for the civil society including funding of labor unions, independent news media and professional associations.

The scope, quality, and effectiveness of US assistance for democracy promotion have been constrained by many factors—the lack of adequate domestic support for promoting democracy abroad, the declining amount of overall foreign aid from $11.6 billion in 1991 to $7 billion in 1999, the need to promote US economic competitiveness (such as in China and many of the countries in the Arab region), and security interests including the need to maintain a predominant military presence throughout the world (including Turkey). Some countries of strategic interest such as Egypt and Pakistan have in the past continued to receive assistance despite their democratic deficit.

The promotion of democratic values is the stated policy of the present US administration. After the terrorist attacks of September 11, 2001, however, the administration had to work with twin objectives—promote democracy and human rights and ensure internal security. Striking a balance between the security objectives and democracy and human rights objectives of the foreign policy is a complex task partly because the administration has needed the support of some of the countries on the frontline of the "war against terrorism"—such as Egypt, Pakistan, and Uzbekistan—which have varying degrees of "guided democracy." Civil society organizations such as Amnesty International and Human Rights Watch have shown concern about the legal and judicial mechanisms used in developing and developed countries to combat terrorism which negatively affect individual rights.

In 2002, the Bush administration created the Millennium Challenge Account (MCA) through which $5 billion per year is to be provided to a small group of countries that are "ruling justly, investing in their people, and establishing economic freedom."[52] In 2003, the administration announced $10 billion in new funding for HIV/AIDS in Africa. These initiatives would not only increase the quantity of aid but would also emphasize, especially in the case of the MCA, the centrality of good governance and democracy. Yet, the MCA will affect only a small number of countries. The countries that need the democracy assistance most—failed and failing states, for example—might not be able to significantly benefit from this initiative. Furthermore, the administration might not be able to deliver funds quickly through the MCA.

The World Bank: Over the past few years, the World Bank studies have examined the importance of good governance and effective public sector institutions, actions needed to improve the performance of governments, and the role of the Bank in improving the capacity of client governments to implement the governance reform agenda.[53] Building effective and accountable institutions to reduce poverty and address development issues is at the "core" of the Bank's activities. The Bank's own analysis shows weaknesses of its past work in this field—a narrow and technocratic view of public sector reform in some of the client countries, reliance on models and "best practices" not suitable to the peculiar setting of the country, Structural Adjustment Loans (SALs) and Technical Assistance (TA) that were based on short-term commitment, and shortages of specialized skills in the client countries.

While the Bank is engaged in many areas of public sector and governance reform, it has developed its niche in the role of the public sector, the structure of government including fiscal decentralization, administrative and civil service reform, public expenditure analysis, anticorruption, legal and judicial reform, and sectoral institution-building. Over the past few years, the Bank has significantly developed its own capacity in the public sector and governance and forged partnerships with other entities.

United Nations: To varying degrees, all parts of the UN system are involved in supporting Member States in strengthening governance capacity at the local, national, regional, and global levels. The United Nations Department of Economic and Social Affairs (UNDESA) contributes to the normative, intergovernmental processes through global level documentation and analysis and sharing of best practices. UNDESA leads the UN system in supporting the Member States dealing with the issues of state governance including the role of the state, public sector management, and civil service reform and chairs the "governance cluster" of the Economic Committee of the Economic and Social Affairs (EC-ESA). It supports comparative research and analysis and facilitates information sharing.

The United Nations Development Programme (UNDP) leads the UN system in providing technical assistance to developing countries in "democratic governance" through its network of over 160 Country Offices. The UNDP supports national processes of democratic transition through policy advice and technical support, capacity development of institutions and individuals, advocacy and communication, the promotion of dialogue and knowledge networking, and sharing of good practices. UNDP services are provided in the following categories of democratic governance—legislatures, electoral systems and processes, access to justice and human rights, access to information, decentralization and local governance, and public administration and accountability. The UNDP Strategic Results Framework for 1999 showed that with UNDP's support 94 countries were strengthening the capacities of key democratic governing institutions, 91 countries were promoting decentralizations, and 75 countries had initiated programs to promote the accountability of the public sector.

Regional Commissions: These commissions, including Economic Commission for Africa and Economic and Social Commission for Asia and the Pacific, promote regional dialogue and intercountry cooperation in governance and public administration reform. UNESCO, ILO, WHO, and UNICEF include governance components in their sectoral programs. The United Nations Programme for Human Settlements (UN-HABITAT) has launched the urban governance campaign among mayors, local government officials, and national-level policy-makers and practitioners. The UN Secretariat supports the Conference of New and Restored Democracies, held every four years, as mandated by the General

Assembly of the United Nations, to review critical issues in sustainability of "new and restored" democracies. The Office of the High Commissioner for Human Rights supports the work of the UN Commission on Human Rights—an intergovernmental body—and coordinates the activities of all entities in the UN system to promote human rights in UN-supported programs and projects. Regional Development Banks—especially in Asia and Africa—provide grants and loans to improve governance systems and processes.

Lessons Learned from Donor Assistance

The results of donor assistance to promote democracy and good governance over the past few decades have been mixed. On the one hand, targeted assistance has enhanced capacity in developing countries in many areas—legislative drafting and procedures, administrative and financial decentralization, increased participation of the civil society organizations due to new legal frameworks, effective and accountable judicial systems, and a more transparent electoral process. Each of these can have a cumulative effect on the consolidation and sustainability of democracy.

There have been some effective interventions by external partners.[54] Some examples of UNDP assistance in effectively developing national capacities are aid coordination in Vietnam, electoral support in Indonesia and Bangladesh, management development in Kyrgyzstan and Mongolia, and modernization of the state in Honduras. Other innovative UNDP assistance programs have included the Global Environmental Facility; decentralization and participatory development in Nepal; human rights training of police and the military and women's participation programs in Latin America; strengthening planning and management processes in the United Arab Emirates; the Africa Governance Forum; and human rights programs in Central and Eastern Europe. To varying degrees, the above programs have strengthened national and local capacities at individual and entity levels, facilitated sharing of innovations and best practices, promoted partnerships between the public sector and civil society organizations, and advocated such global concerns as human rights, the environment, and gender equality.

The United Nations Department of Economic and Social Affairs (UNDESA) —through its support to the intergovernmental process, the World Public Sector Report, the Global Forum on Re-inventing Government, and strategic technical assistance—plays an important role in advocacy of good governance and public administration at the global level. The Office of the High Commissioner for Human Rights, in partnership with governments and civil society organizations, protects vulnerable groups against human rights violations.

As one of the major donors for good governance and public sector reform, the World Bank studies report several cases of successful assistance.[55] The Bank helped countries to combat corruption by advocating integrated approaches in Latvia and Slovakia in Europe; Nigeria, Tanzania, and Uganda in Africa; Argentina, Bolivia, and Ecuador in Latin America; Indonesia, Thailand, and the Philippines in East Asia; the Indian state of Uttar Pradesh in South Asia; and Morocco in North Africa. The Bank provided funding for the Partnership for Capacity Building in Africa (PACT) to support country-based initiatives to strengthen public sector capacity, to interface between the government and the civil society and the private sector, and to support regional and subregional initiatives. Other examples of successful interventions have included the Latvian Revenue Modernization Project, the Institutional and Governance Review in Bolivia, Promoting Partnerships Through Governance Trust Funds, and Indonesia Governance Partnership.

Many bilateral donors including the Netherlands, Sweden, Norway, and the United Kingdom have provided targeted democracy assistance both directly and through multilateral entities. In the case of the United Kingdom, for example, policy advisory services are provided through the Department for International Development (DFID) to improve governance systems and processes. A network of policy advisers at the headquarters and in the field provides support to craft country-level programs. Nordic countries extensively utilize multilateral entities for their democracy promotion programs. They have forged partnerships with entities such as the World Bank and UNDP to provide assistance to developing countries. Bilateral donor support has strengthened local actors—especially those from civil society and the media—in their efforts to hold political leaders and government officials accountable for their actions.

Democracy and good governance assistance has usually been channeled through some combination of the following modalities—workshops and policy seminars, expert consultancies on specific policies and institutional designs and restructuring, skill training courses, study tours to benefit from others' experience, equipment donation, small grants, and infrastructure improvement. Each of these contributes to strengthening the capacity of government and nongovernmental actors. The impact of assistance goes beyond institutional changes. Individuals and national institutions that take part in such programs as legislative strengthening and access to justice are exposed to new ideas and good practices within and outside the country. Partnerships of internal and external actors to undertake policy analysis can influence national policies at the upstream level. External partners provide "seed" grant assistance that can strengthen the hands of innovators within the country.

Despite their positive impacts, the above types of interventions are not sufficient to sustain and consolidate democracy. For example, as examined in earlier sections of this chapter, they do not reshape the internal contextual factors that make democracy work or collapse—culture and ethnicity, the balance of political power including civil and military relations, the incidence of poverty, the media, the vested interests of the ruling elite, regional disparities, and political and historical legacies. Often, national political leaders have to accommodate the interests of the very groups that constrain the effective functioning of democratic institutions. "Democracy aid," argues Carothers, based on his analysis of US experience, "generally does not have major effects on the political direction of the recipient countries."[56]

Some general lessons learned about the effectiveness of the democracy assistance programs of external partners are as follows:

Donor Commitment: The degree of long-term commitment of donors to democracy promotion is constrained by many factors. In most cases, national economic interests get priority over democracy promotion. A major portion of the foreign assistance of each donor, especially in the case of the United States and France, is allocated to a few countries politically and strategically aligned with the donor. The poorest countries, which need the assistance most, are neglected because they are not able to influence groups within the donor country that play a central role in the allocation of assistance. The irony is that in the advanced democracies characterized by competitive political process such as the United States, the most well-organized and financially powerful groups create these inequalities in the allocation of foreign assistance. Furthermore, the priorities of donors keep changing depending upon their new strategic interests. Because democracy promotion requires long-term support, the sustainability of democratic reform initiatives is negatively affected by the short "attention span" of donors.

Partnership Approach: Forging a partnership with the host government, which leads to mutual trust, is a starting point for effective democracy promotion and good governance programs, because such assistance involves a great deal of political sensitivity. The first lesson for the donor community, thus, is to adopt a partnership approach. External partners' lack of adequate understanding of the society and culture of the recipient countries often constrains the emergence of viable partnerships between local actors and external partners.

National Priorities: Recipient countries are more willing to support externally supported governance programs if they are perceived as a means to achieve national goals and priorities. As "allies," external partners must play a constructive role to advance good governance and democracy for human development according to nationally identified priorities. In this regard, they can assist developing countries by providing knowledge, bringing actors together, and supporting advocacy with nonstate actors.

National Ownership and Leadership: Ownership of the reform process is critical, involving political and administrative leadership, public employees, the private sector, and the civil society. Productive democratic governance changes depend upon leaders who are willing to accept the risks that come with challenging the existing internal order, who can mediate between divergent interests, and who can identify a clear vision for the attainment of national goals.

Donor Coordination: A recipient government's capacity to coordinate, manage, and implement governance assistance from external partners is often limited. The absence of effective mechanisms and fora at the country level for dialogue between the recipient government and donors is often a problem, leading to "supply-driven" external assistance. One of the most critical action points to enhance capacity at the country level is to enable the country to be the driving force in coordinating support for external partners.

Political Sensitivities and Donor Conditionalities: For recipient countries, there are significant risks in external assistance for the promotion of democracy.[57] These programs often touch on the sovereignty of individual states and established political and power relationships. The design and conceptualization of effective democracy promotion and good governance projects depend on their understanding and articulated assumptions of project objectives and outputs, with particular attention to ensure that Western and ethnocentric views and values do not override emerging national ideologies and sovereign goals. Restructuring political institutions—parliaments, human rights institutions, and electoral commissions, for example—often takes place in extremely complex sociopolitical contexts, frequently in the aftermath of social upheaval or as a part of efforts to introduce or reintroduce democratic norms in politics.

Some democracy assistance providers and donors add conditionalities to assistance. Most bilateral donors view increasing conditionalities as the trend in the right direction, arguing that debt relief and other incentives should be used to prompt political liberalization, while others worry about separating the "winners" from the "losers" and leaving behind those very countries most in need of help.

CONCLUSION

Internal context does matter a great deal in how democracy works in practice. Ethnic, religious, and cultural heterogeneity influences the route to democracy and good governance in each country—there is no one model that fits all situations. Civil-military relations have an impact on the democratic process and, in turn, are influenced by the process. Freedom of media and the press is an integral part of the efforts to consolidate and sustain democracy. Perhaps the most significant contextual factor is the extent of poverty—which influences the fairness and transparency of the electoral process, the way parliaments perform their primary tasks, the enforcement of human rights legislation, citizens' access to justice, and the capacity and resources of local governments and community groups.

With the spread of democracy around the world over the past few decades, external partners—multilateral organizations such as the United Nations and the World Bank, bilateral donors, and civil society organizations—are providing increasing support to developing countries in their efforts to strengthen capacities of governing institutions and improve the quality of the democratic process. The end of the Cold War, the adoption of the Millennium Declaration, the United Nations Agenda for Peace, and other global factors have contributed to an environment that is conducive to technical cooperation from external partners who use selected entry points to strengthen democracy. Despite many good practices and examples, the overall impact of technical assistance in democracy promotion, however, has been mixed due in part to the political sensitivity of democracy assistance, the lack of long-term commitment of donors, and the lack of national ownership.

ENDNOTES

1. Seymour Martin Lipset, "Prospects for Democracy" (prepared for the Conference of New and Restored Democracies, December 4–6, 2000, Cotonou, Benin), 26.

2. Bernard Lewis, "Islam and Liberal Democracy: A Historical Overview," *Journal of Democracy* 7 no. 2 (1996), 52–63; Samuel Huntington, "The Clash of Civilizations," *Foreign Affairs* 72, no. 3 (1993) 22–49.

3. Samuel P. Huntington, *The Clash of Civilizations and the Remaking of World Order* (New York: Simon and Schuster, 1996).

4. Robert A. Dahl, *Democracy and its Critics* (New Haven, CT: Yale University Press, 1989), 328; Adel Safty, *Global Advance of Democracy in Governance* (New York: Management Development and Governance Division, UNDP, 2000).

5. Alex Hadenius, *Democracy and Development* (Cambridge: Cambridge University Press, 1992), 148.

6. Seymour Martin Lipset, Kyoung-Ryung Seong and John Charles Torres, "A Comparative Analysis of the Social Prerequisites of Democracy," *International Social Science Journal* 45 (May 1993), 159–60; Seymour Martin Lipset, "The Social Requisites of Democracy Revisited," 430–449 in *Comparing Nations and Cultures: Readings in Cross-disciplinary Perspectives,* Alex Inkeles and Masamichi Sadaki, eds. (Englewood Cliffs, NJ: Prentice-Hall, 1996).

7. Samuel Huntington, *The Third Wave: Democratization in the Late Twentieth Century* (Norman, OK: University of Oklahoma Press, 1991), 85.

8. Amartya Sen, "Democracy as a Universal Human Value," *Journal of Democracy* (July 10, 1999), 16; see also Amartya Sen, *Development as Freedom* (New York: Anchor Books, 1999).

9. Samuel Huntington, *The Third Wave,* 76.

10. Seymour Martin Lipset, "Prospects for Democracy" (prepared for the Conference of New and Restored Democracies, December 4–6, 2000, Cotonou, Benin), 26.

11. Freedom House, "Freedom in the World 2001–2002," press release, December 18, 2001.

12. *New York Times,* November 23, 2001, A20

13. Alfred Stepan, "Religion, Democracy and the 'Twin Tolerations,'" *Journal of Democracy* 11, no. 4 (Oct. 2000), 52.

14. Saad Eddin Ibrahim, "Religion and Democracy: The Case of Islam, Civil Society and Democracy," *The Changing Nature of Democracy,* in Takashi Inoguchi, Edward Newman and John Keane, eds. (Tokyo: United Nations University Press, 1998), 225–227.

15. Amin Saikal and Albrecht Schnabel, eds. *Democratization in the Middle East: Experiences, Struggles, Challenges* (Tokyo: United Nations University Press, 2003).

16. Amy Chua, *World on Fire: How Exporting Free Market Democracy Breeds Ethnic Hatred and Global Instability* (New York: Doubleday, 2003).

17. Felipe Aguero, "Toward Civilian Supremacy in South America," in Larry Diamond, et al., eds., *Consolidating the Third Wave Democracies* (Baltimore: Johns Hopkins University Press, 1997), 179.

18. Michael Chege, "Civil-Military Relations in the Transition to Democracy: Patterns and Policy Alternatives" (paper, New York: UNDP, 2001), 10–11.

19. Ibid., 12–20.

20. Huntington, *The Third Wave*, 231–32.

21. Ibid., 238–40.

22. Aguero, "Toward Civilian Supremacy," 179.

23. Ibid., 181.

24. Ibid., 182.

25. Chege, "Civil-Military Relations in the Transition," 20–23.

26. Ibid., 23–28.

27. Huntington, *The Third Wave*, 243–250.

28. UNDP, *Deepening Democracy in a Fragmented World* (New York: Oxford University Press, 2002), 76.

29. Ibid., 76.

30. Alihu Katz, "Mass Media and Participatory Democracy," in *The Changing Nature of Democracy*, Takashi Inoguchi, Edward Newman and John Keane, eds. (Tokyo: United Nations University Press, 1998), 87–100.

31. Ibid.

32. Fareed Zakaria, "The Rise of Illiberal Democracy," *Foreign Affairs* 76 (Nov. 1997), 22–43.

33. Freedom House, *How Free? The Annual Survey of Press Freedom* (New York: Freedom House, 2001), 9–10.

34. Takashi Inoguchi, "Press, Mass Media and Democracy" (paper, New York, UNDP, 2001).

35. UNDP, *Deepening Democracy in a Fragmented World*, 76.

36. Ibid., 77.

37. Ibid., 78.

38. World Bank, *World Development Report 2002* (Washington, DC: World Bank, 2002), 190. Three approaches have been found successful in increasing

access to media—the removal of constraints on entry to new media enterprises, innovations such as newspaper stands to increase the reach of the media, and the development of policy framework including enhanced literacy rates, the establishment of journalism schools, and an increase in technological infrastructure.

39. Ibid., 182.

40. Adam Przeworski, Michael Alvarez, Jose Antonio Cheibub and Fernando Limongi, *Democracy and Development: Political Institutions and Well-Being in the World, 1950–1990* (New York: Cambridge University Press, 2000). For a more in-depth analysis of the relationship between political and economic governance, see Ian Marsh, Jean Blondel and Takashi Inoguchi, eds. *Democracy, Governance and Economic Performance: East and Southeast Asia* (Tokyo: United Nations University Press, 1999); Mihaly Simai, ed. *The Democratic Process and the Market: Challenges of Transition* (Tokyo: United Nations University Press, 1999).

41. Amartya Sen, *Development as Freedom* (New York: Anchor Books, 1999), 147.

42. UNDP, *Deepening Democracy in a Fragmented World*, 83.

43. UNDP, *La Democracia en America Latina* (New York: United Nations Development Programme, 2004).

44. The international dimensions promoting democracy have been recognized even by scholars who have traditionally focused on the significance of internal factors in the process of democratization. Among others, see Philippe Schmitter, "The Influence of International Context Upon the Choice of National Institutions and Policies in Neo-Democracies," *The International Dimensions of Democratization: Europe and the Americas*, Laurence Whitehead, ed. (Oxford: Oxford University Press, 1996).

45. Ibid., 30.

46. United Nations, *Agenda for Development* (New York: United Nations, 1997), 66.

47. Ibid., 66.

48. Among others, see World Bank, *Reforming Public Institutions and Strengthening Governance: A World Bank Strategy* (Washington, DC: World Bank, 2000); "UNDP and Governance—Lessons of Experience" (New York: Management Development and Governance Division, 2000); UNDP, *Human Development Report 2000* and *Human Development Report 2002*; Thomas Carothers, *Aiding Democracy Abroad* (Washington, DC: National Endowment for Democracy, 2000).

49. Among others, see Danish International Development Agency (DANIDA), *Human Rights and Democracy: Perspectives for Development Cooperation* (Copenhagen: Ministry of Foreign Affairs, 1993); DANIDA, *The Nordic Way, Social Summit Special* (Copenhagen: DANIDA, 1995); Finnish International Development Cooperation Agency (FINNIDA), *Human Rights and Good Governance—Some Observations on Finnish Development Cooperation* (Helsinki: 1991); Norwegian Agency for Development Cooperation (NORAD), *NORAD and Norwegian Development Cooperation in the 1990s* (Oslo: NORAD, 1993); Swedish International Development Cooperation Agency (SIDA), *SIDA's Strategy for its Program of Assistance in Support of Democracy and Human Rights* (Stockholm: SIDA, 1993).

50. Bradley Richardson, *Japanese Democracy: Power, Coordination and Performance* (New Haven, CT: Yale University Press, 1997), 7–8.

51. Carothers, *Aiding Democracy Abroad.*

52. Steven Radelet, "Bush and Foreign Aid," *Foreign Affairs,* 82, no. 5 (September/October 2003), 104.

53. Three important studies are *The World Development Report 2000/2001* (Washington, DC: World Bank, 2001); *Attacking Poverty; The World Development Report 1997* (Washington, DC: World Bank, 1997); *The State in a Changing World* (Washington, DC: World Bank, 2000); and *Reforming Public Institutions and Strengthening Governance: A World Bank Strategy* (Washington, DC: World Bank, 2000).

54. UNDP, *UNDP and Governance: Experience and Lessons Learned* (New York: Management Development and Governance Division, 1999).

55. World Bank, *Reforming Public Institutions and Strengthening Governance.*

56. UNDP, *UNDP and Governance.*

57. Carothers, *Aiding Democracy Abroad.*

BIBLIOGRAPHY

Ackerman, Susan Rose. *Corruption and Good Governance.* New York: UNDP (Discussion Paper 3), 1997.

Aguero, Felipe. "Toward Civilian Supremacy in South America." In *Consolidating the Third Wave Democracies,* edited by Larry Diamond, Marc F. Plattner, Yun-han Chu and Jung-mao Tien. Baltimore: Johns Hopkins University Press, 1997.

Anderson, Lisa. Ed. *Transitions to Democracy.* New York: Columbia University Press, 1993.

Archer, Keith. *Voter Registration.* Part of the Administration and Coordination of Elections Project of the United Nations Online Network in Public Administration and Finance (UNPAN). http://www.aceproject.org/.

Asian Development Bank. *Asian Development Bank Anticorruption Policy.* Manila: Asian Development Bank, 1998.

Baaklini, Abdo, Guilain Denoeux and Robert Springborg. *Legislative Politics in the Arab World: The Resurgence of Democratic Institutions.* Boulder, CO: Lynne Rienner, 1999.

Barros, Robert. "Dictatorship and the Rule of Law: Rules and Military Power in Pinochet's Chile." In *Democracy and the Rule of Law,* edited by Jose Maria Maraval and Adam Przeworski. Cambridge: Cambridge University Press, 2003.

Beetham, David. "Democracy and Human Rights: Civil, Political, Economic, Social and Cultural Rights." In *Human Rights: New Dimensions and Challenges,* edited by Janusz Symonides. Brookfield: Ashgate, 1998.

Bisceglie, Robert F. *Types of Electoral Management Bodies.* Part of the Administration and Coordination of Elections Project of the United Nations Online Network in Public Administration and Finance (UNPAN). http://www.aceproject.org/.

Blair, Harry. *Assessing Democratic Decentralization.* Washington, DC: USAID, 1995.

Bratton, Michael. "African Views of Political Parties: Some Cross-National Survey Evidence." Paper presented, Conference on Network Democracy: Enhancing the Role of Political Parties, The Hague, April 24–25, 2001.

Bratton, Michael and Nicolas Van de Walle. *Democratic Experiments in Africa.* Cambridge: Cambridge University Pres, 1998.

Brown, Nathan J. *Mechanisms for Accountability in Arab Governance: The Present and Future of Judiciaries and Parliaments in the Arab World.* New York: UNDP, Programme on Governance in the Arab Region, 2001.

Burdekin, Brian, and Anne Gallagher. *The United Nations and Human Rights Institutions.* Geneva: Office of the High Commissioner for Human Rights, 2001.

Capital Development Fund. *Poverty Reduction, Participation and Local Governance: A Fund for Local and Community Development.* New York: Capital Development Fund, 1995.

Carlson, Scott, Wendy Betts and Greg Gisvold. "The Post-Conflict Transitional Administration of Kosovo and the Lessons Learned in Efforts to Establish a Judiciary and Rule of Law." Paper presented, World Bank Conference on Empowerment, Security and Opportunity through Law and Justice, St. Petersburg, Russia, July 9, 2001.

Carothers, Thomas. *Aiding Democracy Abroad: The Learning Curve.* New York: Carnegie Endowment for International Peace, 1999.

Chege, Michael. "Civil-Military Relations in the Transition to Democracy: Patterns and Policy Alternatives." Paper, 2001. New York: Management Development and Governance Division, UNDP, 2001.

Cheema, G. Shabbir. *Urban Shelter and Service: Public Policies and Management Approaches.* New York: Praeger, 1987.

Cheema, G. Shabbir, John Nellis, and Dennis A. Rondinelli, Eds. *Decentralization and Development: Policy Implementation in Developing Countries.* Beverly Hills: Sage, 1983.

Cheema, G. Shabbir, and Mounir Tabet, "Decentralized Governance for Human Development." In *New Millennium, New Perspectives: The United Nations, Security and Governance,* edited by Ramesh Thakur and Edward Newman. New York: United Nations University Press, 2000.

Chhibber, Pradeep. "State Policy, Rent Seeking and the Electoral Success of a Religious Party in Algeria," *Journal of Politics* 58, no. 1 (1996): 26–48.

Chua, Amy. *World on Fire: How Exporting Free Market Democracy Breeds Ethnic Hatred and Global Instability.* New York: Doubleday, 2003.

Cohen, John. *Administrative Decentralization for the 1990s and Beyond.* New York: United Nations Department for Development Support and Management Services, 1995.

Cranna, Michael. *The True Cost of Conflict.* New York: New York Press, 1994.

Dahl, Robert A. *Democracy and its Critics.* New Haven: Yale University Press, 1989.

————. *On Democracy.* New Haven: Yale University Press, 1998.

Dakolias, Maria. *The Judicial Sector in Latin America and the Caribbean: Elements of Reform.* Technical paper 319, World Bank, Washington, DC, 1996.

Dalpino, Catharin. *Deferring Democracy: Promoting Openness in Authoritarian Regimes.* Washington, DC: Brookings Institution Press, 2000.

Danish International Development Agency. *Human Rights and Democracy: Perspectives for Development Cooperation.* Copenhagen: Danish Ministry of Foreign Affairs, 1993.

————. *The Nordic Way, Social Summit Special.* Copenhagen: Danish Ministry of Foreign Affairs, 1995.

de Castro, Isgani. "Campaign Kitty." In *Pork and Other Perks: Corruption and Governance in the Philippines,* edited by Sheila S. Coronel. Manila: Philippine Centre for Investigative Journalism, 1988.

della Porta, Donatella. "Actors in Corruption: Business Politicians in Italy," *International Social Science Journal* 149 (1996): 349–364.

————. *Working with the Media in Conflicts and other Emergencies.* Issues aper, London: Department for International Development, 2000.

Department for International Development, *Eliminating World Poverty: Making Globalization Work for the Poor,* London: White Paper on International Development, 2000.

Desai, Lord Meghnad, "Poverty and Governance." Paper, New York: Management Development and Governance Division, UNDP, 2000.

Di Palma, Giuseppe. *To Craft Democracies.* Berkeley: University of California Press, 1990.

Diamond, Larry and Marc Plattner, eds. *Civil–Military Relations and Democracy.* Baltimore: Johns Hopkins University Press, 1996.

Diamond, Larry, Mark Plattner, Yun Han Chu and Hung-mao Tien. *Consolidating the Third Wave Democracies: Regional Challenges.* Baltimore: Johns Hopkins University Press, 1997.

Diamond, Larry. *Developing Democracy: Toward Consolidation.* Baltimore: Johns Hopkins University Press, 1999.

————. *Promoting Democracy in the 1990s: Actors and Instruments, Issues and Imperatives.* Report to the Carnegie Commission on Preventing Deadly Conflict. New York: Carnegie Corporation of New York, December 1995.

Dias, Clarence J. "Democracy and Human Rights: The Challenge of Ethnicity and Inclusive Democracy." Paper prepared for the International Conference of New and Restored Democracies, Ulaanbaatar, Mongolia, June 18–20, 2003.

Doig, Alan, and Stephen Riley. "Corruption and Anti-Corruption Strategies: Issues and Case Studies from Developing Countries." In *Corruption and Integrity Improvement Initiatives in Developing Countries,* edited by United Nations Development Programme. New York: United Nations Development Programme and the Organisation for Economic Co-operation in Europe, 1998.

Domingo, Pilar. "Judicial Independence and Judicial Reform in Latin America." In *The Self-Restraining State: Power and Accountability in New Democracies,* edited by Andreas Schedler, Larry Diamond and Marc Plattner. Boulder, CO: Lynne Rienner, 1999.

Doornbos, Martin, Matt Bryden, Richard Koser and June Kane, eds. *War-Torn Societies Project in Somalia.* Geneva: United Nations Research Institute for Social Development, 1998.

Doornbos, Martin, and June Kane, eds. *War-Torn Societies Project in Eritrea.* Geneva: United Nations Research Institute for Social Development, 1998.

Dror, Yehezkel. *Capacity to Govern.* London: Taylor & Francis, 2001.

Elizabeth, V. S. "Law Reform to Combat Domestic Violence in India." Paper presented, World Bank Conference on Empowerment, Security and Opportunity through Law and Justice, St. Petersburg, Russia, July 9, 2001.

Erkens, Rainer. "Some Observations on the Role of Political Parties in the Democratisation Process on the African Continent." Paper presented, Conference on Enhancing the Role of Political Parties, The Hague, April 24–25, 2001.

European Union. "2000 Regular Report from the Commission of Estonia's Progress Towards Accession," http://europa.eu.int/comm./enlargement/Estonia/ (accessed November 8, 2000).

Fearon, James D. "Electoral Accountability and the Control of Politicians: Selecting Good Types Versus Sanctioning Poor Performance." In *Democracy, Accountability and Representation,* edited by Adam Przeworski, Susan C. Stokes and Bernard Manin. Cambridge: Cambridge University Press, 1999.

Feldman, Noa. *After Jihad: America and the Struggle for Democracy.* New York: Farrar, Straus and Giroux, 2003.

Finland Development Agency. *Human Rights and Good Governance: Some Observations on Finnish Development Cooperation.* Helsinki: Finnish Ministry of Foreign Affairs, 1991.

Finnegan, David Louis. "Observations on Tanzania's Commercial Court: A Case Study." Paper presented, World Bank Conference on Empowerment, Security and Opportunity through Law and Justice, St. Petersburg, Russia, July 9, 2001.

Freedom House, "Freedom in the World 2001–2002." News release, December 18, 2001.

Freedom House. *How Free? The Annual Survey of Press Freedom*. New York: Freedom House, 2001.

Friedman, Harry J. "Decentralized Development in Asia: Local Political Initiatives." In *Decentralization and Development: Policy Implementation in Developing Countries*, edited by G. Shabbir Cheema and Dennis A. Rondinelli. Beverly Hills: Sage, 1983.

Garreton, Manuel, and Edward Newman, eds. *Democracy in Latin America*. Tokyo: United Nations University Press, 2001.

Government of Pakistan. *Local Government Plan 2000*. Islamabad: National Reconstruction Bureau, 2000.

Grunberg, Kaul I., and Marc Stern, eds. *Global Public Goods: International Cooperation in the 21st Century*. New York: Oxford University Press, 1999.

Guarnieri, Carlo. "Courts as Instrument of Horizontal Accountability: The Case of Latin Europe." In *Democracy and the Rule of Law*, edited by Jose Maria Maraval and Adam Przeworski. Cambridge: Cambridge University Press, 2003.

Hadenius, Alex. *Democracy and Development*. Cambridge: Cambridge University Press, 1992.

Hammergre, Linn. *Fifteen Years of Judicial Reform in Latin America: Where We Are and Why We Haven't Made More Progress*. Washington, DC: USAID Global Centre for Democracy and Governance, 2002.

Hausermann, Julia. *A Human Rights Approach to Development*. London: Rights and Humanity, 1998.

Hedges, Chris. "Kosovo's Next Masters," *Foreign Affairs* 78, no. 3 (May/June 1999): 24–42.

Heidenheimer, Arnold J., Michael Johnston and Victor T. LeVine, eds. *Political Corruption— A Handbook*. New Brunswick, NJ: Transaction, 1997.

Huntington, Samuel P. "The Clash of Civilizations?" *Foreign Affairs* 72, no. 33 (Summer 1993): 22–49.

————. *The Clash of Civilizations and the Remaking of World Order*. New York: Simon and Schuster, 1996.

————. *The Third Wave: Democratization in the Late Twentieth Century*. Norman, OK: University of Oklahoma Press, 1993.

Ibrahim, Saad Eddin. "Religion and Democracy: The Case of Islam, Civil Society and Democracy." In *The Changing Nature of Democracy*, edited by Takashi Inoguchi, Edward Newman and John Keane. Tokyo: United Nations University Press, 1998.

Inoguchi, Takashi. "Press, Mass Media and Democracy." Draft Paper, UNDP, 2001.

Inoguchi, Takashi, Edward Newman and John Keane, eds. *The Changing Nature of Democracy*. Tokyo: United Nations University Press, 1998.

International Crisis Group. *Kosovo's Ethnic Dilemma: The Need for a Civic Contract*. Brussels: International Crisis Group (Balkans Report no. 143), May 2003.

International Institute for Democracy and Electoral Assistance. "Democracy and Poverty: Is There a Missing Link?" Paper, IIDEA Democracy Forum, Stockholm, Sweden, June 8–9, 2000.

Inter-Parliamentarian Union. *Parliaments of the World*, Geneva: Inter-Parliamentarian Union, 2001.

————. *Ten Years of Strengthening Parliaments in Africa: 1991–2000.* Geneva: Inter-Parliamentary Union, 2003.

International Republican Institute. "IRI Highlights," http://www.iri.org.

Isaak, Robert. *The Globalization Gap: How the Rich Get Richer and the Poor Get Left Further Behind.* New York: FT Prentice Hall, 2005.

Johnson, John K. *Best Practices from the International Conference on Legislative Strengthening.* Washington, DC: USAID, 1997.

Johnson, John K., and Robert Nakamura. *A Concept Paper on Legislatures and Good Governance.* New York: UNDP, 1999.

Johnston, Michael. "Cross-Border Corruption: Points of Vulnerability and Challenges for Reform." In *Corruption and Integrity Improvement Initiatives in Developing Countries,* edited by United Nations Development Programme. New York: United Nations Development Programme and the Organization for Economic Cooperation and Development, 1998.

————. "Public Officials, Private Interests, and Sustainable Democracy: When Politics and Corruption Meet." In *Corruption and the Global Economy,* edited by Kimberly Ann Elliot. Washington, DC: Institute for International Economics, 1997.

Khan, Irshad Hasan. "Judicial System of Pakistan: Measures for Maintaining Independence and Enforcing Accountability." Paper presented, International Conference Legal and Judicial Reform, Washington, DC, June 5–7, 2000.

Kaplan, Robert. "Was Democracy Just a Moment?" *Atlantic Monthly* 280, no. 6 (December 1997): 55–80.

Karam, Azza. "Beijing + 5: Women's Participation: Review of Strategies and Trends." In *United Nations Development Program, Women's Participation and Good Governance: 21st Century Challenges,* edited by UNDP, 15–26. New York: UNDP, 2000.

Katz, Alihu. "Mass Media and Participatory Democracy." In *The Changing Nature of Democracy,* edited by Takashi Inoguchi, Edward Newman and John Keane. Tokyo: United Nations University Press, 1998.

Kpundeh, Sahr J. "Political Will in Fighting Corruption." In *Corruption and Integrity Improvement Initiatives in Developing Countries,* edited by United Nations Development Programme. New York: United Nations Development Programme and the Organisation for Economic Cooperation and Development, 1998.

Kurian, George Thomas, ed. *World Encyclopedia of Parliaments and Legislatures,* Vol. II. Washington, DC: Congressional Quarterly Books, 1998.

Lewis, Bernard. "Islam and Liberal Democracy: A Historical Overview," *Journal of Democracy* 7, no. 2 (1996): 52–63.

Lipset, Seymour Martin. "Prospects for Democracy." Paper, Conference of New and Restored Democracies, Cotonou, Benin, December 4–6, 2000.

————. "The Social Requisites of Democracy Revisited." In *Comparing Nations and Cultures: Readings in Cross-disciplinary Perspectives,* edited by Alex Inkeles and Masamichi Sadaki, 30–49. Englewood Cliffs: Prentice-Hall, 1996.

————. "Some Social Requisites of Democracy: Economic Development and Political Legitimacy," *American Political Science Review* 53 (1959): 69–105.

Lipset, Seymour Martin, Kyoung-Ryung Seong and John Charles Torres. "A Comparative Analysis of the Social Prerequisites of Democracy," *International Social Science Journal* 45 (May 1993): 159–60.

Linz, Juan, and Alfred Stepan. *Problems of Democratic Transition and Consolidation: Southern Europe, South America and Post Communist Europe.* Baltimore: Johns Hopkins University Press, 1996.

Longley, Lawrence D., and Roger H. Davidson. "The New Roles of Parliamentary Committees," *The Journal of Legislative Studies* 4, no 1 (1998).

Lopez-Pintor, Rafael. *Electoral Management Bodies as Institutions of Governance.* New York: UNDP, 2000.

Mabusela, Shirley. "Human Rights and Sustainable Human Development: How Development Is a Necessary Means to Promote and Protect Human Rights," *Human Rights and Human Development,* report of the Oslo Symposium, 54–55, UNDP, 2000.

Maravall, Jose, and Adam Przeworski, eds. *Democracy and the Rule of Law.* Cambridge: Cambridge University Press, 2003.

Marsh, Ian, Jean Blondel and Takashi Inoguchi, eds. *Democracy, Governance and Economic Performance: East and Southeast Asia.* Tokyo: United Nations University Press, 1999.

Mburu, Chris. "Challenges Facing Legal and Judicial Reform in Post-Conflict Environment: Case Study from Rwanda and Sierra Leone." Paper, World Bank Conference on Empowerment, Security and Opportunity through Law and Justice, St. Petersburg, Russia, July 9, 2001.

McClymont, Mary, and Stephen Golub, eds. *Many Roads to Justice.* New York: Ford Foundations, 2000.

Meny, Yves. "'Fin de Siecle' Corruption: Change, Crisis and Shifting Values," *International Social Science Journal* 149 (1997): 309–320.

Messick, Richard E. "Judicial Reform: The Why, What and How." Paper, Conference on Strategies for Modernizing the Judicial Sector in the Arab World, Marrakech, Morocco, March 15–17, 2002.

Molutsi, Patrick, and Anita Inder Singh, "Strengthening Representative Democracy: Parliamentary and Electoral Systems and Institutions." Paper, Fifth International Conference of New and Restored Democracies, Ulaanbaatar, Mongolia, June 18–20, 2003.

Mumtaz, Babar, and Emiel Wegelin. *Guiding Cities: The Urban Management Program.* Paper no. 26, United Nations Center for Human Settlements, UNDP, and World Bank Urban Management Program, Nairobi, 2001.

National Democratic Institute for International Affairs. *Committees in Legislatures: A Division of Labor.* Washington, DC: NDI (Legislative Research Series no. 2), 1996.

————. *Lessons Learned and Challenges Facing International Election Monitoring.* Washington, DC: NDI, 2001.

————. *The Politics of South Africa on Election Day.* Washington, DC: NDI, 1994.

Norwegian Agency for Development Cooperation. *Norwegian Development Authority and Norwegian Development Cooperation in the 1990s.* Oslo: Norwegian Development Authority, 1993.

Office of the High Commissioner for Human Rights. *A Note on the Right to Development.* Geneva: Office of the High Commissioner for Human Rights, 2000.

Olson, David M. *Democratic Legislative Institutions: A Comparative View.* New York: M.E. Sharpe, 1994.

Osborne, David, and Ted Gaebler. *Reinventing Government: How the Entrepreneurial Spirit Is Transforming the Public Sector.* New York: Penguin, 1993.

Oxfam, *Globalization*, London, Oxfam G. B. Policy Paper 5/00, 2000.

Przeworski, Adam, ed. *Democracy and Development: Political Institutions and Well-Being in the World, 1950–1990.* Cambridge: Cambridge University Press, 2000.

Przeworski, Adam, and Fernando Limongi. "Political Regime and Economic Growth," *Journal of Economic Perspectives* 7, no. 3 (Summer 1993): 51.

Przeworski, Adam, Susan Stokes and Bernard Manin, eds. *Democracy, Accountability and Representation.* Cambridge: Cambridge University Press, 1999.

Radelet, Steven. "Bush and Foreign Aid," *Foreign Affairs* 82, no. 5 (September/October 2003): 104.

Reynolds, Andrew S., ed. *Election '94: South Africa—An Analysis of the Results, Campaigns and Future Prospects.* New York: St. Martin's Press, 1994.

Richardson, Bradley. *Japanese Democracy: Power, Coordination and Performance.* New Haven: Yale University Press, 1997.

Rondinelli, Dennis A., G. Shabbir Cheema and John Nellis. *Decentralization in Developing Countries.* Staff working paper, World Bank, Washington, DC, 1984.

Saikal, Amin, and Albrecht Schnabel, eds. *Democratization in the Middle East: Experiences, Struggles, Challenges.* Tokyo: United Nations University Press, 2003.

Safty, Adil. *The Global Advance of Democracy in Governance.* New York: Management Development and Governance Division, UNDP, 2000.

Sandbrook, Richard. *The Politics of Africa's Economic Stagnation.* Cambridge: Cambridge University Press, 1985.

Santiso, Carlos, *Democratic Governance: Economic and Political Development in New Democracies.* Background paper for the International Institute of Democracy and Electoral Assistance. Stockholm: IIDEA, 1997.

Santolaya, Pablo, and Iñiguez, Diego. *Legislative Framework.* Part of the Administration and Coordination of Elections Project of the United Nations Online Network in Public Administration and Finance (UNPAN). http://www.aceproject.org/.

Scallan, Andrew. *Management Considerations: An Introduction.* Part of the Administration and Coordination of Elections Project of the United Nations Online Network in Public Administration and Finance (UNPAN). http://www.aceproject.org/.

Schedler, Andreas, Larry Diamond, and Marc Plattner, eds. *The Self-Restraining State: Power and Accountability in New Democracies.* Boulder, CO: Lynne Rienner, 1999.

Schmitter, Philippe. "The Influence of International Context Upon the Choice of National Institutions and Policies in Neo-Democracies." In *The International Dimensions of Democratization: Europe and the Americas,* edited by Laurence Whitehead. Oxford: Oxford University Press, 1996.

Schwartz, Herman. "Surprising Success: The New Eastern European Constitutional Courts." In *The Self-Restraining State: Power and Accountability in New Democracies,* edited by Andreas Schedler, Larry Diamond and Marc Plattner. Boulder, CO: Lynne Rienner, 1999.

Seketle, Pontso, K. Lekhesa and J. Akokpari. *A Final Report on the Workshop on the Contribution of the Parliamentary Process in Strengthening Governance in Lesotho.* Lesotho: UNDP, 2001.

Sen, Amartya. "Democracy as a Universal Value," *Journal of Democracy* 10, no. 3 (July 1999): 3–17.

———. *Development as Freedom.* New York: Anchor Books, 1999.

———. "What Is the Role of Legal and Judicial Reform in Development?" Keynote address, Global Conference on Comprehensive Legal and Judicial Development, Washington, DC, June 5–7, 2000.

Seoul Metropolitan Government. *Integrity Pact.* Seoul: Seoul Metropolitan Government, 2000.

———. *Clean and Transparent.* Seoul: Seoul Metropolitan Government, 2001.

Silverman, Jerry. *Public Sector Decentralization.* Washington, DC: World Bank, 1990.

Simai, Mihaly ed. *The Democratic Process and the Market: Challenges of Transition.* Tokyo: United Nations University Press, 1999.

Sivaramakrishnan, K. C. *Power to the People? The Politics and Progress of Decentralisation.* New Delhi: Konark, 2000.

Stephan, Alfred. "Religion, Democracy and the 'Twin Tolerations,' *Journal of Democracy* 11, no. 4 (October 2000): 52.

Stremlau, John. *Sharpening International Sanctions: Toward a Stronger Role for the United Nations.* New York: Carnegie Commission on Preventing Deadly Conflict, 1996.

Swedish International Development Agency. *SIDA's Strategy for its Program of Assistance in Support of Democracy and Human Rights.* Stockholm, Swedish International Development Agency, 1993.

Taylor, Harry. "Public Sector Personnel Management in Three African Countries: Current Problems and Possibilities," *Public Administration and Development* 12 (1992): 193–207.

Thakur, Ramesh, and Edward Newman. *New Millennium, New Perspectives: The United Nations, Security and Governance.* Tokyo: United Nations University Press, 2000.

United Nations. "An Agenda for Peace: Preventive Diplomacy, Peacemaking and Peacekeeping." Report of the Secretary General pursuant to the statement adopted by the Summit Meeting of the Security Council, New York, January 31, 1992.

———. *The Global Compact: Corporate Leadership in the World Economy.* New York: United Nations, 1999.

———. *Globalization and the State: World Global Report 2001.* New York: United Nations, 2001.

United Nations Development Programme. *Arab Human Development Report 2002: Creating Opportunities for Future Generations.* New York: Oxford University Press, 2002.

———. *Common Country Assessment for Serbia and Montenegro.* Belgrade: UNDP, 2003.

———. *Conflict and Governance.* New York: UNDP, 2000.

———. *The Contribution of the Parliamentary Process in Strengthening Good Governance in Africa. Report of the Third Africa Governance Forum, 2000.* New York: UNDP, 2001.

————. *Country Assessment in Accountability and Transparency (CONTACT)*. New York: UNDP, 2001.

————. *Deepening Democracy in a Fragmented World.* New York: Oxford University Press, 2002.

————. *Democracy in Latin America.* New York: UNDP, 2004.

————. *Democratic Governance in Mozambique,* Maputo: UNDP, 2000.

————. *Fractured Communities Programme: Summary Report 2001.* New York: UNDP, 2001.

————. "Governance and Conflict Prevention: Proceedings of Expert Group Meeting." Conference, New York, March 7–8, 2000.

————. *Governance Foundations for Post-Crisis Situations.* New York: UNDP, 2000.

————. *Human Development Report 1994: New Dimensions of Human Security.* New York: Oxford University Press, 1994.

————. *Human Development Report 1997: Human Development to Eradicate Poverty.* New York: Oxford University Press, 1997.

————. *Human Development Report 1999: Globalization with a Human Face.* New York: Oxford University Press, 1999.

————. *Human Development Report 2000: Human Rights and Human Development.* New York: UNDP, 2000.

————. *Human Development Report 2003: Millennium Development Goals: A Compact Among Nations to End Human Poverty.* New York: Oxford University Press, 2003.

————. *Human Rights: A Compilation of International Instruments.* New York: UNDP, 2000.

————. *Human Rights and Human Development: Report of the Oslo Symposium.* New York: UNDP, 1998.

————. *Integrating Human Rights with Sustainable Human Development.* New York: UNDP, 1998.

————. *Legislative Committee System.* New York: UNDP, 2000.

————. *The Legislature and Constituency Relations,* New York: UNDP, 2000.

————. *LIFE Programme 1992–1997: Participatory Local Governance.* Technical advisory paper 1, New York, 1997.

————. *Overcoming Human Poverty, United Nations Development Programme Poverty Report 2000.* New York: UNDP, 2000.

————. *Participatory Local Governance.* New York: UNDP, 1997.

————. *Public Sector Management, Governance and Sustainable Human Development.* Discussion paper 1, Management Development and Governance Division, New York, 1995.

————. Report of the Fourth Africa Governance Forum. New York: UNDP, 2000.

————. *UNDP and Governance: Lessons of Experience.* New York: UNDP, Management Development and Governance Division, 2000.

United Nations Research Institute for Social Development. *Rebuilding After War: A Summary of the War-Torn Societies Project*. Geneva: United Nations Research Institute for Social Development, 1998.

————. *War-Torn Societies Project Report*. Geneva: UNRISD, 1998.

United States Agency for International Development. "After the War is Over What Comes Next: Promoting Democracy, Human Rights and Reintegration in Post-conflict Societies." Conference report, Washington, DC, 1997.

————. *Guidance for Promoting Judicial Independence and Impartiality*. Washington, DC: USAID, January 2003.

————. Report on USAID Democracy and Governance Partners Conference, Washington, DC, November 30, 2000.

Waltz, Susan E. *Human Rights and Reform: Changing the Face of North African Politics*. Berkeley: University of California Press, 1995.

Waseem, Mohammad Waseem. *The 1993 Elections in Pakistan*. Lahore: Vanguard Books, 1994.

Weingast, Barry R. "A Postscript to Political Foundation of Democracy and the Rule of Law." In *Democracy and the Rule of Law*, edited by Jose Maria Maraval and Adam Przeworski. Cambridge: Cambridge University Press, 2003.

Weiss-Fagen, June, and June Kane, eds. *War-Torn Societies Project in Mozambique*. Geneva: United Nations Research Institute for Social Development, 1998.

Widner, Jennifer. "Building Judicial Independence in Common Law Africa." In *The Self-Restraining State: Power and Accountability in New Democracies*, edited by Andreas Schedler, Larry Diamond and Marc Plattner. Boulder, CO: Lynne Rienner, 1999.

World Bank. *Reforming Public Institutions and Strengthening Governance: A World Bank Strategy*. Washington, DC: World Bank Office of the Publisher, 2000.

————. *World Development Report 1997: The State in a Changing World*. Washington, DC: Oxford University Press, World Bank Office of the Publisher, 1997.

————. *World Development Report 1998: Knowledge for Development*. Washington, DC: Oxford University Press, World Bank Office of the Publisher, 1998.

————. *World Development Report 1999/2000: Entering the 21st Century*. Washington, DC: Oxford University Press, World Bank Office of the Publisher, 1999.

————. *World Bank Development Report 2000/2001: Attacking Poverty*. Washington, DC: Oxford University Press, World Bank Office of the Publisher, 2000.

————. *World Development Report 2002: Building Institutions for Markets*. Washington, DC: Oxford University Press, World Bank Office of the Publisher, 2002.

Zakaria, Fareed. *The Future of Freedom: Illiberal Democracy at Home and Abroad*. New York: Norton, 2003.

————. "The Rise of Illiberal Democracy," *Foreign Affairs* 76, no. 6 (November/December 1997): 22–43.

Zamora, Rubén I., Christophe Bouvier and June Kane, eds. *War-Torn Societies Project in Guatemala*. Geneva: United Nations Research Institute for Social Development, 1998.

INDEX

Abacha, Sani, 225, 227
Abiola, Mashood A., 225
Accord for Consensual and
  Participatory Democracy, 91
accountability, 51, 89, 98, 120,
  131–32, 178, 187
Adenauer, Konrad, 29
Afghanistan, 107, 194, 197, 205,
  209, 217, 223
Africa, 132, 148, 175, 176, 227
African National Congress
  (ANC), 30, 79, 105
Agenda for Development, 237
Agenda for Peace, 236, 248
Agenda for Peace (Boutros-
  Ghali), 208
Akayev, Askar, 38
Albania, 173
Algeria, 106, 178, 218
Alternative Law Groups
  (ALGs), 181
Alvarez, Michael, 232
American Convention on
  Human Rights, San Jose Pact,
  28
Amin, Idi, 176
Amnesty International, 99, 115,
  238, 242
Angola, 106
Anti-corruption Commission of
  Thailand, 53
anticorruption programs, 70
Arab parliaments, 76
Arab region
  accountability underdeveloped
    for, 178
  country categories in, 76
  democracy difficult in, 3, 220
  gender balance in, 112
  globalization influencing, 216
  groups represented in, 90
  human rights in, 105
  legislatures in, 75
  management improvements
    for, 180
  parliament's budget role in, 83
  policy analysis lacking in, 87
  state owned media in, 231
Area Development Program,
  206
arena legislatures, 74
Argentina, 56, 88, 104, 174, 183,
  203, 204, 205, 224, 226, 233,
  245
armed forces, 205

Asia Foundation, 35
Asian Development Bank, 60
Asian Network for Free
  Elections (ANFREL), 35
Asian values, 215
assistance. *See* democracy assis-
  tance
auditor-general, 84
Australian Electoral
  Commission, 35
authoritarian leaders, 8, 27, 215
authority structures, 132–33

Babaginda, Ibrahim, 227
Bahrain, 105, 216, 218
Balilihan Country Action
  Program (BCAP), 134
Bangladesh, 8, 9, 45, 56, 57, 79,
  83, 181–82, 216, 217, 218,
  223, 233, 244
Bangladesh Environmental
  Lawyers' Association (BELA),
  182
Bangladesh Women Lawyers'
  Association (BNWLA), 181
Beirut Declaration for Justice,
  178
Belarus, 3, 173
Belgium, 76, 193
Belo Horizonte, 129, 135
Benin, 40, 91
Bhutto, Benezir, 124
Bhutto, Zulfiqar, 124
bilateral donors, 245
bipartisan approach, 91
Bolivia, 74, 76, 79, 85, 103, 175,
  183, 184, 235, 245
Bosnia, 193, 199, 203
Botswana, 65–66
Brazil, 45, 79, 88, 99, 103, 113,
  121, 128, 129, 130, 131, 135,
  175, 180, 184, 214, 224, 226
Bretton Woods institutions, 208
bribes, 56, 62, 64
Buddhism, 214
Burkina Faso, 91, 114
Burundi, 106, 198
Bush, George W., 242

Cambodia, 106, 111, 196, 199,
  206
Cambodian Resettlement and
  Reintegration Program
  (CARERE), 111
Campaign Against Gender

Violence in Latin America
  and the Caribbean, 113
Canadian International
  Development Agency
  (CIDA), 28
Carothers, Thomas, 7, 246
Carter Center, 35
Carter, Jimmy, 241
case studies
  corruption with, 65–68
  developing countries with,
    25–26
  elections with, 29–39
  Philippines, 67
censorship, 231
Center for Legislative
  Development, 105
central government, 131, 133–34
central level, 133
Centre for Applied Legal
  Studies (CALS), 182
Chad, 91, 106
checks and balances, 14, 70, 82,
  83, 105, 121, 171
Chege, Michael, 224, 226
Cheibub, Antonio, 232
Chhibber, Pradeep, 59
Chile, 8, 45, 79, 80, 104, 106,
  148, 205, 214, 226, 231
Christian Council of Churches,
  33
Chua, Amy, 8
civic education, 16, 36, 46, 68,
  79–80
civil registry, 41
civil rights, 102
civil servants, 158, 161
civil service, 141
  developing countries weak-
    nesses with, 142–43
  Malaysia reforming, 160
  meritocracy for, 163
  reforms in, 142–43
civil society, 14–15, 108–9, 134,
  135, 136, 154–55
Civil Society Organizations
  (CSO), 132, 137, 179, 197,
  234, 242
  advocacy role for, 237–38,
    244–45
  decentralization and, 121
  human rights role in, 110
  legislatures lobbied by, 80
  political awareness with, 134
  rights violation monitored by,

263

SERIES EDITORS' INTRODUCTION

The Pacific Basin Research Center (PBRC) was created in 1991 by Soka University of America to integrate social science research with enduring values derived from human experience. Its purpose is to engage scholars from around the world in research focused on policies that contribute to the peaceful pursuit of human development.

Over the past decade the PBRC has sponsored research published in nearly a dozen books and in numerous articles and working papers that contributes to our knowledge of international development policy. Its research has examined "great policies" that transcend conventional boundaries of public decision-making and inspire innovation, policies promoting positive human rights, the role of social capital in human development, the impacts of globalization on national sovereignty, and the challenges of nation building in post-conflict societies.

PBRC's current research explores the historic interplay of domestic and international political and economic forces in the Pacific Basin and how, in a period of transition, mutually interactive forces are altering the pace and characteristics of globalization in the region and in the rest of the world. Research sponsored by PBRC seeks to understand how and why governments, social organizations, and private enterprises in Asian, North American, and Latin American Pacific Basin countries are responding to globalization, exercising leadership for development, and protecting and modifying cultural traditions that embody human values as development occurs.

The Pacific Basin Research Center is pleased to include Shabbir Cheema's book, *Building Democratic Institutions: Governance Reform in Developing Countries,* as part of its publication series. Cheema's state-of-the-art survey of knowledge and practice in governance and public sector institution-building in developing countries draws from the experiences of, and provides important lessons for, policymakers in the Pacific Basin. He brings together the latest information about how policymakers in developing countries are democratizing their governance systems to achieve more efficient, effective, participative, and beneficial development for their citizens, and the challenges they face in doing so.

Cheema's book is unified by two important themes that also underlie the PBRC's research agenda: the role of globalization in spreading ideas of democratic governance for development and the role of institutional development in improving public policymaking and implementation. It synthesizes the literature and assesses current practice, connecting the concepts of governance, democracy, and development in ways that are likely to be useful to both scholars and public policymakers.

A virtue of Cheema's book is that it provides a framework not only for understanding how governance, democracy, and development are related but also for assessing the conditions that make democratic governance possible. He examines the importance of elections, of integrity and honesty in government, of parliamentary and judicial reform, and of decentralization and local government in the development process. He explores the impacts of globalization on governance changes in developing countries and of democratization on human rights and citizen participation. He places his discussion of governance and development in the context of the forces needed not only to adopt democratic practices but also to sustain them.

Cheema's book will serve not only as a scholarly reference on the state of the art in governance and development, but also as a valuable guide on democratic institution-building for public policy analysts, government officials, political leaders, and professionals in non-government organizations and the private sector who are pursuing peaceful human development in Pacific Basin countries.

Publication Series

G. Shabbir Cheema, *Building Democratic Institutions: Governance Reform in Developing Countries*, 2005.

Dennis A. Rondinelli
Glaxo Distinguished International
   Professor of Management
University of North Carolina at
   Chapel Hill
Chapel Hill, North Carolina
Director, Pacific Basin Research Center

John M. Heffron
Professor of History
Soka University of America
Aliso Viejo, California
Associate Director, Pacific Basin
   Research Center

John D. Montgomery and Dennis A. Rondinelli (eds.), *Beyond Reconstruction in Afghanistan: Lessons from Development Experience*, 2004.

John D. Montgomery and Nathan Glazer (eds.), *Sovereignty under Challenge: How Governments Respond*, 2002.

John D. Montgomery and Alex Inkeles (eds.), *Social Capital as a Policy Resource*, 2001.

Dennis J. Encarnation, *Japanese Multinationals in Asia: Regional Operations in Comparative Perspective*, 1999.

John D. Montgomery (ed.), *Human Rights: Positive Policies in Asia and the Pacific Rim*, 1998.

Exaltacion E. Lamberte, *Public Health–Human Values Connection*, 1998.

Michael B. McElroy, Chris P. Nielsen, and Peter Lydon (eds.), *Energizing China: Reconciling Environmental Protection and Economic Growth*, 1998.

John D. Montgomery (ed.), *Values in Education: Social Capital Formation in Asia and the Pacific*, 1997.

Michael E. Brown and Sumit Ganguly (eds.), *Government Policies and Ethnic Relations in Asia and the Pacific*, 1997.

John D. Montgomery and Dennis A. Rondinelli (eds.), *Great Policies: Strategic Innovations in Asia and the Pacific Basin*, 1995.

ABOUT THE AUTHOR

G. Shabbir Cheema is Principal Adviser on Governance, Division for Public Administration and Development Management, United Nations. As a senior UN official for the past 15 years, including six years as the Director of the Governance Division of UNDP, he provided leadership in crafting democratic governance and public administration programs at the country level. He also designed global research and training programs in electoral and parliamentary systems, human rights, transparency and accountability of government, urban management, and decentralization. He has taught at the University of Science in Malaysia, University of Hawaii and New York University.

Dr. Cheema has authored or edited eight books and numerous book chapters and journal articles on governance and public administration. His books include *Reinventing Government for the Twenty-First Century: State Capacity in a Globalizing Society*, co-editor (Kumarian, 2003*), Urban Shelter and Services: Public Policies and Management Approaches*, author (Praeger, 1987); and *Decentralization and Development: Policy Implementation in Developing Countries*, co-editor (Sage Publications, 1984).

Also from Kumarian Press...

Governance, International Public Administration

Administrative Decentralization: Strategies for Developing Countries
John M. Cohen and Stephen B. Peterson

Better Governance and Public Policy
Capacity Building for Democratic Renewal in Africa
Edited by Dele Olowu and Soumana Sako

Governance, Administration & Development: Making the State Work
Mark Turner and David Hulme

Managing Policy Reform: Concepts and Tools for Decision-Makers in
Developing and Transitioning Countries
Derick W. Brinkerhoff and Benjamin L. Crosby

Reinventing Government for the Twenty-First Century
State Capacity in a Globalizing Society
Edtied by Dennis A. Rondinelli and G. Shabbir Cheema

International Development, Humanitarianism, Global Civil Society

Creating a Better World: Interpreting Global Civil Society
Edited by Rupert Taylor

Ethics and Global Politics: The Active Learning Sourcebook
Edited by April L. Morgan, Lucinda Joy Peach, and Colette Mazzucelli

Global Civil Society: Dimensions of the Nonprofit Sector, Volume Two
Lester M. Salamon, S. Wojciech Sokolowski, and Associates

Globalization and Social Exclusion: A Transformationalist Perspective
Ronaldo Munck

Human Rights and Development
Peter Uvin

Nation-Building Unraveled? Aid, Peace and Justice in Afghanistan
Edited by Antonio Donini, Norah Niland and Karin Wermester

Ritual and Symbol in Peacebuilding
Lisa Schirch

Visit Kumarian Press at **www.kpbooks.com** or
call **toll-free 800.289.2664** for a complete catalog.

Kumarian Press, located in Bloomfield, Connecticut, is a forward-looking, scholarly press that promotes active international engagement and an awareness of global connectedness.